T O W A R D A
COHERENT
CURRICULUM

1995 YEARBOOK OF THE ASSOCIATION FOR
SUPERVISION AND CURRICULUM DEVELOPMENT

JAMES A. BEANE
EDITOR

ALEXANDRIA, VIRGINIA

Association for Supervision and Curriculum Development
1250 N. Pitt Street, Alexandria, VA 22314-1453
Telephone: (703) 549-9110   FAX: (703) 549-3891

The mission of ASCD, a diverse, international community of educators, is to forge covenants in teaching and learning for the success of all learners.

Printed in the United States of America.

ASCD 1995 Yearbook Committee
James A. Beane, National-Louis University, Evanston, Illinois
Andrew Algren, American Association for the Advancement of Science, Washington, D.C.
Michael Apple, University of Wisconsin, Madison
Frank Betts, ASCD, Alexandria, Virginia
Marion Brady, Cocoa, Florida
Ronald S. Brandt, ASCD, Alexandria, Virginia
Kathleen A. Fitzpatrick, National Study of School Evaluation, Arlington Heights, Illinois
Nathalie Gehrke, University of Washington, Seattle
Gene Harris, Columbus Public Schools, Columbus, Ohio
Greg Morris, Pittsburgh, Pennsylvania
Joan M. Palmer, Maryland State Department of Education, Baltimore
Stephen Tchudi, University of Nevada, Reno
Grant Wiggins, Center on Learning, Assessment, and School Structure (CLASS), Princeton, New Jersey

ASCD Publications Staff
Executive Editor: Ronald S. Brandt
Managing Editor, ASCD Books: Nancy Modrak
Manager, Design and Production Services: Gary Bloom
Print Production Coordinator: Stephanie Justen
Senior Designer: Karen Monaco
Desktop Publisher: Valerie Sprague
Associate Editors: Carolyn Pool, Julie Houtz, Mary McMahon, Margaret Oosterman, Mary Shafer, Ginger Miller

$19.95
ASCD Stock No. 1-95008
ISSN: 1042-9018

Toward a Coherent Curriculum

The Search for Coherence

Commentaries on the Search for Coherence in the Curriculum

Foreword

Early in my career, a consultant introduced me to the term *ambiguity tolerance* as a desirable trait for school administrators to possess. Since then I've found that most educators live in a curricular world where ambiguity tolerance is a valuable commodity. The curriculum in numerous schools lacks clarity and, more important, coherence.

Students move from teacher to teacher and subject to subject along a curriculum continuum that may or may not exhibit planned articulation. The most carefully designed curriculums are often fragmented into various subjects or disciplines. Teachers supply some coherence in terms of how they transform an intended curriculum into an experienced curriculum. Students provide the last measure of coherence, based on mastery of previous material and their ability to relate learnings to other life occurrences.

Real coherence in a curriculum is an elusive theme to capture and may not be possible, at least in the philosophical sense. The pursuit, however, must not slow its pace. The authors of this book point the way for others in describing their own searches for meaning. They elaborate on the problems, while proposing various ways to hold the curriculum together in a unified system. This curriculum "glue" comes in several different bottles for selection by the reader.

This ASCD yearbook deliberately avoids trying to eliminate all the ambiguity that exists with respect to curriculum. The authors, experts in the field, agreed that it would be premature and presumptuous of them to agree among themselves on The Coherent Curriculum. Instead, they have certainly advanced the discussion to new heights and helped educators everywhere move toward a more coherent curriculum. Curriculum development is seen as a dynamic process wherein ambiguity is lessened and coherence increased.

My affiliation with ASCD has been intellectually enriched with stimulating ideas regularly produced and reproduced through its various books, journals, and conferences. Many of the educational concepts or techniques presented are appealing. A few are outside my experience. Most cause me to expand my thinking. The 1995 ASCD Yearbook, *Toward a Coherent Curriculum*, is no exception to the enrichment ASCD offers educators.

ARTHUR W. STELLER
ASCD President, 1994–95

Prologue

The theme for this yearbook emerged from a sense that the curriculum in too many schools consists of a disconnected, fragmented—incoherent—collection of information and skills programs, courses, and so on. This incoherence contributes to the conviction of many young people that their school experiences have no meaning or significance in their lives. Almost anyone who works in or with schools knows the urgency of this problem.

The preparation of the yearbook followed in the tradition of many that ASCD has issued in the past. The work began by convening a Yearbook Committee of ASCD members who represented a variety of backgrounds and perspectives in terms of culture, gender, geography, and professional positions. What they had in common was evidence of previous work that addressed the need for coherence in the curriculum. The committee met for three days in June 1993 and, after much discussion and debate, worked out an organization for the book, including ideas for specific content.

Early in the Committee's deliberations, we realized that our work would not and should not result in a description of *the* or *a* coherent curriculum. In the first place, it appeared unlikely that we could ever reach consensus on a single "model." Even if we could do that, we fully understood that what was coherent for us might not be coherent for others, especially the diverse young people in communities across the country and around the globe. Finally, we understood that commitment to a coherent curriculum depends in part on having a hand in its creation and understanding completely the contributing ideas.

The book that the Committee eventually envisioned, which you now hold in your hands, addresses the possibilities for coherence in three parts. The first part, entitled "What Is a Coherent Curriculum?" raises a number of questions related to the search for coherence in the curriculum as well as some possible features of a coherent curriculum. The second part describes attempts to create coherence in the curriculum. It includes both theoretical perspectives and school stories about such matters as organizing themes, curriculum organization, and assessment. The third part presents commentaries on the previous section. This kind of critique reflects both the seriousness with which the Yearbook Committee took its work and the understanding that real progress toward curriculum improvement must always involve give-and-take about ideas.

Thus, we sought to present in this yearbook a collection of ideas, perspectives, possibilities, and questions that people might use in moving toward coherence in the curriculum. In the end, it is our hope that this yearbook will be used in exactly that way: as a starting point for deliberation and conversation by everyone who has a stake in the curriculum of our schools—educators, parents and other adults in the community, and, of course, the young people whose lives in school are largely defined by the curriculum. If this book makes that kind of contribution, then we will consider our work well worth the effort.

James A. Beane for the
1995 Yearbook Committee

1

Introduction: What Is a Coherent Curriculum?

James A. Beane

I magine that we are faced with a pile of jigsaw puzzle pieces and told to put them together. Our first reaction might well be to ask for the picture. When we put together a jigsaw puzzle, we usually have a picture to guide us. None of the pieces means anything taken alone; only when the pieces are put together do they mean something.

In the beginning, we hold each piece up to the picture to see roughly what space to place it in. Later on, after we have put some pieces together, we look for other pieces to attach to a partly completed section. Even as we put these large chunks together, we still look back at the picture to make sure we're on the right track. It is always the *picture* that guides us. Putting pieces together without the picture can only be a frustrating struggle—at best, a way to kill some time.

This jigsaw puzzle metaphor ought to say something to educators. It is, after all, not unlike how young people experience the curriculum in too many schools. They move from one classroom to another, from one time block to another, from one textbook to another, from one teacher to another, confronted by disconnected, fragmented pieces of information or skills. For these young people, the curriculum is a pile of jigsaw puzzle pieces without a picture. They might ask, "What does all of this mean?" or "What is all of this about?" More often, they simply ask, "Why do we have to do this?" We respond, "Because it will be on the test," or "You'll need it next year," or "You'll find out later in life," or, in exasperation, "Because I said so."

Where is the sense in these responses? Could it be that we ourselves cannot summon a reasonable explanation for what we ask young people to do in the curriculum? Is it possible that we ourselves are unclear or do not know, apart from institutional timelines, what it is that the curriculum is all about? Can it be that the jigsaw puzzle metaphor describes not only the experiences of young people in our schools, but also our own confusion about the curriculum?

This yearbook is about the jigsaw puzzle metaphor. The title, *Toward a Coherent Curriculum,* invites the professional community and others to imagine ways in which we might overcome the problems that metaphor reveals. But this is no leisurely, armchair exercise. The call for coherence insists that we undertake fundamental rethinking of the curriculum. It asks that we abandon our specialized loyalties to particular parts and reconsider what and whom the curriculum is for. This is quite different from most current efforts toward restructuring that seek simply to align or systematize those parts, to demand uniformity, or to tinker with one or more organizational features of the schools. Nor does it simply seek a peaceful coexistence of what is now fragmented and sometimes contentious. Instead, this search for coherence goes to the very center of school life, to the curriculum that defines and mediates the experiences of young people.

The problem of incoherence in the curriculum has a sense of urgency about it. The stakes are high. Increasingly, our students are questioning the purpose and meaning of what we ask them to do. Their lives in school have been deadened by the litany of disconnected facts and skills they face every day. So too are teachers' lives deadened, not only by the students' constant requests for justification, but by their own questions: "Why am I teaching this?" and "If this makes no sense to me, how can I keep asking students to learn it?"

Surely there is no lack of effort being put into the curriculum these days. Talk has heated up about a national curriculum and tests, and countless committees and subcommittees are at work deciding what young people ought to learn in one subject or another. Professional associations of all descriptions are issuing statements trying to put their own stamp on curriculum reform. At least two "umbrella" groups, the Alliance for Curriculum Reform and the Forum on Standards and Learning, are seeking to open dialogue among the fragmented community of professional associations. And hardly a journal issue passes without some suggestion for a "new" curriculum.

Meanwhile, in schools and districts, from classrooms to grade levels to departments to central offices, local curriculum committees are hard at work on a dazzling array of projects that can hardly be said in one breath: outcome-based education, curriculum alignment, interdisciplinary instruction, integrated curriculum, authentic assessment, whole language, multicultural education, thematic teaching, and on and on. There are always some people who love a task of any kind, who thrive on ambiguity, who are willing to simply move from one idea to another. For them, such a flurry of curriculum activity is a pretty picture.

For many local educators, however, it is not. They wonder—and not without reason—what will be next year's topic, or maybe next week's. If they are going to spend time and energy on a project, they want to know that it will make some large and lasting difference, that it is not just a passing fad or some isolated activity that has no connection to a whole. These educators often feel that so many trends are like pieces of a jigsaw puzzle without a picture to guide them. Perhaps this metaphor can help us understand in our own terms how young people experience an incoherent curriculum.

The Meaning of Coherence in the Curriculum

A "coherent" curriculum is one that holds together, that makes sense as a whole; and its parts, whatever they are, are unified and connected by that sense of the whole. The idea of coherence begins with a view of the curriculum as a broadly conceived concept—as *the* curriculum—that is about "something." It is not simply a collection of disparate parts or pieces that accumulate in student experiences and on transcripts. A coherent curriculum has a sense of the forest as well as the trees, a sense of unity and connectedness, of relevance and pertinence. Parts or pieces are connected or integrated in ways that are visible and explicit. There is a sense of a larger, compelling purpose, and actions are tied to that purpose.

The idea of a coherent curriculum is not just another passing fad or this year's "hot topic." It is, in fact, one of the fundamental characteristics of a worthwhile curriculum. Think, for example, about the converse of the preceding definition. An "incoherent" curriculum is one whose parts do not hold together in any way; instead, they are disconnected and fragmented. It lacks a sense of unity, relevance, pertinence, or larger purpose. Actions are simply something people do, not necessarily for any clear or compelling purpose.

Such a stark and negative picture is not meant to imply that the curriculum in our schools is thoroughly incoherent. Rather, it is meant to point out what we want to avoid. At the same time, the negative picture suggests the importance of coherence in the curriculum and the urgency of the work before us. Moving toward a coherent curriculum offers possibilities of unity and connectedness among everyday activities in the school and educational experiences for young people that will make sense in terms of larger purposes.

This kind of coherence will open up possibilities for the integration of educational experiences (Hopkins and others 1937, Dressel 1958). That is, when the curriculum offers a sense of purpose, unity, relevance, and pertinence—when it is coherent—young people are more likely to integrate educational experiences into their schemes of meaning, which in turn broadens and deepens their understanding of themselves and the world. In that sense, we might say that a coherent curriculum is one that offers "unforgettable" experiences to young people. Lacking such coherence, the curriculum is likely to be little more than a smorgasbord of superficial, abstract, irrelevant, and quickly forgotten pieces.

Thus, the search for coherence does not mean simply clarifying purposes in the existing curriculum. Rather, it suggests that creating coherence involves connecting parts or pieces of the curriculum, identifying meaningful contexts for information and skills, and helping young people and adults to make sense of learning experiences. Such conditions, however, are never apart from the politics of curriculum. Moving toward coherence means confronting a variety of views about themes and purposes that might hold the curriculum together, as well as seeking widespread understanding of what the curriculum is about.

We will return to these issues later in considering what is involved in moving toward coherence in the curriculum. For the moment, however, we should realize that thinking about coherence in the curriculum raises several questions:

In what ways is the present curriculum incoherent?
How did it become incoherent?
How might the curriculum be made more coherent?
What might a coherent curriculum look like?
Who should be involved in making a coherent curriculum?

Conditions of Incoherence

Evidence abounds to show that our present curriculum is incoherent. For example, most schools offer a collection of subjects or courses of study that are separate and distinct entities. Their boundaries are virtually etched in stone by schedules, teacher loyalties, and organizational structures like departments, subject area committees, and subject-specific supervisors and chairpersons. The latter, as well as some teachers, define their roles in terms of specialized areas: "I am a language arts (or math, or music, or science, or art, or something else) teacher" or "I like to teach reading more than science."

According to the folklore of education, the problem of incoherence occurs only in middle and high schools. Indeed, these institutions are historical bastions of the separate subject approach, tracked programs, and other instances of fragmentation. Yet elementary schools offer their own version of such problems. After all, the self-contained classrooms in many elementary schools only thinly disguise a day divided into subject or skill time slots, instruction in a long variety of subskills, and specialized instruction in "nonacademic" subjects. And the move toward departmentalization is becoming increasingly popular in the upper elementary grades.

Across all levels of schooling, moreover, any specific or particular concern seems to require a separate program: technical for the supposedly linear and sequential, humanities for the arts, "advisory" for the emotional, academic for college preparation, vocational for work preparation, "exploratory" or "special" for the "nonacademic," and a myriad of thinking, reading, writing, self-esteem, and problem "prevention" programs. When new concerns arise, we simply add new programs with their own scheduling slots, space, specialized teachers, and, often, newly labeled students. In compartmentalizing the curriculum in these ways, we act on our own visions of the presumed fragmentation of knowledge, skill, and human activity.

Young people, too, are disassembled into a collection of disconnected parts. The brain is viewed as having differentiated parts for distinctive functions—one for reasoning, another for feeling, and so on—with relatively little communication among them, but each conveniently matched to a different type of school program. Affective, cognitive, and psychomotor dimensions are acted on in the school as if their differentiation in theoretical discussions were true in real life (Beane 1990).

Furthermore, our views of young people as learners are plagued by a sense that somehow the multidimensional roles in their lives can be differentiated. The well-known Supreme Court reminder that young people do not "leave their rights at the schoolhouse doors" hints at this kind of fragmentation. For example, educators have sought to sharpen their understanding of human growth by assigning "stages of development" to various age groups. While this has supported helpful work in the area of "developmentally appropriate practice," it has also obscured the fact that all young people, regardless of age, live in the larger world. Thus, they experience all of what that means in terms of affluence and poverty, cultural diversity and prejudice, justice and injustice, safety and danger, and so on. In short, their lives are more than just the characteristics associated with some stage of development. The tendency to freeze them in one stage or another not only denies their real lives, but describes only a fragment of young people as whole persons.

Expecting young people to suspend experiences in the larger world contributes to the incoherence that arises from the implication that what happens inside the school has little to do with what happens inside a young person. It is as if there were no out-of-school curriculum from which young people learn about themselves and their world. Worse yet, this perspective implies that the larger world has nothing to offer by way of the "pictures" that show how the pieces of the curriculum hold together.

But what about young people themselves? How does this look to them? Surely they must imagine that there is a reasonable explanation for the disconnection of school from life and the fragmented division of subjects, programs, skills, and activities into separate courses, periods, modules, time slots, tests, projects, worksheets, and so on. Yet they (and we) are nonplussed by the inadequate explanations we offer. Clearly, young people not only sense the incoherence of the curriculum, but know in some way that the incoherence does not make sense.

Isn't it about time that we recognized (or admitted) that the boundaries and categories that fragment the inner life of the school are socially constructed and largely artificial? They do not spring onto the scene from some mystical force. Academic scholars, for example, define the lines that "separate" disciplines of knowledge to secure space in their world and to ease communication among those with similar interests. As Michael Apple (1979, p. 38) has pointed out, "One major reason that subject-centered curricula dominate most schools, that integrated curricula are found in relatively few schools, is at least partly the result of the place of the school in maximizing the production of high status knowledge." Moreover, those who specialize in one or another particular area produce and promote special skill programs. Prevention programs result from interest groups concerned with their own interpretation of one or another particular personal or social problem. And across all of these, the arguments for space and priority in the curriculum have historically been much more about politics than about the quality of educational experiences for young people (Kliebard 1986, Popkewitz 1987, Goodson 1993).

Moving Toward a Coherent Curriculum

The idea of coherence in the curriculum is both compelling and complex and involves a number of issues: design, content, connections, and meaning. The purpose here is to lay out the grounds for these issues.

Subsequent chapters in this book discuss how such issues might be resolved through specific curriculum arrangements.

Coherence in the curriculum involves creating and maintaining visible connections between purposes and everyday learning experiences. When adults plan the curriculum, they have to decide not only what its purposes will be, but what kinds of learning experiences will lead toward those purposes. That those plans seem coherent to adults does not necessarily mean that young people will sense the same coherence. For this reason, young people are faced with the challenge of understanding the larger purposes of the curriculum, connecting particular learning experiences to those purposes and, all along the way, learning about the pieces themselves.

For example, we may say that we want our students to have a sense of the world in which they live, so we introduce statistics to help them understand certain patterns in that world. At every moment in our work on statistics, we risk disconnecting that work from the real world or, in other words, making it simply an abstract exercise in mathematics. The continuing challenge here is to persistently maintain the connection between the larger purpose and the specific activity. Young people also face the simultaneous challenge of learning about statistics, using that learning to broaden their understanding of the world, and continuously maintaining a sense of the connection between the activity and its purpose. Responding to those three challenges is clearly a crucial aspect of curriculum planning and teaching because it offers the possibility that young people will have a sense of what the curriculum is about as a whole.

Moving toward a coherent curriculum involves creating contexts that organize and connect learning experiences. When we are confronted with a problem or puzzling situation in real life, we hardly stop to think, "Which part is mathematics, which physical education, which science, which thinking, which valuing, and so on?" Rather, we sense the problem or situation and then bring to bear whatever we need to know or do without regard for the source. And, of course, if the problem or situation is compelling enough, we are moved to get needed knowledge or skills that we do not already have. Understood this way, knowledge and skills are organically integrated in real life, while their separation in school programs is an artificial and distracting arrangement. Curriculum talk, therefore, frequently includes references to the curriculum being organized around themes. The use of themes helps both adults and young people to see a context for their learning activities and to sense that those activities have some larger purpose.

The repositioning of learning experiences into meaningful contexts is the point of much of the current work on curriculum organization. That work, of course, has taken many different forms. For instance, intradisciplinary efforts bring together smaller pieces of content or skill that are actually parts of a larger discipline of knowledge but that have been disconnected by overspecialization in the curriculum. Here we might place the struggle to create "social studies" out of history, geography, civics, and other aspects of social living (Saxe 1992). Other intradisciplinary examples are the more recent whole language movement and projects in science and mathematics aimed at reconstituting the larger disciplines. A second example is multidisciplinary or multisubject arrangements that involve correlations among two or more areas (Jacobs 1989). In this increasingly popular arrangement, teachers select a theme like "Colonial Living" or "Metrics" from the existing curriculum and then ask what various subject areas might contribute to the theme. Or they might arrange the subjects around some appealing or popular topic like "Kites" or "Whales."

A third example is curriculum integration. Here themes are based on real-life personal issues faced by young people or major social problems like "Conflict" or "Environmental Problems." Knowledge and skills are integrated in the context of the theme and drawn from any pertinent source without regard for subject area lines. This approach blurs or dissolves the boundaries between subject areas or disciplines of knowledge.

A fourth form—actually a variation on the third—involves planning an integrated curriculum with a particular group of young people who themselves identify the issues and problem areas that cluster into themes (Beane 1991, 1993; Brodhagen, Weilbacher, and Beane 1992). This approach extends the jigsaw puzzle metaphor by asking, "Whose picture is it?" When we purchase a jigsaw puzzle, we don't just buy *any* puzzle. We go through the box covers looking for a picture that has meaning to the person who will put the puzzle together, either ourselves or others we know. After all, the work is made more or less enjoyable and compelling by the interest we have in the picture.

Although the term *curriculum integration* is currently used to describe all of these forms of nonseparate subject arrangements, its use with the first two is a relatively recent development. Historically, the term "integration" has most often been reserved for problem-centered themes that help students integrate educational experiences into their ongoing personal and social lives (Hopkins et al. 1937; Dressel 1958; Beane 1993). In short, "integration" was something that young people did for themselves, rather than a simple correlation of various subjects arranged by adults. For our purposes here, though, it is almost redundant to say that a coherent curriculum involves efforts to move beyond a separate subject-matter or skill-area approach and eventually toward more frequent use of integrated arrangements.

Thinking about a curriculum organized around themes, especially those associated with "integration," immediately raises questions about what happens to the content currently covered in schools and its presently conceived sequences. Advocates of thematic designs have taken great pains to demonstrate that they are not abandoning valued content but rather asking how it might be repositioned in the context of themes. But it is also possible that some content presently "covered," as well as subject-centered sequences, could be at risk. This is exactly the point partially made by the idea of coherence in the curriculum. That is, we are currently faced with a good deal of school-based content that is so disconnected from meaningful contexts that it defies clear meaning for anyone. In some cases, there appears to be no purpose beyond games of academic "trivial pursuit." The question before us is whether the concept of coherence is so crucial to worthwhile learning that we are willing to seriously reconsider the place of such content in the school.

It is important to note, however, that the development of a thematic curriculum is not simply a methodological challenge of connecting pieces of the curriculum. Such connections will promote coherence *only if they enhance the sense of purpose and meaning for young people.* Moreover, the matter of whether themes themselves are drawn from topics already found in the subject- centered curriculum, from real-life problems, or from some other source may well influence the degree to which young people find meaning in their learning experiences. And, as we shall see, it also has a great deal to do with the politics of curriculum.

Considering the importance of integration in relation to coherence, *moving toward a coherent curriculum must involve more fully exploring how people make sense out of experiences.* Students of all ages construct schemes of meaning about themselves and their world (Caine and Caine 1991). Such schemes are constructed out of experiences and are shaded by the influences of culture. So it is that any particular experience might have a variety of meanings among young people, depending on race, ethnicity, class, gender, geography, age, family patterns, and many other cultural aspects. Such aspects of cultural diversity may also serve as a kind of "glue" for piecing together experiences to create the "pictures" that are schemes of meaning. In short, the continuous interplay between experience and meaning is a crucial dimension of a sense of coherence. Iran-Nejad, McKeachie, and Berliner put it this way: "The more meaningful, the more deeply or elaboratively processed, the more situated in context, and the more rooted in cultural, background, metacognitive, and personal knowledge an event is, the more readily it is understood, learned, and remembered" (1990, p. 511).

Understanding this leads us toward two final considerations in creating a coherent curriculum. One is that if the curriculum is to be coherent for young people, it must connect with their *present* experiences. This means that the themes or ideas that hold the curriculum together must make space for young people to find points of personal engagement. That is, the curriculum must have room for their own questions, concerns, aspirations, and interests. We may construct glamorous and clever curriculum designs with the most fascinating activities we can imagine; but in the end, if we don't allow room for personal connections, our curriculum will remain remote, superfluous, and incoherent.

Second, a coherent curriculum must account for who young people are. The diverse dimensions of culture are not simply abstract categories in schools. In very concrete ways, young people bring the entire range to school. It is unlikely that adults who also present a range of cultural diversity can construct a curriculum that will have the same meaning for all young people. A coherent curriculum recognizes and honors diversity and ambiguity. By definition, then, our search for coherence is not a search for a single, magical curriculum neatly bound in a three-ring binder or attractive textbook. Instead, it is a "messy" exploration of the ways in which diverse people connect, organize, and make sense out of their experiences.

The Politics of Coherence

The discussion to this point has focused on issues such as organization and design that we might say are "internal" to the process of curriculum planning. These are, of course, crucial to the possibility of moving toward a coherent curriculum. However, as noted earlier, these issues are never apart from the politics of curriculum. After all, curriculum planning is something that is done by real people; and the same diversity among them that enriches the range of meanings also involves tensions and disagreements over purposes, organization, and processes in the curriculum.

The search for coherence involves long-standing issues in the politics of curriculum because it must involve decisions about what ideas or themes will hold the curriculum together. The question of what the "glue" is raises other questions, such as "*Whose* glue is it?" and "Who decides *what* the glue is?" Classical Humanists typically advocate a curriculum of separate, discrete subjects and mastery of what is contained within them (King and Brownell 1966). Such theory asserts that inherent and "ageless" concepts like truth and beauty (Adler 1982) hold these separate subjects together. Religious fundamentalists speak of coherence in terms of a curriculum that is permeated by sectarian values and interpretations that are always based on their own religious beliefs. Those who want the curriculum tied to economic ends would create coherence by continuously placing learning experiences in the context of utilitarian needs of business and industry. And progressives who are interested in democratic schools often call for a curriculum that is held together by contemporary social issues and the instrumental uses of knowledge and skill to take on those issues. Their claims for coherence are grounded in the real-life sources of those issues, their compelling significance, and the use of those issues as contexts for knowledge and skill.

Equally important as naming such differences is noting that the Conservative Restoration of the 1980s has limited the grounds for curriculum conversation mostly to the claims of Classical Humanists, fundamentalist religious demands, and economic interests and has limited the debate over differences to finding overlaps among those three (Apple 1993). Meanwhile, despite its close match with the conditions of coherence, the progressive view has been virtually deleted from curriculum conversations. Thus, the politics of curriculum fragmentation complicate the move toward coherence, especially because that move will require us to reclaim a wider range of views and to seek more than the not-so-peaceful co-existence they presently occupy in the curriculum.

The issue of coherence in the curriculum is multilayered in that the curriculum is experienced by many different groups: young people, teachers, administrators, parents, school boards, and the community at large. While absolutely essential, it is not sufficient to raise the issue of coherence only in terms of the perceptions of young people. The central location of the school as a primary social institution means that even though young people are its initial concern, the curriculum ought to have coherent meaning for others as well. Specifically, those most closely involved with the schools—professional educators—ought to be able to explain the curriculum without resorting to slick campaigns, public relations gimmicks, or esoteric language. Of course, this requires that they themselves have some coherent understanding of what the curriculum is about. Furthermore, silencing the voices of those outside the profession, including young people, when discussing the curriculum only detracts from the possibility for widely understood meaning and is just as much at issue here as is coherence within the curriculum itself.

However, as we concern ourselves with a multilayered understanding of how the curriculum is coherent, we must be careful not to confuse coherence with the more narrow idea of consistency (Buchman and Floden 1992). Much of what has passed for curriculum work in this century has been about the desire for consistency and control. Attempts to align objectives and tests, to mimic work subskills in vocational courses, to identify uniform courses and content, and to design sequential skill "maps" are but a few examples of the obsession with consistency. Moreover, much of the current talk about a national curriculum and tests, as well as that about "tech prep" programs, is but the latest in a long line of such examples. Though the search for coherence does not completely reject the desire for consistency, it has more to do with a sense of wholeness, meaning, and connectedness, while accepting the presence of contradictions, tensions, ambiguity, and diversity.

Distinguishing between coherence and consistency brings us back to the issue of whom the "coherence" is ultimately for. The previous examples of searching for consistency clearly emerge from a perceived need among adults. Consistency of school programs with college expectations, alignment of objectives and tests, and uniform and sequential subject designs have much more to do with the need for institutional order and political slogans than with the quality of learning experiences. Worse yet, it is quite possible to develop highly sophisticated schemes of consistency without creating coherence; we can systematize, align, and sequence all kinds of things without their necessarily making any kind of sense for young people.

Finally, the idea of a coherent curriculum is tied to the long-standing tension between general and specialized education. When we consider what ideas or themes might hold the curriculum together, we confront the question of whether to draw them from common, widely shared concerns or focus on specialized interests or aspirations. Advocates of the separate-subject curriculum, for example, claim that their approach has meaning in relation to the subject specialization found in higher education or academic occupations. Religious fundamentalists may claim meaning for their version of education in relation to their narrow sectarian interests. And young people may insist that nothing has meaning outside of some personal hobby or aspiration. Yet each, in turn, involves increasing specialization that fragments individuals and reduces the curriculum to little more than self-interest.

The idea of coherence, on the other hand, seeks unity and connectedness on all fronts, not only among parts of the curriculum but among those who experience it. The sense of meaning to which coherence refers is, therefore, based on widely shared concerns in the larger society that the schools serve. In other words, particular curriculum arrangements may make sense to young people or one or another special-interest group but may not be sensible in terms of larger educational purposes. It is here, finally, that we may understand that coherence in the curriculum is not simply a methodological issue. It is a philosophical one as well.

The issues raised here are only some of those that are involved in thinking about a coherent curriculum. Yet they illustrate how important and complex such thinking is. And they hint at the politics and tensions that often arise—not the least of which is resistance from those who have deep loyalties to particular pieces of an incoherent curriculum and who may see the move toward coherence as a threat of territorial invasion.

Leaving these tensions for later "commentaries" in this book, we turn next to descriptions of some of the most widely known ideas and projects aimed at creating and sustaining curriculum coherence. Many readers will find here ideas and examples that are familiar in their own schools. That is fully expected because attempts at curriculum coherence, although not necessarily so named, have been of increasing interest among educators. Thus, these chapters may serve the important purpose of showing how to bring many of those very attempts into a coherent focus. For those who have not yet considered the crucial problem of curriculum incoherence, these chapters will undoubtedly offer a challenging set of ideas to consider.

References

Adler, M. (1982). *The Paideia Proposal.* New York: Macmillan.

Apple, M. (1979). *Ideology and Curriculum.* London and Boston: Routledge and Kegan Paul.

Apple, M. (1993). *Official Knowledge: Democratic Education in a Conservative Age.* New York and London: Routledge.

Beane, J. (1990). *Affect in the Curriculum: Toward Democracy, Dignity, and Diversity.* New York: Teachers College Press.

Beane, J. (October 1991). "The Middle School: Natural Home of Integrated Curriculum." *Educational Leadership* 49, 2: 9–13.

Beane, J. (1993). *A Middle School Curriculum: From Rhetoric to Reality.* 2d ed. Columbus, Ohio: National Middle School Association.

Brodhagen, B., G. Weilbacher, and J. Beane. (June 1992). "Living in the Future: An Experiment with an Integrative Curriculum." *Dissemination Services on the Middle Grades* 23, 9: 1–7.

Buchman, M., and R. Floden. (December 1992). "Coherence, the Rebel Angel." *Educational Researcher* 21, 9: 4–9.

Caine, R., and G. Caine. (1991). *Making Connections: Teaching and the Human Brain.* Alexandria, Va.: ASCD.

Dressel, P. (1958). "The Meaning and Significance of Integration." In *The Integration of Educational Experiences,* edited by N. Henry. Chicago: University of Chicago Press.

Goodson, I. (1993). *School Subjects and Curriculum Change.* Philadelphia, Pa.: Falmer.

Hopkins, L.T., and others. (1937). *Integration: Its Meaning and Application*. New York: D. Appleton-Century.

Iran-Nejad, A., W. McKeachie, and D. Berliner. (Winter 1990). "The Multisource Nature of Learning: An Introduction." *Review of Educational Research* 60, 4: 509–515.

Jacobs, H.H., ed. (1989). *Interdisciplinary Curriculum*. Alexandria, Va.: ASCD.

King, A., and J. Brownell. (1966). *The Curriculum and the Disciplines of Knowledge*. New York: John Wiley.

Kliebard, H. (1986). *The Struggle for the American Curriculum: 1893–1958*. Boston and London: Routledge and Kegan Paul.

Popkewitz, T., ed. (1987). *The Formation of School Subjects: The Struggle for Creating an American Institution*. New York: Falmer.

Saxe, D. (Fall 1992). Framing a Theory for Social Studies Foundations. *Review of Educational Research* 62, 3: 259–277.

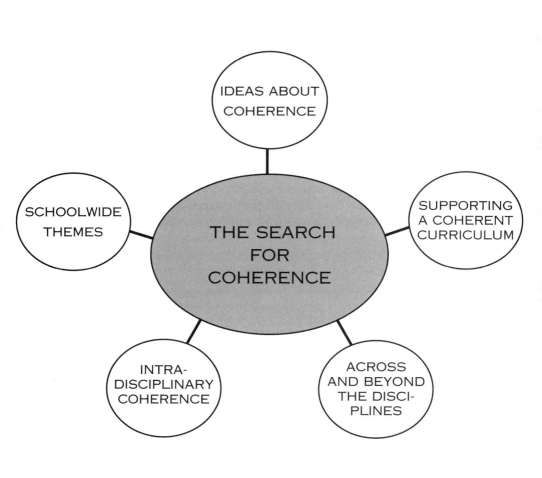

2

The Educated Person

Ernest L. Boyer

A s we anticipate a new century, I am drawn back to questions that have, for generations, perplexed educators and philosophers and parents. What *is* an educated person? What *should* schools be teaching to students?

In searching for answers to these questions, we must consider first not the curriculum, but the human condition. And we must reflect especially on two essential realities of life. First, each person is unique. In defining goals, it is crucial for educators to affirm the special characteristics of each student. We must create in schools a climate in which students are empowered, and we must find ways in the nation's classrooms to celebrate the potential of each child. But beyond the diversity of individuals, educators also must acknowledge a second reality: the deeply rooted characteristics that bind together the human community. We must show students that people around the world share a great many experiences. Attention to both these aspects of our existence is critical to any discussion of what all children should learn.

What, then, does it mean to be an educated person? It means developing one's own aptitudes and interests and discovering the diversity that makes us each unique. And it means becoming permanently empowered with language proficiency, general knowledge, social confidence, and moral awareness in order to be economically and civically successful. But becoming well educated also means discovering the connectedness of things. Educators must help students see relationships across the disciplines and learn that education is a communal act, one that affirms not only individualism, but community. And for these goals to be accomplished, we need a new curriculum framework that is both comprehensive and coherent, one that can encompass existing subjects and integrate fragmented content while relating the curriculum to the realities of life. This curriculum must address the uniqueness of students' histories and experiences, but it also must guide them to understand the many ways that humans are connected.

Some schools and teachers are aiming to fully educate students, but most of us have a very long way to go in reaching this goal. Today, almost all students in U.S. schools still complete Carnegie units in exchange for a diploma. The time has come to bury the old Carnegie unit; since the Foundation I now head created this unit of academic measure nearly a century ago, I feel authorized to declare it obsolete. Why? Because it has helped turn schooling into an exercise in trivial pursuit. Students get academic "credit," but they fail to gain a coherent view of what they study. Education is measured by seat time, not time for learning. While curious young children still ask why things are, many older children ask only, "Will this be on the test?" All students should be encouraged to ask "Why?" because "Why?" is the question that leads students to connections.

In abandoning the Carnegie unit, I do not endorse the immediate adoption of national assessment programs; indeed, I think we must postpone such programs until we are much clearer about what students should be learning. The goal, again, is not only to help students become well informed and prepared for lifelong learning, but also to help them put learning into the larger context of discovering the connectedness of things. Barbara McClintock, the 1983 winner of the Nobel Prize for Physiology–Medicine, asserts: "Everything is one. There is no way to draw a line between things." Contrary to McClintock's vision, the average school or college catalog dramatizes the separate academic boxes.

Frank Press, president of the National Academy of Sciences, compares scientists to artists, evoking the magnificent double helix, which broke the genetic code. He said the double helix is not only rational, but beautiful. Similarly, when scientists and technicians watch the countdown to a space launch, they don't say, "Our formulas worked again." They respond, "Beautiful!" instinctively reaching for the aesthetic term to praise a technological achievement. When physicist Victor Weisskopf was asked, "What gives you hope in troubled times?" he replied, "Mozart and quantum mechanics." Most schools, however, separate science and art, discouraging students from seeing the connections between them.

How, then, can we help students see relationships and patterns and gain understanding beyond the separate academic subjects? How can we rethink the curriculum and use the disciplines to illuminate larger, more integrated ends?

Human Commonalities

In the 1981 book *A Quest for Common Learning,* I suggested that we might organize the curriculum not on the basis of disciplines or departments, but on the basis of "core commonalities." By core commonalities, I mean universal experiences that make us human, experiences shared by all cultures on the planet. During the past decade and a half, my thinking about this thematic structure has continued to evolve. I now envision eight commonalities that bind us to one another.

I. The Life Cycle. As life's most fundamental truth, we share, first, the experience that connects birth, growth, and death. This life cycle binds each of us to the others, and I find it sad that so many students go through life without reflecting on the mystery of their own existence. Many complete twelve or sixteen years of formal schooling not considering the sacredness of their own bodies, not learning to sustain wellness, not pondering the imperative of death.

In reshaping the curriculum to help students see connections, I would position study of "The Life Cycle" at the core of common learning. Attention would go to nutrition, health, and all aspects of wellness. For a project, each student would undertake the care of some life form.

My wife is a certified nurse-midwife who delivers babies, including seven grandchildren of our own. Kay feels special pain when delivering the baby of a teenage girl because she knows that she is delivering one child into the arms of another, and that both have all too often lived for nine months on soda and potato chips. Some young mothers first learn about the birth process between the sharp pains of labor.

Too many young women and young men pass through our process of education without learning about their own bodies. Out of ignorance, they suffer poor nutrition, addiction, and violence. "Maintaining children's good health is a shared responsibility of parents, schools, and the community at large," according to former Secretary of Education William Bennett (1986, p. 37). He urges elementary schools "to provide children with the knowledge, habits, and attitudes that will equip them for a fit and healthy life."

Study of the Life Cycle would encourage students to reflect sensitively on the mystery of birth and growth and death, to learn about body functions and thus understand the role of choice in wellness, to carry some of their emotional and intellectual learning into their relations with others, and to observe, understand, and respect a variety of life forms.

II. Language. Each life on the planet turns to symbols to express feelings and ideas. After a first breath, we make sounds as a way of reaching out to others, connecting with them. We develop a variety of languages: the language of words (written and spoken), the language of symbols (mathematics, codes, sign systems), and the language of the arts (aesthetic expressions in language, music, paint, sculpture, dance, theater, craft, and so on). A quality education develops proficiency in the written and the spoken word, as well as a useful knowledge of mathematical symbol systems and an understanding that the arts provide countless ways to express ourselves.

Our sophisticated use of language sets human beings apart from all other forms of life. Through the created words and symbols and arts, we connect to one another. Consider the miracle of any moment. One person vibrates his or her vocal cords. Molecules shoot in the direction of listeners. They hit the tympanic membrane; signals go scurrying up the eighth cranial nerve. From that series of events, the listener feels a response deep in the cerebrum that approximates the images in the mind of the speaker. Because of its power and scope, language is the means by which all other subjects are pursued.

The responsible use of language demands both *accuracy* and *honesty*, so students studying "Language" must also learn to consider the ethics of communication. Students live in a world where obscenities abound. They live in a world where politicians use sixty-second sound bites to destroy integrity. They live in a world where clichés substitute for reason. To make their way in this world, students must learn to distinguish between deceit and authenticity in language.

Writers and mathematicians have left a long and distinguished legacy for students to learn from. Through words, each child can express something personal. Through symbols, each child can increase the capacity to calculate and reason. Through the arts, each child can express a thought or a feeling. People need to write with clarity, read with comprehension, speak effectively, listen with understanding, compute accurately, and understand the communicative capabilities of the arts. Education for the next century means helping students understand that language in all its forms is a powerful and sacred trust.

III. The Arts. All people on the planet respond to the aesthetic. Dance, music, painting, sculpture, and architecture are languages understood around the world. "Art represents a social necessity that no nation can neglect without endangering its intellectual existence," said John Ruskin (Rand 1993). We all know how art can affect us. Salvador Dali's painting *The Persistence of Memory* communicates its meaning to anyone ever haunted by time passing. The gospel song "Amazing Grace" stirs people from both Appalachia and Manhattan. "We Shall Overcome," sung in slow and solemn cadence, invokes powerful feelings regardless of the race or economic status of singer or audience.

Archaeologists examine the artifacts of ancient civilization—pottery, cave paintings, and musical instruments—to determine the attainments and quality of a culture. As J. Carter Brown (1986) observes, "The texts of man's achievements are not written exclusively in words. They are written, as well, in architecture, paintings, sculpture, drawing, photography, and in urban, graphic, landscape, and industrial design."

Young children understand that the arts are language. Before they learn to speak, they respond intuitively to dance, music, and color. The arts also help children who are disabled. I once taught deaf children, who couldn't speak because they couldn't hear. But through painting, sculpture, movement, and rhythm, they found new ways to communicate.

Every child has the urge and capacity to be expressive. It is tragic that for most children the universal language of the arts is suppressed, then destroyed, in the early years of learning, because traditional teaching does not favor self- expression and school boards consider art a frill. This is an ironic deprivation when the role of art in developing critical thinking is becoming more widely recognized.

Jacques d'Amboise, former principal dancer with the New York City Ballet, movie star, and founder of the National Dance Institute, offers his view on how art fits into education: "I would take the arts, science and sports, or play, and make all education involve all of them. It would be similar to what kindergarten does, only more sophisticated, right through life. All of the disciplines would be interrelated. You dance to a poem: poetry is meter, meter is time, time is science" (Ames and Peyser 1990).

For our most moving experiences, we turn to the arts to express feelings and ideas that words cannot convey. The arts are, as one poet has put it, "the language of the angels." To be truly educated means being sensitively responsive to the universal language of art.

IV. *Time and Space*. While we are all nonuniform and often seem dramatically different from one another, all of us have the capacity to place ourselves in time and space. We explore our place through geography and astronomy. We explore our sense of time through history.

And yet, how often we squander this truly awesome capacity for exploration, neglecting even our personal roots. Looking back in my own life, my most important mentor was Grandpa Boyer, who lived to be one hundred. Sixty years before that, Grandpa moved his little family into the slums of Dayton, Ohio. He then spent the next forty years running a city mission, working for the poor, teaching me more by deed than by word that to be truly human, one must serve. For far too many children, the influence of such intergenerational models has diminished or totally disappeared.

Margaret Mead said that the health of any culture is sustained when three generations are vitally interacting with one another—a "vertical culture" in which the different age groups are connected. Yet in America today we've created a "horizontal culture," with each generation living alone. Infants are in nurseries, toddlers are in day care, older children are in schools organized by age. College students are isolated on campuses. Adults are in the workplace. And older citizens are in retirement villages, living and dying all alone.

For several years, my own parents chose to live in a retirement village where the average age was eighty. But this village had a day-care center, too, and all the three- and four- year-olds had adopted grandparents to meet with every day. The two generations quickly became friends. When I called my father, he didn't talk about his aches and pains, he talked about his little friend. And when I visited, I saw that my father, like any proud grandparent, had the child's drawings taped to the wall. As I watched the two of them together, I was struck by the idea that there is something really special about a four-year-old seeing the difficulty and courage of growing old. And I was struck, too, by watching an eighty-year-old being informed and inspired by the energy and innocence of a child. Exposure to such an age difference surely increases the understanding of time and personal history.

The time has come to break up the age ghettos. It is time to build intergenerational institutions that bring together the old and young. I'm impressed by the "grandteacher" programs in the schools, for example. In the new core curriculum, with a strand called "Time and Space," students should discover their own roots and complete an oral history. But beyond their own extended family, all students should also become well informed about the influence of the culture that surrounds them and learn about the traditions of other cultures.

A truly educated person will see connections by placing his or her life in time and space. In the days ahead, students should study *Western* civilization to understand our past, and they should study *non-Western* cultures to understand our present and our future.

V. Groups and Institutions. All people on the planet belong to groups and institutions that shape their lives. Nearly 150 years ago, Ralph Waldo Emerson observed, "We do not make a world of our own, but rather fall into institutions already made and have to accommodate ourselves to them." Every society organizes itself and carries on its work through social interaction that varies from one culture to another.

Students must be asked to think about the groups of which they are members, how they are shaped by those groups, and how they help to shape them. Students need to learn about the social web of our existence, about family life, about how governments function, about the informal social structures that surround us. They also must discover how life in groups varies from one culture to another.

Civic responsibility also must be taught. The school itself can be the starting point for this education, serving as a "working model" of a healthy society in microcosm that bears witness to the ideals of community. Within the school, students should feel "enfranchised." Teachers, administrators, and staff should meet often to find their *own* relationship to the institution of the school. And students should study groups in their own community, finding out about local government.

One of my sons lives in a Mayan village in the jungle of Belize. When my wife and I visit Craig each year, I'm impressed that Mayans and Americans live and work in very similar ways. The jungle of Manhattan and the one of Belize are separated by a thousand miles and a thousand years, and yet the Mayans, just like us, have their family units. They have elected leaders, village councils, law enforcement officers, jails, schools, and places to worship. Life there is both different and very much the same. Students in the United States should be introduced to institutions in our own culture and in other cultures, so they might study, for example, both Santa Cruz, California, and Santa Cruz, Belize.

We all belong to many groups. Exploring their history and functions helps students understand the privileges and the responsibilities that belong to each of us.

VI. Work. We all participate, for much of our lives, in the commonality of work. As Thoreau reminds us, we both "live" and "get a living." Regardless of differences, all people on the planet produce and consume. A quality education will help students understand and prepare for the world of work. Unfortunately, our own culture has become too preoccupied with *consuming*, too little with the tools for *producing*. Children may see their parents leave the house carrying briefcases or lunch pails in the morning and see them come home again in the evening, but do they know what parents actually do during the day?

Jerome Bruner (1971) asks: "Could it be that in our stratified and segmented society, our students simply do not know about local grocers and their styles, local doctors and their styles, local taxi drivers and theirs, local political activists and theirs? . . . I would urge that we find some way of connecting the diversity of the society to the phenomenon of school" (p. 7). A new, integrative curriculum for the schools needs to give attention to "Producing and Consuming," with each student studying simple economics, different money systems, vocational studies, career planning, how work varies from one culture to another, and with each completing a work project to gain a respect for craftsmanship.

Several years ago when Kay and I were in China, we were told about a student who had defaced the surface of his desk. As punishment, he spent three days in the factory where the desks were made, helping the woodworkers, observing the effort involved. Not surprisingly, the student never defaced another desk.

When I was Chancellor of the State University of New York, I took my youngest son, then eight, to a cabin in the Berkshires for the weekend. My goal: to build a dock. All day, instead of playing, Stephen sat by the lake, watching me work. As we drove home, he looked pensive. After several miles, he said, "Daddy, I wish you'd grown up to be a carpenter—instead of you-know-what!"

VII. Natural World. Though all people are different, we are all connected to the earth in many ways. David, my grandson in Belize, lives these connections as he chases birds, bathes in the river, and watches corn being picked, pounded into tortillas, and heated outdoors. But David's cousins in Boston and Princeton spend more time with appliances, asphalt roadways, and precooked food. For them, discovering connectedness to nature does not come so naturally.

When I was United States Commissioner of Education, Joan Cooney, the brilliant creator of *Sesame Street*, told me that she and her colleagues at Children's Television Workshop wanted to start a new program on science and technology for junior high school kids. They wanted young people to learn a little more about their world and what they must understand as part of living. Funds were raised, and *3–2–1 Contact* went on the air. To prepare scripts, staff surveyed junior high school kids in New York City, asking questions such as "Where does water come from?"—which brought from some students the disturbing reply, "The faucet." They asked, "Where does light come from?" and heard, "The switch." And they asked, "Where does garbage go?" "Down the chute." These students' sense of connectedness stopped at the VCR or refrigerator door.

Canadian geneticist David Suzuki, host of *The Nature of Things*, says: "We ought to be greening the school yard, breaking up the asphalt and concrete. . . . We have to give children hand-held lenses, classroom aquariums and terrariums, lots of field trips, organic garden plots on the school grounds, butterfly gardens, trees. Then insects, squirrels—maybe even raccoons and rabbits—will show up, even in the city. We've got to reconnect those kids, and we've got to do it very early. . . . Our challenge is to reconnect children to their natural curiosity" (Baron Estes 1993).

With all our differences, each of us is inextricably connected to the natural world. During their days of formal learning, students should explore this commonality by studying the principles of science, by discovering the shaping power of technology, and, above all, by learning that survival on this planet means respecting and preserving the earth we share.

VIII. Search for Meaning. Regardless of heritage or tradition, each person searches for some larger purpose. We all seek to give special meaning to our lives. Reinhold Niebuhr said, "Man cannot be whole unless he be committed, he cannot find himself, unless he find a purpose beyond himself." We all need to examine values and beliefs, and develop convictions.

During my study of the American high school, I became convinced ours is less a school problem and more a youth problem. Far too many teenagers feel unwanted, unneeded, and unconnected. Without guidance and direction, they soon lose their sense of purpose—even their sense of wanting purpose.

Great teachers allow their lives to express their values. They are matchless guides as they give the gift of opening truths about themselves to their students. I often think of three or four teachers, out of the many I have worked with, who changed my life. What made them truly great? They were well informed. They could relate their knowledge to students. They created an active, not passive, climate for learning. More than that, they were authentic human beings who taught their subjects and were open enough to teach about themselves.

Service projects instill values. All students should complete a community service project, working in day-care centers and retirement villages or tutoring other students at school. The North Carolina School of Science and Math develops an ethos of responsible citizenship. To be admitted, a child must commit to sixty hours of community service per summer and three hours per week during the school year (Beach 1992, p. 56).

Martin Luther King, Jr., preached: "Everyone can be great because everyone can serve." I'm convinced the young people of this country want inspiration from this kind of larger vision, whether they come across it in a book or in person, or whether they find it inside themselves.

Values, Beliefs, and Connections

What, then, does it mean to be an educated person? It means respecting the miracle of life, being empowered in the use of language, and responding sensitively to the aesthetic. Being truly educated means putting learning in historical perspective, understanding groups and institutions, having reverence for the natural world, and affirming the dignity of work. And, above all, being an educated person means being guided by values and beliefs and connecting the lessons of the classroom to the realities of life. These are the core competencies that I believe replace the old Carnegie units.

And all of this can be accomplished as schools focus not on seat time, but on students involved in true communities of learning. I realize that remarkable changes must occur for this shift in goals to take place, but I hope deeply that in the century ahead students will be judged not by their performance on a single test but by the quality of their lives. It is my hope that students in the classrooms of tomorrow will be encouraged to create more than conform, and to cooperate more than compete. Each student deserves to see the world clearly and in its entirety and to be inspired by both the beauty and the challenges that surround us all.

Above all, I pray that Julie and David, my granddaughter in Princeton and my grandson in Belize, along with all other children on the planet, will grow to understand that they belong to the same human family, the family that connects us all.

Fifty years ago, Mark Van Doren wrote, "The connectedness of things is what the educator contemplates to the limit of his capacity." The student, he says, who can begin early in life to see things as connected has begun the life of learning. This, it seems to me, is what it means to be an educated person.

References

Ames, Katrine, and Marc Peyser. (Fall/Winter 1990). "Why Jane Can't Draw (or Sing, or Dance . . .)." *Newsweek* Special Edition: 40–49.

Baron Estes, Yvonne. (May 1993). "Environmental Education: Bringing Children and Nature Together." *Phi Delta Kappan* 74, 9: K2.

Beach, Waldo. (1992). *Ethical Education in American Public Schools.* Washington, D.C.: National Education Association.

Bennett, William J. (1986). *First Lessons.* Washington, D.C.: U.S. Department of Education.

Boyer, Ernest L. (1981). *A Quest for Common Learning: The Aims of General Education.* Washington, D.C.: Carnegie Foundation for the Advancement of Teaching.

Brown, J. Carter. (November/December 1983). "Excellence and the Problem of Visual Literacy." *Design for Arts in Education* 84, 3.

Bruner, Jerome. (November 1971). "Process of Education Reconsidered." An address presented before the 16th Annual Conference of the Association for Supervision and Curriculum Development.

Rand, Paul. (May 2, 1993). "Failure by Design," *The New York Times,* p. E19.

3

A Supradisciplinary Curriculum

Marion Brady

A few days ago, an algebra-teaching friend of mine heard a familiar question from that legendary voice at the back of the classroom: "What good," it asked, "will quadratic equations do me?"

"I don't know," she answered, "but isn't solving them fun?"

My friend told the story with a hint of pride. She obviously felt her response was an effective put-down.

A good many teachers share my friend's educational perspective. Wrapped up in their disciplines, they find their work inherently satisfying. That what they teach has little bearing on real life doesn't much concern them. Algebra, world history, chemistry, government—the courses are in the catalog. From that fact, all else—books, lectures, demonstrations, homework, exams—follows automatically.

Most teachers, of course, can offer some sort of rationale for the study of their fields. My friend believes that studying algebra is "good for the mind." Pressed, she might even be able to lay out a scenario in which solutions to quadratic equations came to someone's rescue. But an objective observer of education in the United States would surely conclude that much of what takes place in our classrooms is ritual. If we ask ourselves, "Does this help me make more sense of my experience?" the answer is, "No."

Consider the apparent complexity of my immediate reality. Asked to describe it, I'd probably say, "I'm sitting at my computer, trying to write a piece for the 1995 ASCD Yearbook."

This is true, but not a thorough description. "Sitting at my computer, trying to write" doesn't begin to encompass what's happening here at this moment. I touch the keys on my computer keyboard. Switches close, the closings are converted into a data pattern inside the keyboard, the coded signal passes through a cable to the computer, the computer interprets the code, stores it as the next item in a sequence in memory, and generates a character pattern for the monitor. This character pattern passes through another cable where it turns an electron beam off and on. When the beam is on it stimulates a phosphor coating on the back of my monitor screen, making it glow.

I've still hardly scratched the surface of what's happening. As I write, I glance beyond the monitor, out a window, past the branches of a hickory tree, across the Indian River. A mile out, a tug is pushing a fuel oil barge up the Intracoastal Waterway toward an electrical generating plant a few miles north. I stop thinking about what I'm writing and wonder for perhaps the fiftieth time how long it takes the bow wave of a vessel in the Waterway to reach my dock. My thoughts move from that to the generating plant where the oil will be burned. Decades-old memories return of Babcock and Wilcox boilers and General Electric steam turbines and generators in an electrical generating plant in Ohio where I once worked.

I think, momentarily, about the oil being converted to heat to produce steam to power turbines to rotate generators to generate electricity to come back down transmission lines along U.S. Route 1 to power my computer. "Up the river, back down the road." Sounds like a country music song title, I think, as a Regulator clock in another part of the house strikes nine times.

That's still only a small part of my immediate reality. I wasn't conscious of it as I wrote those paragraphs, but part of my experience was the room's temperature and humidity, the faint throb of the tug's diesel engines, the angling of the sun through the open, river-facing windows, a lingering taste in my mouth of a sip of tea . . . .

How do I begin to understand—make coherent—such varied experience? We make sense of experience by breaking it into intellectually manageable pieces, pieces we call occurrences, events, incidents, accidents, happenings, movements, situations, things, actions, eras, ages, this moment. When we want to be more specific, we give these parts of reality more precise conceptual labels—call them wars, volcanic activity, elections, chemical reactions, marriages, writing articles. When we want to be even more specific, we name the parts: The Battle of Bull Run, Mount Saint Helens' eruption, Woodrow Wilson's margin of victory, the World Trade Center bombing, "that Charles and Di thing," a piece for the 1995 ASCD Yearbook called "A Supradisciplinary Curriculum."

That done—the "what" identified—we fill in the picture with answers to the other four simple questions high school journalism students know so well: Who was involved? When did it happen? Where? Why? Understanding a particular experience, making it coherent, requires information about (a) time, (b) environment, (c) participants, (d) action, and (e) motive (if humans are involved). These five areas, and the relationships between them, are a *supradiscipline:* an integrated conceptual structure encompassing and organizing not merely all that lies within the boundaries of the disciplines, but all reality. A particular experience seems coherent only when we've acquired, at a useful level of generality, information about each of our supradiscipline's major categories.

Pedants may prefer the same idea in different words: There is a perception of coherence in the elements of a particular segment of reality when, in relation to that segment, data are presented that (1) provide an image of a milieu sufficiently detailed to identify its component elements' relationship to events occurring within it, (2) identify actors on the basis of their action(s) and cognitive state(s) within the segment of reality, (3) posit or imply actor cognitive state(s) leading to meaningful actor action, (4) describe actual physical behavior growing out of or consistent with actor cognitive state, and (5) fix the whole in appropriate time parameters. The criterion for inclusion of any particular element or characteristic of milieu, actor, cognitive state, or action in an account of a particular segment of reality is the extent of that element's or characteristic's systemic relationship to other elements in the system, the question being whether or not that relationship is sufficient to cause change, and if so, to what degree, in one or more of those elements.

In other, much simpler words: Experience is coherent when we know who did what, when, where, and why.

Figure 3.1 shows a supradisciplinary view of reality, which makes a natural base for the general education curriculum.

Figure 3.1
Supradisciplinary View of Reality

REALITY: OCCURENCES, EVENTS, INCIDENTS, ACCIDENTS, ETC.

Some will think I'm belaboring the obvious; others, that I'm laying out an approach to curriculum at a level of sophistication appropriate only for small children. Nothing could be further from the facts. The overarching purpose of education is to make sense of human experience. "Making sense" means expanding our awareness of patterns, structures, and relationships of, within, and between elements of reality. We perceive reality as having five distinct elements, each of which exhibits myriad patterns that we sense and convert into a mental model of reality. As shown in Figure 3.1, these five elements are environment, actors, action, thought, and time. Each is a starting point for an incredibly vast conceptual framework, a framework that encompasses and organizes everything we know. The exploration of possible relationships between components of this framework is the basic process underlying the expansion of human knowledge.

When I say that each of the five is a starting point for a vast conceptual framework, I mean nothing esoteric. For example, in our attempt to understand the environment, we use the concepts "primary" and "secondary." If we move out from the primary conceptual branch, climate is one of a half-dozen or so further branchings. Climate, in turn, has its own elaborate system of branches, of which wind is one. One of wind's many conceptual branchings is trade winds, and one of trade winds' branchings is direction. All concepts related to the environment—thousands upon thousands of them—are thus organized and related. Figure 3.2 shows this idea in graphic form.

Figure 3.2
Examples of Conceptual Branchings

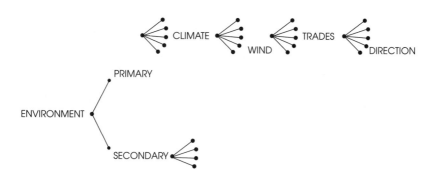

The conceptual branching of reality that begins with environment, actors, action, thought, and time encompasses all reality. Nothing that's now being taught in any classroom in America falls outside the boundaries of the conceptual framework. Nothing about which we know is excluded.

But human experience can't be made coherent merely by labeling its parts, locating them on a conceptual framework, and studying them in isolation. The interactions *between* the parts and the resultant systemic changes must be explored. If, for example, the direction of trade winds affects the growing season, the growing season affects crop yields, crop yields affect levels of wealth, levels of wealth affect economic patterns, economic patterns affect political institutions, and political institutions affect who lives and who dies, it follows that this string of relationships is important and should be understood. If ideas about causation affect medical research initiatives, medical research initiatives affect treatment modes, treatment modes affect mortality rates, mortality rates affect intergenerational competition for resources, and intergenerational competition for resources affects societal stability, it follows that this string of relationships is important and should be understood. There are hundreds of thousands, no, perhaps an infinite number of such relationships. The more we're aware of them, the more our experience makes sense, and the more control we have over our individual and collective fates. That's what coherence is all about.

In between the very general concepts of pattern, structure, and relationship and the narrower concepts that are the tools of the academic disciplines lie the fifty or so familiar, academically neglected concepts that we most frequently use in dealing with ordinary experience. Figure 3.3 shows these concepts, which lie in the middle range of generality and take in most aspects of perceived reality. About thirty more concepts, drawn mostly from general systems theory (such as element, feedback, lag, cause), help us think about relationships and interactions within and between the other fifty concepts. Together, these eighty or so concepts make up most of our model of reality. They are the framework of our "natural" supradiscipline. Their clarification and elaboration ought to be the primary content of instruction.

The supradiscipline pictured in Figure 3.3 is implicit in our thinking. It's embedded in our language. It's the basic conceptual organizer of our perceptions of reality. If we make this discipline explicit, we have the basis for a curriculum that's absolutely comprehensive and totally integrated— exactly as comprehensive and integrated (as coherent) as the experience it represents.

Figure 3.3
Supradiscipline Elements

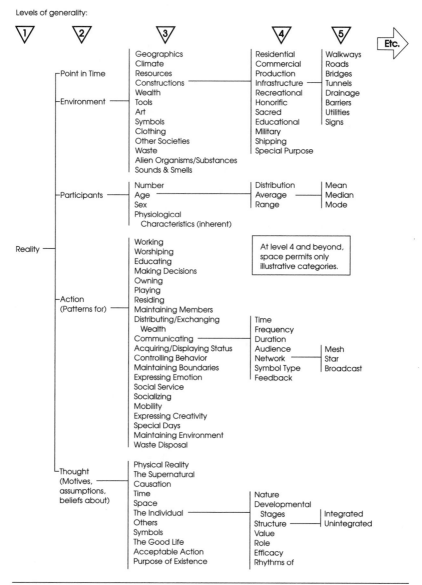

Levels of generality:

| ① | ② | ③ | ④ | ⑤ | Etc. |

	Point in Time	Geographics	Residential	Walkways
		Climate	Commercial	Roads
		Resources	Production	Bridges
		Constructions ——	Infrastructure ——	Tunnels
	Environment ——	Wealth	Recreational	Drainage
		Tools	Honorific	Barriers
		Art	Sacred	Utilities
		Symbols	Educational	Signs
		Clothing	Military	
		Other Societies	Shipping	
		Waste	Special Purpose	
		Alien Organisms/Substances		
		Sounds & Smells		

	Participants ——	Number	Distribution	Mean
		Age ————————	Average ——	Median
		Sex	Range	Mode
		Physiological Characteristics (inherent)		

Reality ——

At level 4 and beyond, space permits only illustrative categories.

	Action (Patterns for)	Working	
		Worshiping	
		Educating	
		Making Decisions	
		Owning	
		Playing	
		Residing	
		Maintaining Members	
		Distributing/Exchanging Wealth	Time
		Communicating ——	Frequency
		Acquiring/Displaying Status	Duration
		Controlling Behavior	Audience —— Mesh
		Maintaining Boundaries	Network —— Star
		Expressing Emotion	Symbol Type —— Broadcast
		Social Service	Feedback
		Socializing	
		Mobility	
		Expressing Creativity	
		Special Days	
		Maintaining Environment	
		Waste Disposal	

	Thought (Motives, assumptions, beliefs about)	Physical Reality	
		The Supernatural	
		Causation	
		Time	Nature
		Space	Developmental
		The Individual ——	Stages —— Integrated
		Others	Structure —— Unintegrated
		Symbols	Value
		The Good Life	Role
		Acceptable Action	Efficacy
		Purpose of Existence	Rhythms of

31

Our society's supradisciplinary conceptual framework can be made the basis for the curriculum with minimal institutional wave making. Its adoption requires no new teachers, no new books, no new organizational structures, no new schedules, no additional investment except perhaps a bit of inservice teacher education. What teachers need is something they should have learned in school but didn't: the general nature of their model of reality.

Ask today's discipline-oriented teacher what he or she was hired to do and the response will probably be something like "Teach biology." Ask tomorrow's supradiscipline-oriented teacher the same question, and the answer will be longer but far, far richer: "I teach about systemic conceptions of reality. I spend most class time dealing with biological subsystems, but I constantly relate what I do to the structure and functioning of the whole system, the system our society thinks of as 'reality.' "

Teachers who think in those terms—whether they teach biology, art, physics, language, mathematics, music, or anything else—are providing their students with a comprehensive, integrated picture of reality. The totality won't be well balanced unless all teachers within a school system put their specializations in the same supradisciplinary perspective, but any teacher in any discipline can provide students with the basic conceptual structure of their society's model of reality.

Anyone who thinks that bringing a different conceptual structure to our familiar reality isn't revolutionary should remember Copernicus. He didn't change the earth and sun, just the way people looked at them. Modern astronomy resulted.

Teachers who put their disciplines in a supradisciplinary context will gradually make changes in content organization and emphasis. They'll see nearby conceptual territory that could profitably be absorbed. They'll be far more aware of conceptual framework, lessening the diversionary attractiveness of facts for facts' sake. Mathematics, linguistic, and graphics skills activities will tie to matters of significance. Students will connect what they're learning to other discipline-oriented instruction, creating a self-reinforcing structure. And what is arguably the most important idea students can learn—that reality is systemic—will be inescapable.

The benefits of making our implicit model of reality explicit and using the resultant supradiscipline to select, organize, and integrate knowledge aren't limited to the model's ability to help us do better what we're currently attempting. *Making our model of reality explicit allows us to examine, criticize, and change it—the basis for a quantum leap toward freedom.* The model provides a formal cognitive system for organizing, and thereby making more accessible in memory, all thought. It permits the creation of a much more compact general education curriculum, thereby freeing instructional time for student specializations not now possible. The model makes it clear that specific instructional content is mere means to the larger end of building conceptual structure, thereby defusing paralyzing conflict over the canon and other instructional materials and specific facts. The model's conceptual nature ensures that the curriculum constantly evolves—a near impossibility when the content of instruction is specific "cultural knowledge." And our model of reality's disclosure of the systemic nature of reality makes it far more difficult for its users to formulate poor policy as a consequence of oversimplifying human experience.

Finally, a formally adopted model of reality, with its elements clearly identified, pushes students to explore relationships between those elements, giving them a powerful intellectual tool that alters in fundamental ways the nature and thrust of schooling. Traditional education is static; it emphasizes student retention of existing knowledge. Relationship exploration is dynamic; it emphasizes the creation of new knowledge.

We can cope with a little incoherence; we can even find it delightful. When Vladimir Nabokov and Gabriel García Márquez juxtapose in clever ways the elements in our model of reality, as they did in their novels *Ada* and *One Hundred Years of Solitude,* the resulting disorientation is stimulating and thought-provoking. But when we're trying to understand human experience as we confront it moment by moment, we want it to be coherent. And it is coherent. Unfortunately, the traditional curriculum—the curriculum we've fashioned to explore reality and help students understand their experience—isn't coherent. We won't have a coherent curriculum until we recognize the supradisciplinary conceptual framework implicit in our perception of reality and make that framework the organizer of the curriculum.

4

It *Must* Have a Name:
Coherence In and Through
English and Language Arts

Stephen Tchudi

The field of English—the home base of reading and writing, phonics and grammar, *Little Women* and *Catcher in the Rye*, spelling rules and usage faults, literary heritage and kiddie lit, red pencils and reading miscues, English as a second language (ESL) and bilingual education, and myriad other bits and pieces—is deeply engaged in the search for coherence within the classroom and across the K–12 curriculum. The names for the new movements in the field provide a clue to the range of approaches being employed in the quest to find a solid center: *whole language, integrated language arts, communication arts and skills, language experience, reading and writing in the content areas, reading and writing workshop, student-centered English, holistic English, language across the curriculum,* and *interdisciplinary English.*

Despite the diversity of those terms and expressions—there *must* be a name for it—English and language arts teachers have been steadily moving toward common goals and methodologies for what is arguably the messiest of the school disciplines (and, also arguably, the most encompassing).

Language interpenetrates the daily lives of adults and children to an astonishing degree; language is *always* with us, guiding us, and allowing us to guide, persuade, provoke, amuse, and entertain others. From a sneeze ("gesundheit") to a lecture ("My fellow Americans . . .") to an expression of intimacy ("d-e-l-e-t-e-d"), we conduct our daily business in words. And over the years, the ubiquitous and omnipresent nature and function of language has caused problems and incoherence in English and language arts programs. Do we teach classic literature or help kids learn to read? Is the purpose of writing to reinforce spelling rules or to help youngsters become good citizens? If we allow second-language speakers to use their first language in class, are we still teaching "English"? Are we teaching a liberal art or a job skill? Are we sharing values or information? Where does journalism fit in? speech? drama? computer keyboarding? Why do *we* always have to do the yearbook? What is "English" anyhow? If we want to succeed at creating a coherent program for English and language arts, we have to explore all those questions.

The Quest for Coherence

The story of the current search for coherence goes back to the early 1960s, when English, like many other fields, was searching for new disciplinary centers. The then-standard "tripod" curriculum—based on the three supposedly equal legs of *language, literature,* and *composition*—began to totter. However, most teachers were paying far more attention to the literature leg of the tripod than the more labor-intensive and less popular legs of composition and grammar. And further, the favored child of literary study was just a weak copy of the disciplinary approach taken in the colleges, with emphasis on mastering literature and reading through selected classics approached through literary functions and forms: poetry, fiction, and drama; rhyme, plot, and rising action; symbol and "deeper meanings." Efforts at finding a "new English" analogous to the new math and the new science—new structures for ordering the discipline—led to a host of competing formulas, with two new grammars, several new rhetorics, and a smorgasbord of alternate patterns for structuring literature, plus sometimes nasty arguments over the comprehensiveness of each new schema.

However, at a paradigm-busting conference held at Dartmouth College in 1966, educators from the United Kingdom and the United States fought their way to the conclusion that—to phrase it in terms of this yearbook—coherence was *not* to be found in diverse language disciplines lumped together under the heading of *English.* Rather, participants at the Dartmouth seminar argued that the core of English teaching lay elsewhere, both in the nature of language itself and also in the growth and development of people who use that language.

In reporting the proceedings of that conference, John Dixon wrote, "English is a quicksilver among metals—mobile, living, and elusive. Its conflicting emphases challenge us today to look for a new, *coherent* definition" (1967, p. 1, italics added). He argued for a coherence centered on language-in-action in the classroom: "To sum up: Language is learnt in operation, not by dummy runs." He and his colleagues argued for an experience-centered classroom where "pupils meet to share their encounters with life, and to do this effectively they move freely between dialogue and monologue—between talk, drama, and writing; and literature, by

bringing new voices into the classroom, adds to the store of shared experience" (p. 13).

James Moffett was one of the first of the post-Dartmouth English
educators to translate those ideas into plans for a coherent curriculum. His
student-centered program was a paradigm buster that integrated experiences in language through a sequence of increasingly sophisticated discourse forms for reading and writing that he saw as corresponding to the
intellectual and linguistic sophistication of young people (Moffett 1968a,
1968b). He was able to sketch out a coherent program that began with
show-and-tell for the youngest children and evolved toward reportage and
research (a more sophisticated show-and-tell) for the high schoolers. Literature flowed naturally into writing and vice versa, through language arts
programs deeply steeped in an oral language base. Many schools adopted
Moffett's program in whole or part, and today many elements of his
program still survive in progressive schools seeking a model for curricular
coherence (Moffett 1990).

Another approach developed in the 1960s also provided a useful model
for integrating programs, especially at the elementary level. The *language-
experience* model of Dorris Lee and Roach Van Allen (1963) follows a
naturalistic learning approach that begins with young people's conversation on familiar topics, moves them toward writing about those topics with
the teacher's support, and then helps them learn to read through their own
writing. Thus, the approach provides a tight connection between the
traditional language arts elements of reading, writing, listening, and speak-
ing as anchored in children's experience. Van Allen's work, like Moffett's,
still influences language arts programs in a great many schools.

In the 1970s, the work of Donald Murray (1968) and Donald Graves
(1983) on *process writing* become widely known. They argued that rather
than focusing on the forms or structures or "products" of writing, teachers
should give attention to the processes that children go through as they
compose. Children who have mastered the process, goes the argument, will
naturally produce the kinds of quality writing products that people want to
see. The coherence of a writing-process approach is found, once again, in
the experiential "anchors" that children bring to the classroom. Instead of
structured writing topics, the teacher offers a wide range of choices, and
children choose increasingly difficult writing products as an outcome of
the program.

Although process writing in itself does not provide an integrated
writing *and* reading curriculum, many educators found the approach
linked by analogy to the work of Louise Rosenblatt on "response to literature" (1968). Her argument that readers create (or "compose") new texts

for themselves by drawing on their own experiences leads to an elegant, coherent flow between reading and writing programs centered on workshop approaches. Such integration currently goes under the umbrella term of *whole language,* which is certainly the strongest integrated elementary curriculum movement in language arts worldwide (Goodman 1992).

One other new strand of English curriculum development needs to be discussed in this brief history of the quest for coherence. In 1975, James Britton and his colleagues at the University of London introduced the idea of *language across the curriculum.* For instruction in language to be valid, they pointed out, all classrooms must reinforce language and language learning. In the United States, their work was popularized through approaches variously labeled *writing in the content areas, reading in the content areas,* and *writing across the curriculum.* And through efforts at reaching out to engage colleagues in other fields in the enterprise of language, many English and language arts teachers became "interdisciplinized" themselves, finding points of connection, not only in language, but also in content learning. Thus, the range of readings in English and language arts has expanded beyond the usual classics to include a great range of multidisciplinary and multicultural materials; writing topics have grown beyond the old standby of "My Summer Vacation" to permit exploration of history, science, mathematics, and the fine and applied arts.

Where Are We Today?

In retrospect, we can see clearly that the theoretical framework for a coherent language curriculum (or coherent curriculum*s,* to be more precise) has been in place in the minds and practices of many theoreticians and practitioners for more than twenty years. A 1987 gathering of English educators under the aegis of the National Council of Teachers of English and the Modern Language Association found widespread agreement on the principles of English and language arts instruction, from kindergarten through college. Those principles emphasize:

- Whole texts
- Multiethnic and multicultural literature
- Writing in diverse modes for personal and public purposes
- The classroom as community, functioning for its own instructional purposes while preparing students to participate as literate citizens in a democracy (Jensen 1988, Elbow 1990, Lloyd Jones and Lunsford 1989)

At the same time, traditional fragmentation of English and language arts programs continues in all too many schools. In the mid-1990s, we commonly find advocates of an integrated-writing workshop or language-experience approach sending home spelling lists of isolated words learned by rote out of context. Or see the process-centered pedagogy of the writing workshop dismissed in reading class, where phonics and skill drills rule the day. Or find the traditional and largely discredited structures of expository prose (e.g., the five-paragraph theme) imposed on a process or discovery approach. Factions in English and language arts often oversimplify one another's positions, making intelligent discussion difficult and leading to stereotypes: the whole-language teacher who has children "let it all hang out," ignoring grammar and punctuation; or the traditional "Miss Fidditch," a rod-and-rule ideologue who crunches young minds in a Procrustean bed of 17th century grammatical, rhetorical, and literary structures.

The National Writing Project, which has done so much to popularize the process-writing approach, has nevertheless steadfastly declined to integrate literature in its program (largely for fear that teachers' desire to teach literature would drive out writing, a not unfair worry). We now see, in many schools, the irony of separate and independent writing projects and literature projects operating concurrently and incoherently, each evangelizing its participants in new, presumably "integrative" approaches.

Probably the two most successful, widespread efforts at curriculum coherence in English today are *whole language* (Weaver 1990) and *language across the curriculum* (Fulwiler and Young 1990, Tchudi 1993). Whole-language programs are operating most powerfully at the elementary school level (Peetoom 1993). There, a concern for teaching writing and reading through workshop approaches has oozed into the curriculum so that for many teachers, *whole language* has become synonymous with *whole learning*, cutting across disciplinary lines and integrating the elementary school subjects through thematic or topical units as diverse as dinosaurs, family, mythology, world geography, and pets and animals. Whole language takes advantage of the self-contained classroom with its open blocks of time and its potential for flexible scheduling.

Language across the curriculum has developed mainly at the secondary and college levels, where traditional disciplinary boundaries make the unity and coherence of the self-contained classroom difficult to achieve. Here, too, an initial focus on writing has, by curricular osmosis, generated interest not only in language, but also in *learning* across the curriculum. It has led to team-taught courses by teachers of English, social studies, science, and other areas, as well as courses taught from within an English framework that take on an interdisciplinary character (Mathers 1993; Carvellas, Blanchette, and Parren 1993).

Where Are We Headed?

It might be a bit difficult for the educator outside the field of English and language arts to see coherence in the diverse and sometimes misleadingly named approaches to language instruction. Coherence in this area will come, however, not from identifying common learnings (e.g., a list of core great books) or writing forms to be mastered level by level, but from developing diverse content and by recognizing the common denominators of language learning. The National Council of Teachers of English has, in a summary document, agreed that those common denominators include language instruction that is:

- Inextricably linked to critical thinking
- Social and interactive
- A process of constructing meaning from experience, including print as vicarious experience
- Based on and emerging from students' prior knowledge
- Linked to problem solving
- A means of empowering students as functioning citizens
- Intended to help students become "theorizers" about their own learning and language

If we examine those assumptions and aims, we can see that they share a great deal with other disciplines where a search for coherence and more effective instruction is taking place. Like science, English and language arts are concerned with careful observation, generalization, and expression of "results" in a community of learners. Like math, English and language arts focus on detail and precision even while emphasizing fundamental processes that carry a learner well beyond "the right answer." Whether we are talking about science, math, history, social studies, fine arts, or even applied and vocational skills, educators are concerned less with content area mastery and more with such processes as thinking creatively and critically, solving problems, constructing knowledge, and theorizing about our own learning.

To date, the successes of integration and coherence in English and language arts have taken place primarily within individual classrooms. The professional literature abounds with discussions of applications to a range of classrooms:

- Technology education (Conroy and Hedley 1990)
- Learning disabled (Clary 1992, Rencik 1992)
- Teacher education (Short and Burke 1989)
- ESL and bilingual education (Heu Pai Au and Kawakami 1990)

Successful efforts at K–12, K–8, middle school, or high school curriculum development are emerging but still less common (Hassler 1991, Swiggett 1991, Kuykendall 1991).

To predict how English and language arts curriculum integration can or will cohere in the next five or ten years would be risky business indeed. In the past two decades, this curriculum area has been subjected to intense public and legislative pressures, and clear lines of development are often interrupted. (Witness the high school "elective" movement of the early '70s, an effort at curricular coherence through student and teacher empowerment, that died a quick death at the hands of the back-to-basics movement and led to the restoration of the clearly antiquated teaching-by-anthology that persists in many schools.)

An Avenue Toward Coherence Across the Curriculum

Without prophesying, I would like to close this chapter with some speculation about the potential of English and language studies, not only to become coherent in themselves, but also to offer an avenue toward coherence across the curriculum. The language discipline can and should:

• Continue to seek coherence within its own elements, not only by seeking integrative theories of language learning, but also by continuing to explore practical curricular approaches to ending the isolation of subject components

• Reconcile its traditional dichotomies—skills versus process, literature versus reading, creative writing versus expository, rote learning and situational learning—through theories and practices that foster authentic learning

• Develop more sophisticated ways of documenting student growth in language through whole-language, integrative approaches, in particular, demonstrating that methods of alternative assessment generally provide more information about the holistic nature of language than do standardized tests

• Search for and evaluate coherent sequences of instruction

In contrast to some disciplines, English and language arts curriculum study will never establish a single program, pattern of instruction, list of books to cover, or prescribed set of writing activities for all children. Good, coherent programs can be sequenced around themes, literary works (arranged by student interests and growth), composing processes and skills, and even the nature of language itself. What won't suffice for the future are curriculums formed by eclectic or smorgasbord approaches that lead to the imposition of contradictory philosophies or approaches.

In addition, I believe English and language arts teachers must continue to reach out and support schoolwide curricular coherence through language-across-the-curriculum programs, *not* for the purpose of passing on the "burden" of language instruction to others, but to show teachers in all disciplines that language is a common denominator of instruction and that attending to language is a matter of attending to the quality of learning. English teachers should look for connections with the themes and strands of other disciplines, as illustrated, say, by Science 2061 or the Bradley Commission report in history. They will find in the themes and recurring concerns of other disciplines topics that are easily and naturally integrated in and through language study.

Perhaps the greatest hope and challenge for English and language arts in the 21st century will be a matter of growth or, more accurately, *out*-growth. First, the language discipline must outgrow its ancient reputation of being concerned only with grammatical correctness and the niceties of poetry. Without necessarily abandoning its traditions, it must find ways to show that it can integrate its various components to renew itself as a study that finds coherence in the needs for human creativity, expressiveness, imagination, and explanation through language. Second, it must continue to grow outward, offering its knowledge as a means of integration and coherence for teachers in all disciplines. Such outgrowth can preserve and earn a place for English and language arts in the coherent curriculum of the future.

But what can we call this 21st century holistic, integrated, interdisciplinary, student-centered, multicultural field that centers on the learning and use of language?

It *must* have a name.

References

Britton, James, Doublas Barnes, Nancy Martin, Harold Rosen, and Robert Parker. (1975). *The Development of Writing Abilities* (pp. 11–18). London: Macmillan Educational.

Carvellas, Betty, Brad Blanchette, and Lauren Parren. (1993). "Science and Society: Escape to the Real World." In *The Astonishing Curriculum: Language in Science and Humanities*, edited by Stephen Tchudi. Urbana, Ill.: National Council of Teachers of English.

Clary, Linda. (May-June 1992). "Integrated Language Arts for Adolescents with Learning Disabilities." *Clearing House* 5, 5: 315–319.

Conroy, Michael T., and Carolyn Hedley. (January 1990). "Communication Skills: The Technology Student and Whole Language Strategies." *Clearing House* 63, 5: 231–235.

Dixon, John. (1967). *Growth Through English*. London and Urbana, Ill.: National Association for the Teaching of English and National Council of Teachers of English.

Elbow, Peter. (1990). *What Is English?* Urbana, Ill., and New York: National Council of Teachers of English and Modern Language Association.

Fulwiler, Toby, and Art Young, eds. (1990). *Programs That Work: Models and Methods for Writing Across the Curriculum*. Portsmouth, N.H.: Boynton/Cook.

Goodman, Kenneth. (September 1992). "Why Whole Language Is Today's Agenda in Education." *Language Arts* 9, 5: 354–363.

Graves, Donald. (1983). *Writing: Teachers and Children at Work*. Portsmouth, N.H.: Heinemann.

Hassler, Lillian. (1991). "The Fairbanks Writing Project." In *Planning and Assessing the Curriculum in English Language Arts*, edited by Stephen Tchudi. Alexandria, Va.: Association for Supervision and Curriculum Development.

Heu Pai Au, Kathryn, and Alice J. Kawakami. (October 1990). "Experiences with Literature: A Thematic Whole-Language Model for the K–3 Bilingual Classroom." *Language Arts* 67, 6: 609.

Jensen, J.N., ed. (1988). *Stories to Grow On: Demonstrations of Language Learning in K–8 Classrooms*. Portsmouth, N.H.: Heinemann.

Kuykendall, Carol. (1991). "Project ACCESS." In *Planning and Assessing the Curriculum in English Language Arts*, edited by Stephen Tchudi. Alexandria, Va.: Association for Supervision and Curriculum Development.

Lee, Dorris, and Roach Van Allen. (1963). *Learning to Read Through Experience*. New York: Appleton, Century, Crofts.

Lloyd Jones, Richard, and Andrea Lunsford, eds. (1989). *The English Coalition Conference: Democracy Through Language*. Urbana, Ill., and New York: National Council of Teachers of English and Modern Language Association.

Mathers, Kathy. (1993). "When Decades Collide." In *The Astonishing Curriculum: Language in Science and Humanities*, edited by Stephen Tchudi. Urbana, Ill.: National Council of Teachers of English.

Moffett, James. (1968a). *A Student-Centered Language Arts Curriculum, K–13*. Boston: Houghton Mifflin (subsequent editions 1976 1990).

Moffett, James. (1968b). *Teaching the Universe of Discourse*. Boston: Houghton Mifflin (subsequently reprinted by Boynton/Cook 1984).

Moffett, James. (1990). *Harmonic Learning: Keynoting School Reform*. Portsmouth, N.H.: Heinemann.

Murray, Donald. (1968) *A Writer Teaches Writing*. Boston: Houghton, Mifflin.

National Council of Teachers of English. (n.d.). *NCTE's Position on the Teaching of English: Assumptions and Practices*. Urbana, Ill.: National Council of Teachers of English.

Peetoom, Adrian. (1993). "Little Children Lead the Way." In *The Astonishing Curriculum: Language in Science and Humanities*. Urbana, Ill.: National Council of Teachers of English.

Rencik, Patricia R. (March-April 1992). "A Whole-Language Approach in an LD Classroom." *Clearing House* 5, 4: 206–209.

Rosenblatt, Louise. (1968). *Literature as Exploration*. New York: Noble and Noble (subsequent edition 1983).

Short, Kathy G., and Carolyn L. Burke. (November 1989). "New Potentials for Teacher Education: Teaching and Learning as Inquiry." *Elementary School Journal* 90, 2: 193–207.

Swiggett, Betty. (1991). "Using Language for Learning Across the Curriculum." In *Planning and Assessing the Curriculum in English Language Arts*. Alexandria, Va.: Association for Supervision and Curriculum Development.

Tchudi, Stephen. (1991). *Planning and Assessing the Curriculum in English Language Arts*. Alexandria, Va.: Association for Supervision and Curriculum Development.

Weaver, Connie. (1990). *Understanding Whole Language: From Principles to Practice*. Portsmouth, N.H.: Heinemann.

5

Attempting Curriculum Coherence in Project 2061

Andrew Ahlgren and Sofia Kesidou

Project 2061 is a long-term initiative of the American Association for the Advancement of Science (AAAS)—in collaboration with school-district teams—to transform K–12 science education. Under the convenient label of *science*, we include natural and social science, mathematics, and technology—and the connections among these fields. The rationale for this inclusiveness is that these fields are so closely related that reform of education in any one requires close attention to the others as well. Project 2061 has commissioned the Council for Basic Education to develop a "blueprint" paper, "Curriculum Connections," to consider the relations of these fields with other parts of the curriculum.[1]

To increase the variety of options available to schools (and avoid the creation of a new orthodoxy), Project 2061 is not designing a single new K–12 curriculum model. Rather, we are developing tools that local curriculum designers can use to assemble their own curriculums.

Science for All Americans (*SFAA*) (Rutherford and Ahlgren 1990), the first Project 2061 tool, describes and recommends science literacy goals for high school graduates—what knowledge and skills in science, mathematics, and technology students should retain after graduation from high school. Consistent with the Project 2061 premise that the useful knowledge people possess is richly interconnected, *SFAA* softens the boundaries between traditional subject areas. For example, *SFAA* describes what students should know about the physical setting and the living environment, but not within the explicit categories of chemistry, physics, geology,

---

[1]Some of the teams working with us are attempting to design completely integrated K–12 curriculums. We currently view such comprehensiveness as an interesting option—although we are perhaps already too ambitious in purporting to include social sciences, mathematics, and technology.

astronomy, or biology. *SFAA* also asks students to become aware of the similarities between the natural and social sciences and to learn about some of the interdependencies of science, mathematics, and technology.

The second tool, *Benchmarks for Science Literacy* (AAAS 1993), elaborates the *SFAA* recommendations in terms of the progress students should make toward each of the learning goals in *SFAA*—specifically, what students should know and be able to do by the end of grades 2, 5, 8, and 12. Figure 5.1 shows the sequence of benchmarks through which students might progress to understand the *SFAA* literacy goal that both culture and heredity influence human behavior.

Next, Project 2061 teams are in the process of identifying useful current materials, constructing larger-scale "curriculum blocks" and making sketches of "curriculum models." Curriculum blocks are coherent units of instruction that target a collection of benchmarks. Curriculum models illustrate alternative configurations of curriculum blocks that account for all benchmarks. To maintain coherence in blocks and models over thirteen years of schooling, Project 2061 design teams typically work in cross-grade and cross-subject groups instead of in traditional isolation by grade level and subject matter.

Beyond these basic tools, we have commissioned a dozen "blueprints," such as the one mentioned earlier by the Council for Basic Education, that recommend how other aspects of the schooling system—assessment, teacher education, school organization, and so forth—will accommodate new curriculum models. And further still, we will design computerized systems that will connect Project 2061 tools to a variety of materials and resources, allowing curriculum designers to draw on them in a coordinated, guided way.

Approach to Curriculum Design

As the work on curriculum models got underway, Project 2061 staff gave the following charge to the school-district team members:

> If we invest our energies in selecting and/or inventing activities and placing them intuitively at different grade levels, we will fall short of the quality of innovation that Project 2061 intends. The job is rather to first think through the entire K–12 flow of ideas to be learned, including the major connections among ideas, and only *then* to identify the kinds of learning experiences that would optimally contribute to students growing along those lines. The Project 2061 intent is, we recognize, outside the experience of most curriculum developers—including the 2061 teams and the 2061 staff. But educators in schools have a better chance than anyone else to do a valid and credible job. Not because they already know how to do it, but because

Figure 5.1
Benchmark Progression Toward the Literacy Goal "Culture and Heredity Influence Human Behavior"

Human behavior is affected both by genetic inheritance and by experience. The ways in which people develop are shaped by social experience and circumstances within the context of their inherited genetic potential (*SFAA*, Ch. 7, "Human Society").

By the end of the 2nd grade, students should know that
• Offspring are very much, but not exactly, like their parents and like one another (*Benchmarks*, Ch. 5, "The Living Environment," Sec. B, "Heredity").
• People can learn from each other by telling and listening, showing and watching, and imitating what others do (*Benchmarks*, Ch. 6, "The Human Organism," Sec. D, "Learning").
• People often choose to dress, talk, and act like their friends, do the same things they do, and have the same kinds of things they have. They also often choose to do certain things their own way (*Benchmarks*, Ch. 7, "Human Society," Sec. A, "Cultural Effects on Behavior").

By the end of the 5th grade, students should know that
• Some likenesses between children and parents, such as eye color in human beings, or fruit or flower color in plants, are inherited. Other likenesses, such as people's table manners or carpentry skills, are learned (*Benchmarks*, Ch. 5, "The Living Environment," Sec. B, "Heredity").
• People can learn about others from direct experience, from the mass communications media, and from listening to other people talk about their work and their lives. People also sometimes imitate people—or characters—in the media (*Benchmarks*, Ch. 7, "Human Society," Sec. A, "Cultural Effects on Behavior").

By the end of the 8th grade, students should know that
• Some animal species are limited to a repertoire of genetically determined behaviors; others have more complex brains and can learn a wide variety of behaviors. All behavior is affected by both inheritance and experience (*Benchmarks*, Ch. 6, "The Human Organism," Sec. D, "Learning").
• Each culture has distinctive patterns of behavior, usually practiced by most of the people who grow up in it (*Benchmarks*, Ch. 7, "Human Society," Sec. A, "Cultural Effects on Behavior").

By the end of the 12th grade, students should know that
• Heritable characteristics can be observed at molecular and whole-organism levels—in structure, chemistry, or behavior. These characteristics strongly influence what capabilities an organism will have and how it will react, and therefore influence how likely it is to survive and to reproduce (*Benchmarks*, Ch. 5, "The Living Environment," Sec. B, "Heredity").
• Differences in the behavior of individuals arise from the interaction of heredity and experience—the effect of each depends on what the other is. Even instinctive behavior may not develop well if the individual is exposed to abnormal conditions (*Benchmarks*, Ch. 6, "The Human Organism," Sec. D, "Learning").
• Cultural beliefs strongly influence the values and behavior of the people who grow up in the culture, often without their being fully aware of it. Response to these influences varies among individuals (*Benchmarks*, Ch. 7, "Human Society," Sec. A, "Cultural Effects on Behavior").
• Heredity, culture, and personal experience interact in shaping human behavior. Their relative importance in most circumstances is not clear (*Benchmarks*, Ch. 7, "Human Society," Sec. A, "Cultural Effects on Behavior").

Sources:
American Association for the Advancement of Science. (1993). *Benchmarks for Science Literacy.* New York: Oxford University Press.
Rutherford, F.J., & A. Ahlgren. (1990). *Science for All Americans.* [*SFAA*]. New York: Oxford University Press.

their interests, sensitivities, and experiences best suit them to learn how to do it.

Thinking carefully through the K–12 flow of ideas requires two things: (1) gaining a deep understanding yourself of the ideas that you want students to learn, including major connections among them, and (2) imagining the steps of increasing sophistication by which students would come eventually to understand those ideas. These two requisites for high-quality curriculum planning are the indispensable basics of the 2061 teams. Without them we have no pretense of being different from any of dozens of other curriculum projects. Without having thought through how students are supposed to grow in understanding, activities for topics are hit-or-miss, shotgun curricula, without a coherent rationale.

Making Progression-of-Understanding Maps

So how does a team think through a broad-reaching progression of understanding? Our proposition was to begin by considering one *SFAA* literacy goal at a time. For each goal, a team was to start with the ideas students are likely to bring to primary school and then imagine how students' ideas would gradually progress toward that goal. The sketch of K–12 development of increasing sophistication came to be called a "progression-of-understanding map."[2] The best scope for a map is an open issue and differs from one map to another. Figure 5.2 (see the next page) shows a progression-of-understanding map for the *SFAA* literacy goal "Culture and Heredity Influence Human Behavior." This map is already a composite that includes portions of what could be separate maps for Heredity, Learning, and Culture.

Some colleagues have found that a good way to begin making a progression-of-understanding map is to start at the earliest grades, speculating on the simplest possible idea that would start students toward an understanding of the 12th grade idea. The beginning-level idea is then built on to produce a sequence of increasingly sophisticated statements. In building this sequence, people also typically think of many links to other ideas—when some increases in sophistication require that several simple ideas be put together, or when two distinct ideas are mutually supporting. For example, the combination of two simpler ideas "magnifiers often show that things have unexpectedly small parts" and "small parts can be put together to make all sorts of different things" contributes to understanding

---

[2]Our use of the term *map* for that endeavor is risky, because of the several different meanings of "map." The popular "concept map" was considerably different—a depiction, mostly hierarchical, of connections among scientific terms.

Figure 5.2
Progression-of-Understanding Map for the Literacy Goal "Culture and Heredity Influence Human Behavior"

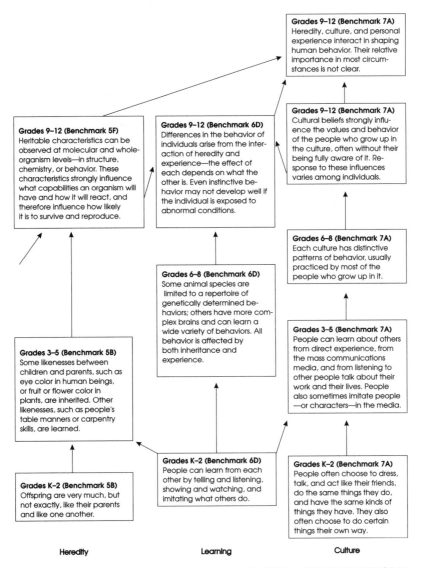

Grades 9–12 (Benchmark 7A)
Heredity, culture, and personal experience interact in shaping human behavior. Their relative importance in most circumstances is not clear.

Grades 9–12 (Benchmark 5F)
Heritable characteristics can be observed at molecular and whole-organism levels—in structure, chemistry, or behavior. These characteristics strongly influence what capabilities an organism will have and how it will react, and therefore influence how likely it is to survive and reproduce.

Grades 9–12 (Benchmark 6D)
Differences in the behavior of individuals arise from the inter-action of heredity and experience—the effect of each depends on what the other is. Even instinctive be-havior may not develop well if the individual is exposed to abnormal conditions.

Grades 9–12 (Benchmark 7A)
Cultural beliefs strongly influ-ence the values and behavior of the people who grow up in the culture, often without their being fully aware of it. Re-sponse to these influences varies among individuals.

Grades 6–8 (Benchmark 7A)
Each culture has distinctive patterns of behavior, usually practiced by most of the people who grow up in it.

Grades 6–8 (Benchmark 6D)
Some animal species are limited to a repertoire of genetically determined be-haviors; others have more com-plex brains and can learn a wide variety of behaviors. All behavior is affected by both inheritance and experience.

Grades 3–5 (Benchmark 5B)
Some likenesses between children and parents, such as eye color in human beings, or fruit or flower color in plants, are inherited. Other likenesses, such as people's table manners or carpentry skills, are learned.

Grades 3–5 (Benchmark 7A)
People can learn about others from direct experience, from the mass communications media, and from listening to other people talk about their work and their lives. People also sometimes imitate people —or characters—in the media.

Grades K–2 (Benchmark 5B)
Offspring are very much, but not exactly, like their parents and like one another.

Grades K–2 (Benchmark 6D)
People can learn from each other by telling and listening, showing and watching, and imitating what others do.

Grades K–2 (Benchmark 7A)
People often choose to dress, talk, and act like their friends, do the same things they do, and have the same kinds of things they have. They also often choose to do certain things their own way.

Heredity   Learning   Culture

Source of benchmarks: American Association for the Advancement of Science. (1993). *Benchmarks for Science Literacy.* New York: Oxford University Press.

the more advanced idea "things are made of huge numbers of invisibly small pieces." Such cross-connections may occur within the same map or between ideas in related maps. *Benchmarks for Science Literacy* provides elements for making maps, but seldom is explicit about the connections among them.

Coherence in Activities

A progression-of-understanding map for a concept in *SFAA* is the basis for designing experiences for students—during thirteen years of schooling—that will enable them to understand that concept adequately. Such a sequence of experiences constitutes a curriculum "strand." Although progression-of-understanding maps may be very similar from one development team to the next, the corresponding curriculum strands developed from them may be very different.

When should we propose certain kinds of experiences for learning particular ideas? Should we start to attach kinds of activities as soon as a progression-of-understanding map takes shape? Or should we spot conceptual links between progression-of-understanding maps, weave them together to find commonalities and convergences, and only then start to attach kinds of activities? Surely thoughts about possible activities arise inevitably as part of making any progression-of-understanding map, and people making these maps should keep notes along the way—not only about activities, but about cross-connections, or "hooks," to other maps.

Conceivably, curriculum developers could focus on curriculum strands for one progression-of-understanding map at a time. For example, curriculum designers could develop strands for separate maps on diversity of life, origin of variation among organisms, natural selection, or evolution. That strategy, however, might lead to a fragmented curriculum much like what most schools have now. This danger would be particularly likely in the earlier grade ranges, because the relationships between ideas may not be evident until later grades—say, when they together contribute to understanding a more advanced concept.

So what are possibilities for coherence in identifying activities? Figure 5.3a is an abstract representation of a progression-of-understanding map that relates ideas labeled A1, A2, A3, A4, A5, and A6. A set of activities chosen to serve this progression of understanding would have long-term, *developmental coherence* (for developers, anyway) because they lead eventually to the 12th grade learning goal A6. If there were multiple steps in increasing sophistication of a single idea within a single grade level, activities could have a conceptual coherence for students. But for the common situation depicted in Figure 5.3a, the activities would lack conceptual coherence for students within the grade K–2 span by itself because there would be as yet no evident connections among the targeted ideas A1, A2, A3.

Rather than consider only one map at a time, developers could identify conceptually related maps, as depicted in Figure 5.3b, and then identify one activity (or more) that would target both the cross-connected ideas. Activities that make these connections evident would provide conceptual *cross-connection coherence*. Finding or inventing activities that make such connections, however, could be a demanding task for the design team.

A more feasible strategy might be to first identify an activity for a particular idea in one map, and then consider what other ideas that activity could serve—regardless of what map those ideas might be found in. For example, for learning about the diversity of life, curriculum developers might suggest a series of trips for students to observe organisms in a nearby field or plot of land. Curriculum developers might suggest how this activity could also contribute to learning goals on measurement, describing data, and testing hypotheses. So the observing activity could be augmented into a unit that includes data-analyzing and hypothesizing activities. In this case, the unit would derive its coherence from the common context in which the activities are embedded—say, field trips to observe organisms. Figure 5.3c is an abstract representation of two maps that have no conceptual cross-connections, but contain ideas that could be served within the same context—which therefore provides *context-based coherence* for student learning.

Coherence in Curriculum Blocks

On how large a scale is coherence in the curriculum needed (or tolerable)? A K–12 curriculum could well be a pile of singly chosen activities, or a patchwork of one-map-at-a-time strands, or a jungle of multiple-map-connecting strands. At one extreme, we do not want every activity to be unconnected to the previous one and the next one (perhaps all too common in the lower grades)—that way, each is too easily forgotten. At the other extreme, however, we do not favor a completely rationalized, thirteen-year curriculum in which every piece is elaborately connected to others. That type of curriculum allows too little local flexibility to adjust to different circumstances and to mobile populations.

In one stage of our planning of curriculum models, a group of consultants told us that a major problem of science education in the elementary and middle school is its activity-to-activity incoherence—one activity fol-

Figure 5.3a
A Progression-of-Understanding Map Relating Ideas A1–A6

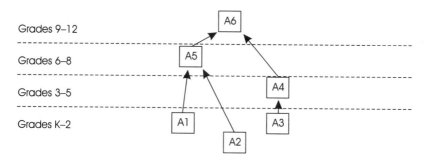

Figure 5.3b
Two Progression-of-Understanding Maps with Conceptual Cross-Connections

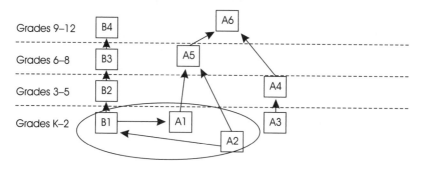

Figure 5.3c
Two Progression-of-Understanding Maps with No Conceptual Cross-Connections

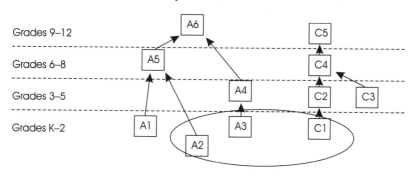

lows another with no rhyme or reason. In current practice, there is often no explicit communication to the student about the purpose for learning science (although we may still give implicit messages such as "We learn science because it is correct" or "We learn this to get ready for the next course"). Even approaches in which activities are clustered by contexts (such a field trip to observe organisms) or superficial "themes" (such as whales) may not enhance the sense of purpose and meaning of these activities for students.

We resolved to build curriculum with coherence on a larger scale than was typical, designing patterns of activity—curriculum blocks—that would have a comprehensible (and, we hope, motivating) unity for students. A curriculum block could occupy from a few minutes a day to entire school days and last from days to months or even years. One example would be measuring temperature for a few minutes daily over two annual cycles. Another example would be spending all day for a solid week on designing and testing a better waste-disposal process for the cafeteria. The essential criterion for a block, however, is that it have *coherence of purpose*.

What are suitable purposes for curriculum blocks from the students' point of view? Reflecting on the ways science-literate people use their knowledge, we have adopted four purposes for a curriculum block:

• Finding out about how something in particular in the world works (description and explanation)
• Solving a practical problem (design)
• Reflecting on some enduring human concern (issues)
• Learning about how we know what we know (inquiry)

A curriculum block should have *one* of these purposes. The purpose for the whole block, however, does not dictate what instructional format(s) it should include. A "design" block, for example, might well include experiments, seminars, and surveys of social opinions, all of which would contribute to the design. It is a design block because the orienting purpose of undertaking the set of activities is to solve some practical problem. To the question "Why are we doing this today?" students would answer, "Because it will help us to make Y happen." The same question for a "description and explanation" block would elicit answers like "To find out how X works." For an "issues" block, the answer would be "To learn what both sides of the argument about Z are." The answer for an "inquiry" block would be "To account for why we believe Q."

Curriculum models are to provide a vision of the ways literate people use knowledge and skills. Any complete curriculum model should therefore include blocks for each rationale. Moreover, students' appreciation of the whole set of rationales might be served well by maintaining the rationales' separate identities. A singular focus of a curriculum block provides a basis for closure—hence satisfaction—for the student: "We've finished the investigation, produced and tested our design, made recommendations on an issue, and used our knowledge to explain a new (to us) phenomenon." On a general level: "I've used my science knowledge and skills for these purposes so I know what science is useful for."

A singular purpose for a curriculum block also improves coherence by helping the block designer make choices about which benchmarks to include (and which to leave out). We can imagine, for example, different blocks that would target benchmarks about the germ theory of disease. A "design" block on germs might also target benchmarks about physical health and the nature of technology (students might design a sanitary inspection system for a restaurant). An "inquiry" block on germs might instead target the history and nature of science (say, through a seminar on how beliefs about what causes disease changed in the past century). An "issues" block on germs might target benchmarks on human society, such as cultural effects on behavior and social trade-offs. A "description and explanation" block on germs might include the interdependence and evolution of life. All four curriculum blocks would likely also target benchmarks for mathematics and common themes (systems, models, patterns of change, and scale).

Next Steps

Project 2061 cannot hope to produce the necessary pool of hundreds of diverse curriculum blocks needed for building alternative K–12 curriculums. Rather, with the help of our school-district teams, we plan to provide some examples that will help curriculum developers produce the kinds of curriculum blocks that are needed for their state, province, region, district, or local schools. To illustrate that it is possible to design thirteen years of schooling to achieve literacy in science, mathematics, and technology, Project 2061 is working on alternative curriculum models. Team members will suggest possibilities for planning curriculum and instruction and will show the degree to which models can vary and still provide a common core of instruction aimed at science literacy.

If Project 2061's vision of reform is realized, science curriculums in the future will be quite different from those of today.

First, an identifiable *common core* of learning in science, mathematics, and technology will focus on science literacy as its main goal and be closely allied with a common core of learning in the arts and humanities.

Educators will justify instructional units by referring to grade-level learning goals derived from expectations for what adults should retain. A comparison of this new core curriculum with the traditional curriculum would show many fewer topics than before, so that students can concentrate on learning well a basic set of ideas and skills that will lead to science literacy—and optimally promote further learning.

Second, schools will be able to plan K–12 curriculums so that teaching and learning are coordinated over long spans of time and across subjects. (The National Science Teachers Association recommends doing just that in its "Scope, Sequence, and Coordination" projects.) K–12 teams will have planned for continuity of experiences, and cross-discipline groups will have ensured connections. Designers will not have to develop a curriculum from scratch but will be able to select from many instructional blocks that foster *SFAA* goals while matching the needs of the local community.

Finally, students will have many opportunities for the reflective thinking that enables them to make sense of their experiences—including connecting ideas among science, mathematics, and technology, and between these disciplines and the arts and humanities. Students' activities and reflections will engage them in using their knowledge in ways characteristic of literate adults—to explain everyday phenomena, to solve practical problems, to inform decisions about issues, and thereby to learn more and have more personal satisfaction.

References

American Association for the Advancement of Science (1993). *Benchmarks for Science Literacy*. New York: Oxford University Press.

Rutherford, F.J., & A. Ahlgren. (1990). *Science for All Americans*. New York: Oxford University Press.

6

Interdisciplinary Curriculum—Again

Joan M. Palmer

Education is forever awash in words. We speak of interdisciplinary curriculum, integrated curriculum, connected curriculum, and curricular connections as though they were completely different, complex models. We fail to understand that by doing so, we risk losing sight of the basic reason for looking for coherence in the curriculum: to discover and uncover commonalities in what teachers are expected to teach and students are expected to learn. To isolate curriculum from the context of teaching and learning sets up a false dichotomy of content versus practice. Contrary to the impression given by much of the current rhetoric, interdisciplinary curriculum is not a "thing." Interdisciplinary curriculum is both process and product, providing on one hand a philosophic framework and approach to decision making in the all-important arena of "What to Teach" and, on the other, an instructional focus that results in lessons that demonstrate the connectedness of knowledge and life.

We have long known that making connections between and among the disciplines provides the setting for increased understanding, retention, and application; but we have not been able to "pull it off" in school systems in an organized and sustained manner. Developing interdisciplinary curriculum emerges as a rallying point at regular intervals, only to fade away when the difficulties become overwhelming or other "promising practices" take the field. A few hardy souls in a few schools or districts continue the effort; but as a profession, we have reverted to the apparently easier task of isolating content from its natural habitat—the cultural and societal milieu that gives it texture and meaning. That has been an illusory compromise, however, for it is "easier" only in the short run, in the isolation of the schoolhouse. When students function outside of that bubble, the reality of the seamlessness of knowledge sets in, and they are often not prepared to recognize or deal with all of the interacting factors. The mentality that has led education to the side-by-side theory (teach history directly before or after language arts and they will "get" the connections) just doesn't work for the majority of students. They need to be consciously guided to see, discuss, internalize, and then discover the nature of the connections in what they are studying.

The Messages

The difficultly in making curriculum connections has obviously not been the result of ill-will or lack of effort, but rather a lack of understanding of the wholeness of the process of education. We have paid attention to only a piece of the problem. The goal is not just to develop interdisciplinary curriculum but, more importantly, to implement it. And that is accomplished through the teaching/learning interaction with the curriculum as intermediary. Unfortunately, the messages sent to teachers in this regard are confusing and sometimes contradictory.

Typically, interdisciplinary curriculum is developed by a team of teachers who possess a depth of understanding of their content and recognize the need to show students the interdependency of knowledge. With great enthusiasm (at least by the writers), the curriculum is introduced in the district in a full-day workshop. Teachers are then sent back to their schools with the well wishes of all and the ringing tones of "Have a good year!" echoing in their ears.

Back in their classrooms, however, teachers rarely find time set aside in the day for planning with an interdisciplinary team. Time is at a premium, and there is no room in the schedule— a clear signal about priorities. Nor do they always receive help, support, and encouragement from supervisors or resource teachers. The lingering suspicion that integrated teaching and learning might deflect from time and focus on specific disciplines sometimes (often?) causes concern for the subject area supervisor, which is quickly communicated in subtle or even overt ways. Seldom, too, is well-designed staff development available at the school level to prepare and support faculties in their efforts.

Again, time and money (and it is difficult to separate the two) are cited as barriers. So dedicated teachers meet before school, after school, and in planning periods to write integrated lessons, share ideas, develop materials, and coach each other as best they can. In some instances, they are joined by equally fervent administrators and supervisors; but other duties demand their attention if curriculum integration is not a district focus. And after a while they all become tired—especially the teachers. Eventually the flurry of activity in the field dies down; the focus shifts to a different priority. A new instructional approach or a mandate from a local, state, or federal agency takes the stage and absorbs the time and energy of those grappling with the issues of interdisciplinary teaching for learning. The struggle is unequal and frustrating, so gradually practice reverts to the study of discrete content, with perhaps some ongoing attempts to make connections through long-term assignments or cross-curricular projects.

In the presence of such conditions and mixed messages, is it any wonder that interdisciplinary curriculum has failed to take hold in our nation's schools? Unless we recognize the components of successful implementation—planning time, administrative and supervisory support, staff development, and appropriate materials—it is fruitless to begin.

The Modes

Even with the elements for successful institutional implementation in place, obstacles remain. Interdisciplinary curriculum is problematic for many teachers, particularly those trained as subject area experts. Teachers feel threatened, fearing that they will be asked to teach material unknown to them; their own area of expertise might become undervalued and shortchanged in the process; or they could be bound to team-teaching or other structures with which they are uncomfortable or unfamiliar. All of this exists within the national focus on goals and outcomes often interpreted as a mandate for facts, figures, and formidable testing. And people's perception of mutual exclusivity between interdisciplinary curriculum and achievement on both criterion-referenced and standardized tests is widespread.

A curriculum guide or resource bulletin developed at a central level will seldom answer all of the questions or solve the problems inherent in planning for interdisciplinary teaching (although if well designed, it can certainly make life easier). The only lasting way to institutionalize an interdisciplinary, integrated, or cross-curricular approach to teaching and learning, whatever the format of curriculum in a district, is to *empower teachers to make decisions about the connections*. Teachers need to identify and plan how and when to make the connections. If they are to be held accountable for results, they must be given the opportunity to structure the means.

Just as there is no single way to teach all children, there is no single model for organizing curriculum for integrated teaching and learning. The essence of any model that has a chance of becoming institutionalized must revolve around teacher decision making. Making connections in the classroom has to do with relating natural, normal, and appropriate core curriculums. It is the *overt* linking of pertinent outcomes and objectives within essential curriculum, whether it is called interdisciplinary, integrated, or cross-curricular. Only teachers, planning together, can make that happen.

Teachers and students need to know where they have been, where they are going, and why. For transfer and understanding to occur, students need *conscious* practice in recognizing and applying concepts and skills across disciplines. And to be effective, integration must be both vertical and horizontal—that is, across content areas and between grade levels. That can only happen at the school level, teacher by teacher, team by team, faculty by faculty.

Empowering teachers to make decisions about the integration of curriculum is not without its difficulties and pitfalls. Making curricular connections is a matter of *negotiation*, and that requires the ability to work as a team, listen to another point of view, and change long-held practices or beliefs. But basic to all of that is the necessity for flexible curriculum that lends itself to movement. Flexible curriculum does not mandate content by months; it identifies expected outcomes. We need to rethink the "chronology of curriculum" so that teachers understand that they have the option to move content to make natural, normal, and appropriate connections, coupled with the accountability for student achievement of those systemwide outcomes.

Negotiating Curriculum

The idea of "negotiating curriculum" is frightening for some. The term does not mean, however, a process of deleting or dismissing the district curriculum. It simply means that the process of planning for integrated teaching and learning requires some give and take on all sides and is achieved over time and within a trusting collegial situation.

Take, for example, a team developing a unit around a theme (or a question, concept, etc.) that requires the English teacher to introduce students to appropriate documentation of sources in November. This is an experienced teacher who has, for years, taught documentation in February, as part of learning to write a research paper. To make the desired time shift, the other team members must convince the teacher that it would (1) be good for the *teacher* (we are human, after all) and (2) be good for the students. An understanding that such a schedule would give the teacher another chance to present the information and provide a context for using the skills in a variety of situations usually does the trick, but not quickly. Unless the is curriculum is flexible, however, either in reality or in perception, it will not work. Curriculum must be designed and understood in such a way that teachers are able to move objectives around to meet their students' instructional needs—always within the understanding that they are accountable in the end for the required goals and objectives of the course or subject.

Developing a Model

Even in the best of conditions—with sufficient planning time, staff development, and flexible curriculum—there is still a basic need for a way to get started—a structure for identifying, scrutinizing, and putting the pieces together. As Tanner[1] reminds us,

> There is a biological principle that structure determines function, from which is derived the architectural principle that form follows function. This is no less valid for the curriculum. Integrative curriculum designs are needed to counter the isolation and fragmentation of knowledge that plagues the traditional curriculum.

In the public school system in Howard County, Maryland, we found that a simple "Planning Wheel" provided a visual organizer as well as a symbol of what we were about, representing the seamlessness and interaction among the variables of content, teaching, and learning. As more teachers started using the approach, the pitfalls in planning for curriculum connections became apparent. The first wheel was simple (Figure 6.1), designed simply to show the integrating focus in the center and the content to be related in one of each of the wedges. Team planning took it from there. What we soon found, however, was that success could sow the seeds of failure. Contrary to expectations, some teachers were finding they could not teach the content for which they were responsible; students were enjoying the activities, but not retaining the "right things."

A sense of frustration led us to take a critical look at some of the Planning Wheels and follow-up lessons. We soon recognized what had happened: Planning was occurring at the *activity* level, not at the *objective* level. As a result, students and teachers were involved in exciting, motivating activities without a clear focus or connections to an essential objective. In other words, great instruction and interactive learning were taking place around content that was sometimes trivial—a major issue at all times, but especially so in the context of increasing accountability. We recognized that we needed to find a way to keep on track, staying focused on identified, agreed-on outcomes.

---

[1] Daniel Tanner, "A Brief Historical Perspective of the Struggle for an Integrative Curriculum," *Educational Horizons* (Fall 1989) 68, 1: 6–11.

Figure 6.1
A Planning Wheel for Making Curricular Connections

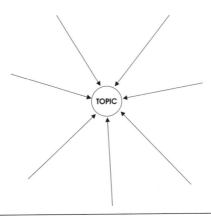

The solution was to modify the Planning Wheel so that it clarified and emphasized the necessary planning steps evolving from the central focus to the identification of the related objectives, to the enabling thinking skills, to the assessment design, and then and only then to the activities that would bring it all about (Figure 6.2). That process facilitated responsible connections between and among curriculums.

Since that breakthrough, teachers have continued to find new and creative ways to make connections. They involve students in the planning, get parents involved in schoolwide projects, and use the Wheel as an assessment device for groups and individuals. As curriculum is written and revised, curriculum "maps" are included to facilitate planning across subjects and through levels. Sample Wheels are also provided, but only for use as models, not as givens; for the strength and power of the approach is as much in the planning as in the presentation.

New Learnings

Interdisciplinary teams involved in making connections for students learn the interconnections themselves. They recognize the vast possibilities for applying knowledge; understanding and appreciating each other's expertise, they share teaching techniques and strategies. The result is a focused approach to attaining the goals of interdisciplinary teaching: students who will see, understand, and articulate connections; students

Figure 6.2
A Planning Model for Making Curriculum Connections*

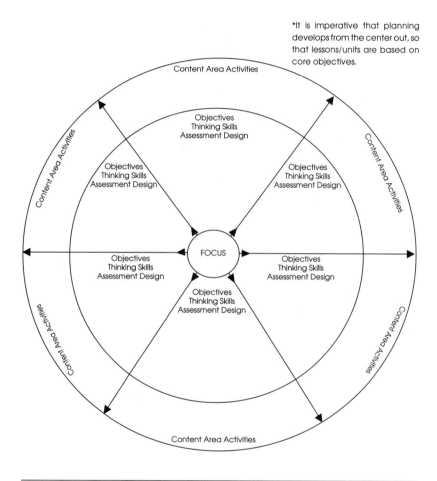

*It is imperative that planning develops from the center out, so that lessons/units are based on core objectives.

Content Area Activities

Objectives
Thinking Skills
Assessment Design

Objectives
Thinking Skills
Assessment Design

Objectives
Thinking Skills
Assessment Design

Objectives
Thinking Skills
Assessment Design

FOCUS

Objectives
Thinking Skills
Assessment Design

Objectives
Thinking Skills
Assessment Design

Content Area Activities

Content Area Activities

Content Area Activities

Content Area Activities

Content Area Activities

who are able to apply knowledge and skills across content; and students who will, themselves, consciously look for and make connections between and among the content and skills they are taught both as young people and as adults—in other words, students who think.

Perhaps the most important learning of all has been the understanding that there is no *one way* to approach integrated teaching and learning. Teachers understand this and are eager to explore new avenues; they only want the necessary time and support to help them reach that goal.

7

Creating Coherence Through Curriculum Integration

P. Elizabeth Pate, Karen McGinnis, and Elaine Homestead

Dissatisfied with the failure of traditional schooling to connect curriculum with the needs of students and teachers, three educators embarked on an educational quest for coherent curriculum. Through discussion, research, and reflection, we explored integrated curriculum as a vehicle for making schooling relevant. Our quest for coherent curriculum led us to make significant changes to connect the curriculum to the needs of all involved.

During one summer break, Karen and Elaine (two middle school teachers), and Elizabeth (an assistant professor of middle-level education) met to discuss curriculum issues, two-member teams, flexible scheduling, teaching and learning strategies, and student and teacher motivation. We reflected on the ideas of Beane (1990), Dewey (1938), Jacobs (1989), Wigginton (1986), and those suggested by the Carnegie Council on Adolescent Development (1989). We discussed and debated schooling. We began to plan significant changes in our curriculum. Our quest for coherent curriculum had begun.

A Quest for Coherence

The following school year brought significant changes for the two middle school teachers. We became teachers on a two-member (rather than our former five-member) 8th grade team. Developing a democratic classroom, one that actively involves students in decision making, was a top priority. We did not leave implementing an integrated curriculum to chance. We actively pursued our goal of connecting all aspects of the curriculum—the working world, subject content and skills, and social skills—for students and teachers. We devoted weeks and sometimes months to curriculum themes such as human migration, human interactions, human and civil rights and responsibilities, leadership, and communities of the future. We adopted block scheduling to better meet students' physical and academic needs. Within the block time, we embedded advisor-advisee relationships, making time for teachers and students to talk about students' social and emotional needs and concerns. That arrangement permitted us to address these needs and concerns as they occurred.

That next summer, we met to reflect on the previous school year. We identified several key components of a coherent curriculum: identifying goals, creating a democratic classroom, integrating content, making connections, using traditional and alternative assessments, determining appropriate pedagogy, personalizing learning, enhancing relationships, communicating, developing effective scheduling and organizational structures, and reflecting.

Though we discuss these components separately, in reality they are intertwined. An integrated curriculum looks different in every classroom and across years. The components described here are ones we consider necessary in an integrated curriculum to facilitate coherence.

Components of a Coherent Curriculum

Identifying Goals. Goals are an important component of coherent curriculum: They guide the curriculum, shape how it is taught and learned, and provide a sense of purpose to schooling. Some of our goals included:

- Developing a curriculum that gave students and teachers a deeper understanding of content,
  - Making connections between school and the outside world,
  - Teaching students how to learn,
  - Encouraging students to accept responsibilities,
  - Learning to work effectively with a diversity of people,
  - Encouraging students to take risks and learn from mistakes,
  - Teaching students to become effective problem solvers,
  - Developing expertise in self-expression, and
  - Discovering that learning can be fun.

In our unit "Human Interactions," all our goals were addressed. This unit was a study of social issues and concerns that affected us personally, as well as issues that have affected societies in the past. Some issues our students wanted to investigate included racism, abortion rights, animal testing, and world hunger. The students developed questions for research, determined how they would share their information with others, kept journals, and constructed their own alternative assessments. For example, one group of students were concerned about world hunger. They wanted to make a difference in the lives of children in Somalia. They formulated a plan to collect money, wrote a proposal seeking approval, made speeches to every homeroom in the school asking for support, established collection sites around the school, held contests, and ultimately collected $250 to send to a relief agency working in Somalia. The students really felt proud of their efforts because they had made a difference in the lives of others. When students are involved in working with personally meaningful and relevant issues, goals are realized, thus facilitating curriculum coherence.

Creating a Democratic Classroom. Democracy in our classroom included student and teacher collaboration on the team management plan, grading policy, parent communication, and curriculum. It meant providing opportunities for student choice. It did not mean letting students dictate everything that went on.

In a democratic classroom, students realize how important their input is. For example, in the unit on human and civil rights and responsibilities, we examined the relationships between past, present, and future human and civil rights issues from the 1600s to the present. We asked students to develop a timeline as an assessment to demonstrate their understanding. The classroom became totally silent. Students looked at each other and then at us. They said they had learned too much for a "simple" timeline. So we asked them how *they* wanted to demonstrate what they had learned. The students brainstormed, and ideas started flowing. They all wanted to "do something big." The students ended up constructing a "Living History Timeline" based on historical events of human and civil rights. They chose issues and events to reenact. They wrote scripts and created scenery backdrops. The "Living History Timeline" depicted eleven events ranging from the Salem Witch Trials to Bosnia/Herzegovina.

Democracy promotes self-worth and encourages student ownership in team decisions. It ensures a classroom environment where students feel comfortable questioning and stating their opinions. The "Living History Timeline" was a result of democracy at work in the classroom.

Integrating Content. In our previous teaching years, we observed that traditional teaching had not ensured overwhelming student success in content retention. One of our goals in our quest for coherent curriculum was to make content more meaningful for our students. Content in our curriculum meant many things. It encompassed the content facts and skills of science, social studies, mathematics, language arts, and the fine arts. It also encompassed the social skills necessary for students to become responsible citizens—for example, the ability to relate well with a diversity of people. Some facts and skills that we believe are important are not always interesting to students. But integrated into the context of significant themes, such as human interactions or communities of the future, these facts and skills begin to take on real meaning for students. This integration of content enhances curriculum coherence.

The Human Interactions theme was expanded to include students' concerns about the environment. We discussed environmental issues— ozone pollution, erosion caused by clear-cutting ("selective harvesting"), acid rain, and air and water quality and their relationship to our environment. In exploring this theme, the students wanted to find out who was responsible (locally and nationally) for regulating and monitoring the environment. The students formed small "environmental concern groups" and educated other students through multimedia presentations. The students realized they needed extensive content background in earth science and social studies (e.g., chemical structure of ozone, erosion and deposition, underground water systems, local and state agencies and their duties and responsibilities in maintaining a safe environment, demographics, map skills) to better understand their concern, teach others, and devise plans to help make a difference.

The students sought information from their textbooks and current outside-the-classroom resources. They scoured the media center for information; invited guest speakers; and contacted state agencies for up-to-date information. The students wrote a proposal to the principal, who then funded an on-line computer information service; and they planned fact-finding missions off-campus.

This kind of meaningful schoolwork that integrates content within a significant theme is fundamental to developing curriculum that is coherent for students and teachers.

Making Connections. Making connections is another fundamental component of a coherent curriculum. It means several things in our classroom. It means organizing a curriculum with no artificial boundaries between content areas. For example, connecting all the social studies disciplines as they relate to a theme—government, economics, history, or geography—gives more meaning to the whole concept of social studies.

By making connections, we also relate to students how content and skills can or will be important outside of school. Finding connections among the students, subject-area content, and the outside world makes for more meaningful, coherent learning.

Making connections, as informal assessments, also helped us understand how students perceived instructions, teacher expectations, and their own feelings about particular assignments or themes.

Using Traditional and Alternative Assessments. Assessment was an integral part of the integrated curriculum. Matching assessments to themes, activities, and students' needs ensures a more coherent curriculum. Thus, we combined traditional and alternative assessments, as well as formative and summative assessments. For example, in our community-of-the-future theme, we used these assessments:

- Worksheets
- Vocabulary quizzes
- Pop tests
- Essays
- Observations
- Brochures,

- Journal writings
- Portfolios
- Models
- Posters
- Presentations

We collaborated with our students in ways to assess their learning. We often used rubrics. A rubric is a scaled set of criteria clearly defining what a range of performances look like. Sometimes we developed the rubrics, and at other times the students generated their own rubrics. In an interview, one student said:

> Designing my own rubric affected my project preparation by letting me know what I was going to be graded on, and I got first-hand information on how to do things. I feel that using rubrics for assessment is wonderful, because I can learn more stuff this way.

Using traditional and alternative assessments, appropriate to the themes, provided even more coherence to the curriculum for our students and ourselves.

Determining Appropriate Pedagogy. Determining appropriate pedagogy connects the curriculum to students' needs. We found that our curriculum was more coherent when we used a variety of strategies. Sometimes students taught each other, collaborated in small or large groups, or worked individually. Occasionally, when appropriate, we lectured. Sometimes we spent the day in the library, went to the computer lab, or invited guest speakers to our classroom. We based our strategies on our knowledge of the students; the mood of the class; the time of the year; and current local, state, national, and international events.

For example, in the unit on human and civil rights and responsibilities, we used various strategies, including questioning, discussion, imagery, and reflection. We wanted our students to understand, as much as possible, the horror of the Holocaust and its connection to human and civil rights. We wanted them to "experience" the Holocaust individually before we discussed it as a large group. First, each student received background lecture notes. Then, we set up a gallery of Holocaust posters from B'nai B'rith. Under each photograph was a probing question—for example, "Look into the eyes of this child and tell what you think he is feeling." The students then individually responded to twenty probing questions and photographs. They "experienced" the Holocaust during their visit to this gallery. As a result, they were eager to learn more about the social, political, religious, and cultural aspects of the era. Incorporating appropriate pedagogy in this theme allowed meaningful learning to occur.

Personalizing Learning. Knowledge of the student is essential to personalizing learning and promoting coherence in the curriculum. Personalizing learning includes:

- Identifying learning styles,
- Determining strengths and weaknesses in content and social skills,
- Researching background and family information,
- Recognizing personal interests and concerns,
- Exploring career interests, and
- Determining student expectations from school.

For example, one student—we'll call him "Robert"—had been previously identified as a "slow learner." After working with him, we recognized persistence as one of his strengths. In his earlier school years, Robert performed poorly with traditional methods of teaching and evaluation. But he blossomed with integrated curriculum, partly because we encouraged his input in decisions on how he wanted to demonstrate his learning. In an interview, he said: "I'm not a person who has a lot of ideas, but I can do what people tell me to do. I'm a hard worker." We placed Robert with a group of students who recognized his talents and were willing to work with him. He learned about himself and other people. Other students began to perceive Robert in a new light, as a contributor to the class. As one student said aloud in class one day, "You should hear the idea Robert just had!" Robert just beamed. As a result, his self-concept and self-esteem improved greatly.

In integrated curriculum, knowledge of the student is essential to personalizing learning and promoting coherence.

Enhancing Relationships. During our quest for a coherent curriculum, a variety of relationships formed between students and teachers. Our students viewed us as facilitators for their learning rather than as "teachers." Open, nonjudgmental, supportive, and trusting relationships emerged between students and with students and teachers. Student relationships with other adults also matured.

The professional relationship between the three of us was also unique: Our strengths were complementary. We benefitted from excellent collaboration and an effective team-teaching experience. Open communication, respectful conversations, and consideration of feelings were some outcomes of our quest for coherent curriculum.

Communicating. Curriculum integration—because it is unfamiliar to students, parents, and many administrators—requires open and frequent communication. At the beginning of the school year, we met with our students, their parents, and our administrator to discuss integrated curriculum. We discussed what we were planning and why. During the year, we provided curriculum updates in newsletters that we developed with our students. We had numerous student-teacher-parent conferences throughout the year to keep everyone informed. In addition, through team meetings, surveys, and journal writings, we solicited input from students on the integrated curriculum.

However, integrating the curriculum and making it coherent is no easy feat. After about eighteen weeks of integrated curriculum, our students told us that they felt they weren't learning enough facts and figures from textbooks. They said they felt they learned more the traditional way, "like in 6th and 7th grades." So during lunch that day, we went to the 7th grade teachers to find out what main concepts our students had been taught in science and social studies. The teachers told us they had studied plant and animal cells and the geography and culture of the Middle East.

After lunch, we told our students they were going to have a pop test. When they complained, we replied:

> Oh, you know the information. You studied this last year. Get out a piece of paper, and put your name at the top. On the front of the paper, list the countries of the Middle East and North Africa bordering the Mediterranean Sea. Don't worry, you don't have to name the capitals or their GNP, even though we know you studied that last year. Then, on the back, draw and label the main parts of a plant cell and an animal cell. Don't worry about naming the functions of each part.

For ten minutes, our students sweated and squirmed. No one passed the pop test.

We asked the students, "Since you spent most of your 7th grade school year studying these facts through a traditional approach to teaching and learning and you still haven't learned them, what was the point?" One student replied, "Yeah, if I want to know about the rivers of Africa, I can look them up in an atlas." "Right," we agreed, "you need to learn *how* to learn, not just memorize the facts."

Not long after the pop test, a parent told us during a conference that she was concerned her child was not getting a traditional education. She thought the way her daughter was taught in the 7th grade was the best way. We showed the parent her daughter's almost blank pop test. This opened up a discussion about the need for a variety of teaching strategies to facilitate meaningful learning. Instances like this conference reinforce the necessity of open communication. With open communication, teachers, students, parents, and administrators can more clearly see the benefits of an integrated, coherent curriculum.

Developing Effective Scheduling and Organizational Structures. During our quest for coherent curriculum, having just two teachers on the team enabled us to have fewer students. With fewer students, we could get to know each one on a more personal level and therefore more effectively meet their needs. Having fewer students on a team gives each student more opportunities for input. Also, arranging for off-campus study trips was more manageable for 60 students than for 150 students.

In our classrooms, we used flexible grouping of student desks and tables. That way, all 60 students could gather in one area during team meetings, content lectures, and large-group sessions.

We began each day with both of us teaching a math skills class. After math, our students had two exploratory classes while we had planning time. Students then returned to our team for the three and a half hours remaining in the school day. During this block time, we worked on thematic units and scheduled content skills classes as needed. For example, if students needed to work on specific science content or skills (e.g., effects of acid rain) or language arts content or skills (e.g., interviews), then we held classes to address those areas.

Sometimes we split the team, and one of us took thirty students for an activity while the other teacher took the other thirty for another activity. Then we swapped students. For example, as a large-group activity, we developed a rubric for assessing the "Living History Timeline" presentation. After this large-group activity, we had some students working on backdrops for their skits in one room while other students practiced their skits in another room.

Providing for flexible scheduling and organization allowed us to respond more flexibly to our students' needs. Developing effective scheduling and organizational structures helps support coherent curriculum because we can then continue work uninterrupted.

Reflecting. Reflection means to stop and look back. What worked? What didn't work? What did we learn? What connections were made? What would we do differently? We responded to these and other questions during large- and small-group discussions with students, individually as teachers, and among the three of us. Because curriculum integration was so new to us and to the students, we stopped and reflected frequently. Asking our students to respond to such questions—"How do you like curriculum integration?" or "If you could change the grading policy or classroom management plan, how would you change it?"—helped them articulate their thoughts and feelings.

One student's response summed up what he felt about curriculum integration: "I like integrated curriculum because it's more fun than just regular class, just like that mixed juice, Twister, with the mixed fruits."

References

Beane, J.A. (1990). *The Middle School Curriculum: From Rhetoric to Reality*. Columbus, Ohio: National Middle School Association.

Carnegie Council on Adolescent Development. (1989). *Turning Points: Preparing American Youth for the 21st Century*. Washington, D.C.: Carnegie Corporation.

Dewey, J. (1938). *Experience and Education*. Bloomington, Ind.: Kappa Delta Pi.

Jacobs, H.H., ed. (1989). *Interdisciplinary Curriculum*. Alexandria, Va.: Association for Supervision and Curriculum Development.

Wigginton, E. (1985). *Sometimes a Shining Moment: The Foxfire Experience*. Garden City, N.Y.: Anchor Press/Doubleday.

8

The Case for a Culturally Coherent Curriculum

Beverly E. Cross

In U.S. schools, the curriculum is bounded by culture in explicit (primarily content) and implicit (the structures of schools) ways. In almost every school, curriculum is built on the framework of Euro-American cultural experience, which is generally perceived to be neutral, universal, and appropriate. The typical curriculum works to "deculturalize" (Boateng 1990) children of minority groups, to make them part of a common Euro-American learning, perceiving, valuing, and acting community. The pedestrian perspective on which such a curriculum is based goes largely unchallenged, even though it involves questionable assumptions about power, superiority, domination, and inequality among peoples.

There is an alternative to a curriculum based on the assumptions of a single cultural group that sees itself as superior to and dominant over other racial, ethnic, and cultural groups. We can develop a curriculum that reflects the heritage of all the children in our schools, one that promotes the study of diverse cultures. This new curriculum would acknowledge the cultural assumptions underlying it within a historical and sociocultural context.

A Question of Values

Sixty years ago, Woodson (1933) asked, "Will schools remain a questionable factor in the life of minority people?" Some may be alarmed to know we still struggle with the basic question of equality of education that concerned Woodson in 1933. Others are untroubled by the way inequality is woven into the fabric of American society and into our schools. Despite efforts to create multicultural curriculums, too many children spend years in school without seeing their own race, culture, or ethnic group reflected in their studies. Still other children never explore or understand the diversity of our society. "Too often the best-case scenario is that cultural diversity is absent or invisible; the worst-case scenario is that it is actively resisted and denied" (Gay 1994, p. 72). Given the research linking a culturally relevant curriculum to the success of children in minority groups (Lomotey 1990, Boateng 1990, Gay 1994), these scenarios are extremely troubling. They are troubling also because they work against our need to understand and support one another as human beings, a goal that is perhaps the very essence of education.

Will current school reform efforts abolish these scenarios and ensure that schools educate rather than *mis*educate children? Throughout our history, periods of educational reform have called into question what we as a country value. The current period of reform is no different. As debate ensues, questions of "power and control necessarily surface" (Jones-Wilson 1990, p. 31). In the United States, questions of value are debated within a context of power situated around disparate racial, cultural, and ethnic groups. Our decisions about what we value and consider ideal in our education system will in great part determine the attitudes and behaviors that we will pass on to our children and what our children will in turn pass on to their children. We need to determine how to center children within their cultural framework and to touch their psychological centers. If we do not, we will continue to destroy the spirit of children of minority groups (Asante 1992).

We need to take advantage of the current school reform movement to look beyond the dominant Euro-American cultural perspective and advance equitable consideration for other racial, ethnic, and cultural perspectives. Whether we can succeed in our efforts depends not so much on our knowledge and ability to redefine the curriculum, but on our will to do so.

Toward Culture to Achieve Curriculum Coherence

Educators have a responsibility to ensure curricular equality for all children. Although numerous influences on schooling are beyond our control, we do oversee many things that significantly affect the lives of children. Even in times of great external influence and standardization, we have some control over shaping the curriculum. We have the opportunity to imagine, to experiment, and to use knowledge to bring about a more coherent curriculum. But do we have the courage to amass the social, political, and economic will to use culture to do so?

In *Going to School,* Lomotey (1990) analyzes four theories about why African American children are not succeeding in school: cultural differences, structural inequalities, social deficits, and genetic deficits. He suggests that cultural differences leave minority children out of the curriculum and that structural inequalities in schools produce inequalities in student achievement. He concludes that a synthesis of these two theories could be useful in understanding how to better educate minority children. Both theories are at the core of using culture to achieve a coherent curriculum. The curriculum must be reshaped around content (what is included in, and excluded from, the curriculum) and structure (how the curriculum shapes the school and determines what children experience). The curriculum should bring culture into students' educational experiences in a systematic, truthful, integrated, and meaningful manner.

Many educators recognize the influence of cultural differences and structural inequalities on the achievement of minority children. Reports based on a year of study in Ohio (Governor's Commission on Socially Disadvantaged Black Males 1990) and Milwaukee (Milwaukee Public Schools 1990) provide evidence. Both studies conclude that a cultural perspective lends support to advancing academic achievement for African American children. The reports suggest the following important considerations for schools: (1) a shift from a deficit view of African Americans to one that integrates into the curriculum their world view and cultural experiences; (2) coherent, consistent strategies to improve education; (3) an analysis of the role of the curriculum; (4) an analysis of the role of teachers; (5) an identification of supports needed; and (6) a focus on how minority children view themselves in our schools and in our society. These same considerations are essential to developing a coherent curriculum built on the framework of culture.

The first step in developing this curriculum is to rethink what curriculum is all about. Figure 8.1 offers two perspectives on curriculum that represent different points on a continuum of views rather than a dichotomy. In the next three sections, I'll explore the ideas listed in this figure and show that a coherent curriculum organized around the study of diverse cultures cannot evolve from the traditional linear view of curriculum; it must be the product of a dynamic process that engages children and teachers in constructing curriculum for themselves.

Developing Purposeful and Connected Curriculum. Chapter 1 poses a question about what the curriculum means and what it is all about. Should the purpose of schools be to control and manage what children learn? Or should their purpose be to engage children in criticism and inquiry about knowledge and its relationship to the human experience?

Figure 8.1
Curriculum Perspectives

Traditional Views of Curriculum	Alternative Views of Curriculum Coherence Through Culture
Curriculum as exclusively a tangible document	Curriculum as the constructed and lived experiences of children and teachers
Curriculum as prescriptive, single, absolute, universal, and managed	Curriculum as socially constructed Curriculum as multiple, inclusive, and subjective Curriculum as a basis for inquiry by teachers and children investigating big ideas Curriculum as the result of decisions Curriculum as potentially liberating, rather than dominating
Curriculum as a compilation of fragmented and independent disciplines, boundaries, topics, and ideas	Curriculum as a whole Curriculum as interrelated experiences Curriculum as framed around the human experience
Curriculum as value-free, neutral, and objective	Curriculum as value-bound, prioritized, subjective, and inequitable Curriculum content as not universal (when focused on dominant cultures) Curriculum as a means to become more truthful, representational, and valid Curriculum as framed around multiple realities and views that ensure that children view the world through diverse eyes and diverse realities
Curriculum as neutral in context and time	Curriculum as contextually specific, time-situated, and culturally bound Curriculum as the means to present and validate the entire human experience through analysis of diverse perspectives, contexts, and times
Curriculum as a means to control and dispense knowledge	Curriculum as a means of empowering children through their culture and the culture of others Curriculum as what children understand and interpret
Curriculum as composed of static, linear knowledge	Curriculum as primarily dialogic, participatory, and engaging Curriculum as driven by inquiry, reflection, questions, and challenges for increased understanding, action, and empowerment Curriculum as relevant, pertinent, meaningful, and compelling Curriculum as a means of stirring students' and teachers' imagination, intellect, emotion, and creativity Curriculum as complex, lifelike, personally challenging, and enriching

Embedded in these questions are curricular assumptions and somewhat oppositional views about what constitutes knowledge, what truth is, what children should learn in school, what reality is, and what recognition diversity will hold in the curriculum.

Culture can serve as a framework for rethinking some of our curricular confusion and ambivalence. It can be the *whole* that unifies and connects the content of the curriculum. It can aid us in moving away from the socially constructed boundaries of current curriculum. As culture moves to the foreground, the boundaries between the schools, the lives of children, and larger society become blurred; knowledge and skills come together, and cognitive, affective, and psychomotor development are viewed as inseparable parts of the whole person.

A curriculum organized around culture is based on two underlying beliefs: (1) children need to see themselves and others in the curriculum; (2) the identity of children is inseparable from the curriculum of schools and from cultural contexts. Imagine a curriculum experience that engages students in studying their own community before studying the people of their state, nation, and world. In this learning environment, students use multiple resources (community members, official records, tours, newspapers) to trace the economic, social, cultural, and political transitions of their community. They learn how these compare to larger contexts, what patterns are significant, and what human experiences were meaningful. Students become researchers, interviewers, and document analysts. They connect information in textbooks with their own findings about the people in their community. They hear and understand how various members of the community experience and view life and how they interpret the world.

To view culture as a framework for curriculum coherence is to think of the curriculum as a structure that allows children to view the world through multiple perspectives or "through diverse others' eyes" (Greene 1993, p. 13). By "learning to look through multiple perspectives, children may be helped to build bridges among themselves; attending to a range of human stories, they may be provoked to heal and to transform" (Greene 1993, p. 17). Children begin to understand themselves and each other, how their current experiences are connected to their past, and how they fit into a larger society. The curriculum becomes a means of connecting "book learning" to larger ideas, to humanity, to life. What could be more unifying, relevant, and pertinent than the human experience? What could give the curriculum more meaning and connect it to a larger purpose than a grounding in culture? Through studying the diversity of cultures, children can come to understand what it means to know oneself and to be part of humanity.

Choosing Meaningful Content for the Curriculum. Should the content of curriculum be designed to transmit a single set of knowledge valued by a single culture—knowledge that is fragmented and independent and viewed as value-free, neutral, and objective? Should the curriculum be used to teach cultural superiority? Or should the content of curriculum be multiple, diverse, integrated, and constructed by children and teachers? Should it be acknowledged as value- and culture-bound, subjective, and not universal? Should the curriculum lead children to understand their existence in society and their role in shaping their world? Should the curriculum be based on real-world problems, issues, and knowledge? Should it be focused on constructing meaning?

The curriculum of many schools is discipline-bound and often framed around "the manipulation of information, including propaganda and disinformation, primary tactics employed in the domination process" (Hilliard 1992, p. 12). Framing the curriculum around diverse cultures moves beyond such miseducation to recognize that curriculum is created as children and teachers relate to one another and negotiate meanings. Such a curriculum is recognized as multiple, inclusive, and subjective. Banks (1994) describes several approaches to multicultural curriculum, including the social action approach, which involves framing curriculum around big issues such as justice, freedom, equality, and human rights and moves toward using culture to achieve curriculum coherence. Through such a curriculum, teachers and children can began to understand that "human culture is the product of the struggles of all humanity" (Hilliard 1992, p. 13), rather than a set of discrete, singular facts to be transmitted. From the perspective of those seeking an integrated curriculum, culture is an important means of organizing and connecting studies. Through curriculum framed around multiple cultures, races, and ethnicities, children and teachers can begin to understand that "cultural difference is fundamental to appreciating individuality and humanity" (Gay 1994, p. 66). Theorists argue that including content about diverse racial, ethnic, and cultural groups is important in creating a multicultural curriculum, but they emphasize that it is only a first step (Banks 1994, Pine and Hilliard 1990).

A reality-based and problem-centered curriculum organized around culture can help children make sense of their experiences and connect them with other learnings. Through analysis, synthesis, criticism, and metacognition, children are led to derive greater meaning from what they experience through the curriculum. Moreover, through wrestling with complex, engaging, compelling, and often controversial matters, children begin to confront reality and truth and to make meaningful connections. Through understanding themselves and others, they begin to understand important concepts: truth, peace, conflict, human tensions, interdependence, responsibility, change, order, and justice—topics that transcend disciplines and relate to human existence.

Imagine an integrated curriculum focused on the concept of perceptions and points of view. The questions guiding the curriculum might be: What is a perception or point of view? How is a perception or point of view developed and influenced? How do people react to each? How does each perception affect problem solving and decision making? Since the integrated curriculum should have a major impact on students' lives and their thoughts about their existence, this unit could be designed to aid students in understanding how their lives inform their perceptions of others. Further, students could be aided in developing general skills for understanding their perceptions, communicating them, analyzing them, defending points of view, compromising, showing tolerance and respect for various perceptions and points of view, and making decisions.

Determining the Context of the Curriculum. Should the curriculum be viewed as a tangible repository of static, linear knowledge that requires children to passively receive information without inquiry, challenge, and criticism? Or should the curriculum be viewed as a dynamic learning process constructed by teachers and students, a process that empowers students by helping them make connections between their culture and their schooling? The answers to these questions determine the context of the curriculum. A curriculum built on the framework of culture results in three context-related changes.

First, the context for curriculum becomes participatory, inquiry driven, dialogic, and critical. Hilliard (1992, p. 13) suggests that to foster truth,

> we must facilitate in students the assumption of a critical orientation. [This] implies an awareness of all cultural alternatives and a thoughtful and honest examination of those alternatives. No cultural tradition can be regarded as immune to criticism.

Such a curriculum requires understanding that "culture is not static: neither is it necessarily positive or negative" (Nieto 1992, p. 279).

Second, the curriculum becomes situated around big ideas, real life, personal and societal issues, choices, and emotional issues. Fragmented facts are replaced with integrated ideas, concepts, issues, topics, tensions, arguments, and dilemmas. Passive children are replaced with inquiring, challenging, debating, and action-oriented children. Disciplines become connected through analysis, observation, thinking, contrasting and comparing, evaluation, judgment, and synthesis. The context for curriculum becomes shaped around connections between meaningful experiences and ideas. Children are expected to construct, examine, and extend meaning. They become constructors of knowledge. In the earlier example of an integrated unit on perceptions and points of view, students would likely be researchers, authors, debaters, mediators, persuaders, and evaluators.

Third, the context expands beyond the classroom and textbooks. Sources of knowledge are not limited to textbooks, teachers, and the written curriculum, but instead include the knowledge and experiences students gain outside of school. The curriculum expands to acknowledge students' past, present, and future. Families, communities, and schools are also more likely to be part of the curriculum.

Malcolm X Academy

Malcolm X Academy in Milwaukee, Wisconsin, uses African and African American culture to achieve curriculum coherence. This focus is the result of a study of the academic achievement of African American males conducted by the school district (Milwaukee Public Schools 1990). The study prompted a district task force to make significant recommendations for improving the quality of education for minority children, including the following:

- restructuring schools
- developing strong self-images/self-concepts among minority children
- developing alternative discipline programs
- revising curriculum in all disciplines to include the true story of minorities
- enhancing family support for minorities
- increasing parents and caregivers' abilities to support their children's education
- increasing the involvement and support of both the minority and Anglo-American communities in the education of all children

These recommendations reflect the underlying assumptions about why schools with traditional structures are not meeting the needs of minority children.

Themes Shaping the Curriculum. Heritage and pride are two major themes shaping the ideals of Malcolm X Academy. The school's staff promotes these themes by weaving the concepts of self-esteem, self-awareness, cultural awareness, and academic success throughout the curriculum. They try also to create an aesthetically pleasing, sensitive, caring, safe, and positive environment.

The curriculum, tailored toward the cultural and social needs of the children, is composed of thematic units framed by organizing questions culled from the work of Asa Hilliard (1990): Who are my people? What have my people done? What are my people like (cultural description)? What was done to my people? What is the status of my people? A statement in the school manual reads:

> The infusion of the curriculum with African-American content is the largest battle being fought in the education of black children. The heavy munitions in this fight are the two buzzwords Afrocentrism and multiculturalism. Each is loaded with enough emotional weight to start yet another academic war (Malcolm X Academy 1994).

The school district's mandated curriculum is adapted and enriched with African American culture and heritage. The school staff explains that this focus results from "our belief that African American children must understand that language arts, history, mathematics, science are a part of their rich cultural background." The curriculum is aimed at decreasing generalizations, perceptions, ethnocentrism, sensationalism, and exploitation through careful study of Africa, America, and the people of both.

The mandated curriculum is enriched, strengthened, and diversified as children study African American entrepreneurs, careers in which African Americans are underrepresented, and the communities in which students now live. Children learn the "Black National Anthem" in addition to "The Star-Spangled Banner." They participate in rites of passage that direct them to recognize their inner resources, choose elders who will guide them, and become initiated into their culture. They design and display shields representing aspects of society. They learn about the Kente cloth and Kwanzaa. Extracurricular activities include a culturally enriched media center, Kuumba Dancers, Imani Gospel Choir, Damali Art Gallery, History Makers/Mentors Program, African American Festival, Male/Female Summits, and Parent Conference Center. All of these curriculum expectations are tied to the aim of students becoming responsible decision makers, critical thinkers, and socially and politically active adults.

A Teacher's Story. The following piece by Anne White, a teacher at Malcolm X Academy, paints a clear picture of the creativity and commitment of teachers who have accepted the challenge of building a curriculum on the framework of culture.

> I teach at Malcolm X Academy, a middle school in Milwaukee, Wisconsin. Our approximately 600 children are 99.9 percent African American. Our school became an African American Immersion curriculum school in 1991 as the result of a task force report showing that schools operating within the traditional structure were not meeting the educational needs of African American males. Our curriculum is designed to promote self-es-

teem, self-awareness, cultural awareness, and academic success. Our purpose at Malcolm X is not one of ethnic superiority, but of excellence. We strive to legitimate the African and African American story. Our curriculum is not a "feel good" curriculum; it is designed to tell the whole truth.

My own approach to the curricular integration process has its roots in two awakenings in my life. The first occurred in 1991 when I heard Asa Hilliard speak on the Portland Baseline Essays. The second awakening was when I read an article by Gloria Ladson-Billings describing research she had conducted on what makes effective teachers. She concluded that all the teachers who were perceived to be effective were engaged in what she refers to as "culturally relevant teaching."

I began to feel I needed to be reeducated to be culturally relevant and to be effective and truthful. I now approach my curriculum planning in three ways to achieve a curriculum that is coherently organized around culture. First, I analyze what I know about African and African America culture and how it fits into my curriculum. Then I look at my mandated curriculum to determine what I need to teach. I then analyze what I need to learn in order to integrate my curriculum with the mandated curriculum. For example, I determine what I need to learn to replace the missing pages of history or the silent/silenced voices. Then I look to the experts like Hilliard, Banks, and Ladson-Billings.

My personal approach to curriculum has its foundation in the classroom format. I use a multifaceted approach. I focus the curriculum on events, concepts, and topics. I am mindful of whose perspective I am presenting. To provide diverse perspectives, I use what I loosely refer to as supplementary materials that are correlated with the mandated text. These materials include, for example, *Black History for Beginners, Lessons from History: A Celebration in Blackness* and *The African-American Experience: A History.* I ensure I use diverse historical accounts through *The Unfinished March, A Glorious Age in Africa, Quest of the African Past,* and *Great Kingdoms of the African Past.*

Next I organize my curriculum around schoolwide themes: Who Am I and Who are My People?; Values/Rites of Passage; and Entrepreneurship and Community, Social, Political Responsibility. An example of how I approach the second and third themes includes discussing the Kwanzaa values, exploring the political process and its importance to the African American community, analyzing grass-roots organizations as a means to achieving social justice, and promoting volunteerism.

Finally, my curriculum also involves special topics. Some examples include: Nations of Africa; Nonviolence and Direct Action; Malcolm X Learning Stations; Thank You Africa: African Culture Story.

The bottom line of any curriculum effort is the impact it has on children's performance and attitude. We've had test scores go up slightly and the school climate improve. These are signs to build on as we continue to create a coherent curriculum organized around culture.

Lessons from Malcolm X Academy. What can we learn from Malcolm X Academy about achieving curriculum coherence through the framework of culture? The lessons are significant; and some reiterate what we know about the importance of culture, identity, and schooling.

1. Children need to see and benefit from seeing themselves in the curriculum. Children know whether they are valued through their representation in the curriculum. Adding to the traditional curriculum content on the contributions, holidays, and heroes of various cultural, racial, and ethnic groups does not make children feel truly valued. A curriculum rebuilt on the diversity of culture, however, shows children that they are important to the school and that they can contribute to what occurs there.

At Malcolm X Academy, cultural identity is integrated into a curriculum that is explicitly framed around diverse cultures. In particular, African and African American heritage and culture are emphasized, in addition to the traditional curriculum of American schools. The school staff believes the integration connects self-esteem, self-awareness, and cultural awareness to the academic success of its predominately African American student body. The identity, competence, and psychological and academic development of the children are interrelated through the curriculum. For example, the students study African shields, languages, and cultural practices. The band plays African instruments, and their dancers perform African dance. The students complete Rites of Passage at predetermined stages of their program. Families, community members, and businesses are involved in educational activities to further expose children to the work and community involvement of their own cultural, ethnic, and racial members.

2. Children benefit from seeing people of diverse cultures in the curriculum. A curriculum framed around diverse cultures allows children to learn about themselves and about others. Children learn to view the world through multiple lenses; they learn that they count and that everyone counts; and they begin to understand multiple social, cultural, and value systems.

The children at Malcolm X Academy benefit from studying various American and African cultures. These cultural groups are used to open doors to the study of other groups through social, political, and economic connections within a global context. Students learn how different groups experience the world and how these experiences are interrelated and distinguished. They learn to view the world through a variety of eyes. The experiences of people and their existence in the world become central to the curriculum. Learning to understand diverse viewpoints prepares students to examine what they can do to create a more equitable and humane world. The school is furthering this goal by developing plans to institute student service projects that will increase students' sense of community, social responsibility, community involvement, ownership, and pride. As students develop this sense in their own communities, they will expand its use to larger, global contexts.

3. The multicultural practices now used in many schools fall short of ensuring that the curriculum does not result in the "mis-education of minority children." Achieving curriculum coherence through culture moves beyond the addition of cultures to a complete transformation of the curriculum. Efforts to construct an integrated curriculum framed around diverse perspectives and big ideas move schools closer to becoming a learning community that is better able to meet the educational needs of all children. A curriculum built on the study of various cultures, ethnicities, and races can lead children to understand the human experience and to understand important ideas like freedom, equality, and justice.

The children at Malcolm X Academy study cultures in an effort to seek truth about people and their existence in the world. Thus, their studies are primarily guided not by textbooks, but by numerous resources, research, and analyses. The curriculum is shaped around themes that are broad in scope and integrated throughout the academic year and the grade levels. The schoolwide themes unify students and teachers in the school. Individual teams of teachers develop curriculum and subthemes to fit the educational aims and needs of the students. This design requires daily curriculum planning, which promotes systematic integration of cultures, rather than the use of short, discrete units that often trivialize and distort a culture.

4. School reform efforts benefit from refocusing on the identity of children as a central ideal, rather than viewing children as future workers. Viewing curriculum and children in a utilitarian way distorts both. School reform will be only as successful as its ability to advance equality and achievement for all children. In a curriculum organized around culture rather than preparation for work, job skills are replaced by truth, morality, consciousness, critical inquiry, social action, equality, justice, and freedom.

At Malcolm X Academy, students study what has happened to people through social injustice and inequality. They learn about the struggles of people from a historical perspective and about their struggles today. For example, students study the historical and cultural patterns in employment trends in different communities and among different groups of people. They develop systems to understand the social, political, and economic impact of employment, unemployment, entrepreneurship, and occupational access within various communities and groups of people. They begin to understand the influence their own lives may have on these issues. And they begin to develop social action commitments through the curriculum and experiences of the school.

5. Viewing curriculum as singular and standardized endangers curriculum equality for all children. The current efforts to control and standardize curriculum through uniform content and assessment conflict with diversity at multiple levels. Diversity of ideas, of children, and of curriculum does not fit with standardized notions. Yet standardization and uniformity are embedded in many reform ideals. The reform movement of the last few decades will fall short of achieving its targeted educational excellence if it ignores the role of cultural diversity in schooling.

At Malcolm X Academy, the move to an integrated curriculum, teacher teaming for curriculum planning and teaching, the use of small groups, the idea of teachers as advisors to students, participatory learning, team-based learning, and problem-based learning are reform efforts systematically tied to a curriculum built on the framework of culture. Culture is the center around which these reform efforts support and organize learning experiences for students.

6. Structuring curriculum around culture has implications for children's life in classrooms, for what children will learn, and for what they want for their future and the future of others. To achieve equal educational outcomes for all children, the curriculum must complement rather than oppose diverse cultures (Hale-Benson 1990, p. 210). When cultures frame the coherent curriculum, the potential emerges to concurrently validate, make relevant, and improve the quality of the education experience for all children. To realize this potential, educators must really know children, not just have a cursory understanding of generalized developmental theories. They must understand children as sociocultural beings. They must recognize that children bring knowledge to the classroom with them, that they are members of cultural groups that influence how they think, perceive, act, and value. They must further understand and develop an appreciation for the interrelationships of culture and the curriculum.

At Malcolm X Academy, the curriculum is designed to build the self-esteem and social competence of students. Students and their existence in the world are constant backdrops to the study of subjects such as algebra, technology, the arts, and writing. One priority for the staff continues to be restructuring the mathematics, science, and technology curriculum for better instructional integration and expanded cultural and historical understanding of these subjects. As active learners and inquirers, students engage in inquiry, validation of truth, and connecting what they learn. As they do so, they see the purpose of school differently. They see its relevance, and they see it as a place where their learning is at the center. Students who have this view of school are prepared to pursue additional education, to interact within a diverse society, to find out how they fit into society, and to think about the rest of their lives.

7. Improvement of teachers' knowledge and skills should occur, along with the development of a curriculum organized around culture. To teach a coherent curriculum organized around culture, the nation's teaching force needs to understand diverse cultures and different views of the world. They need to understand their own cultural being. They need to ignite in their students an interest in studying cultures different from their own. And they need to learn how to develop coherent curriculum." To achieve these improvements, we will likely have to revamp teacher education programs and offer new forms of professional development to inservice teachers.

At Malcolm X Academy, the teachers are involved in professional development at various levels. They are engaged in extensive curriculum development. They are taking university courses in African studies, developing integrated curriculum, teaching African American adolescents, conducting action research, and analyzing African Americans in American society. They are also involved in professional associations. Many teachers attend and present at conferences, workshops, and institutes to expand their preparedness to teach a culturally coherent curriculum. And they meet daily in teams to develop curriculum, to monitor integration, and to assist one another with curriculum planning. The school has an extensive professional library, offers internships in community-based organizations to teachers, and provides courses on home relations for parents and teachers together. This model for professional development not only serves the school but also informs the preparation of future teachers through school-university collaboration.

What Will Our Answer Be?

Let's return to our opening question: "Will schools remain a questionable factor in the life of minority people?" (Woodson 1933). This question is most important, for we are at a unique historical moment in educating children of minority groups. Despite years of research, study, and reform, we may have to answer yes to this question. If we fail to consider the relationship between culture and curriculum, if we continue to deny the role of race, ethnicity, and culture in the curriculum, we will have to answer, "Yes, the schools are still not adequately serving minority students."

"Schools need to accommodate diversity in more humane and sensitive ways than they have in the past" (Nieto 1992, p. 272). To continue to deny the significance of culture in the curriculum, especially the culture of minority groups, is to "foster mediocre classroom experiences and exacerbate existing barriers to the attainment of academic success" for minority children (Lomotey 1990, p. 6). We must acknowledge that the curriculum has a profound and lasting effect on children. We must also recognize that children and who they are have a profound effect on the curriculum. Children and curriculum mutually inform each other. Educators must be agents in recognizing culture's potential for making the curriculum coherent. We must also recognize our professional responsibility to garner the political will and moral imperative to support these ideals and to affect the political, social, and policy systems for educational change. The education of children from minority groups is the most critical issue facing educators today. Let's use our imagination, creativity, and knowledge to make a difference. All of America's children deserve no less.

References

Asante, M.K. (December/January 1992). "Afrocentric Curriculum." *Educational Leadership* 49, 4: 28–31.

Banks, J.A. (1994). *An Introduction to Multicultural Education.* Boston: Allyn and Bacon.

Boateng, F. (1990). "Combatting Deculturalization of the African-American Child in the Public School System: A Multicultural Approach." In *Going to School: The African-American Experience,* edited by K. Lomotey. Albany: State University of New York Press.

Gay, G. (1994) *At the Essence of Learning: Multicultural Education.* West Lafayette, Ind.: Kappa Delta Pi.

Governor's Commission on Socially Disadvantaged Black Males. (1990). *Ohio's African-American Males: A Call to Action.* Columbus, Ohio: Office of Black Affairs.

Greene, M. (January/February 1993). "The Passions of Pluralism—Multiculturalism and the Expanding Community." *Educational Researcher* 22, 1: 13–18.

Hale-Benson, J. (1990). "Visions for Children: Educating Black Children in the Context of Their Culture. In *Going to School: The African-American Experience,* edited by K. Lomotey. Albany: State University of New York Press.

Hilliard III, A.G. (November 1990). Presentation to the Milwaukee Public Schools' African-American Immersion School Implementation Committee, Milwaukee, Wisconsin.

Hilliard III, A.G. (December/January 1992). "Why We Must Pluralize the Curriculum." *Educational Leadership* 49, 4: 12–15.

Jones-Wilson, F.C. (1990). "The State of African-American Education. In *Going to School: The African-American Experience,* edited by K. Lomotey. Albany: State University of New York Press.

Lomotey, K., ed. (1990). *Going to School: The African-American Experience.* Albany: State University of New York Press.

Malcolm X Academy. (1994). *African American Immersion Manual.* Milwaukee, Wisc.: Malcolm X Academy.

Milwaukee Public Schools. (May 1990). *Educating African-American Males: A Dream Deferred.* Milwaukee, Wisc.: Milwaukee Public Schools.

Nieto, S. (1992). *Affirming Diversity: The Sociopolitical Context of Multicultural Education.* New York: Longman.

Pine, G.J., and A.G. Hilliard III. (April 1990). "Rx for Racism: Imperatives for America's Schools." *Phi Delta Kappan* 71, 8: 593–600.

Woodson, C.G. (1933). *The Mis-education of the Negro.* New York: AMS Press.

9

Designing Schools and Curriculums for the 21st Century

Willard M. Kniep and Giselle O. Martin-Kniep

What knowledge and skills do students need to face the 21st century? How should curriculums be organized to address students' needs? Are today's schools capable of preparing students for the future? Those are some of the questions that drive the systemic redesign of educational systems, the approach that we believe will result in different kinds of schools with different, more coherent, kinds of curriculums. This approach places students and their needs in a changing world squarely at the center of systemic redesign.

For the past several years, we and colleagues at the American Forum for Global Education have worked in partnership with local communities to totally redesign schools in the light of changing world conditions. Since 1987, seven diverse communities in different parts of the United States have begun this effort, called Education 2000.[1] As a partner with local communities, we have offered a process for design, helped develop the local capacity for design, and supported the local leadership in carrying out the process (see Kniep 1992). At the center of the systemic design effort is the creation of an "educational blueprint" that provides a coherent, overarching conceptual framework (see Figure 9.1). That educational blueprint defines the domains as well as the comprehensiveness and balance that students' curricular encounters should reflect (see Goodlad 1987).

On one level, Education 2000 is a curricular design effort. On another level, the project is about systemic change. As a process for curricular design, Education 2000 has drawn heavily from the best of other reform strategies, especially standards-based education and alternative approaches to assessment. We have focused on identifying the desired out-

---

[1]Education 2000 is not affiliated in any way with America 2000 or its successor, Goals 2000.

Figure 9.1

Elements of the Educational Blueprint: Education 2000

Shared Vision

The foundation of the blueprint is the community's shared vision of the kinds of schools and schooling its children will need to prepare them for the 21st century.

Goals

Based on the shared vision, goals represent the community's most fundamental educational values, describe a desired state or condition for all students, and answer the question "Prepared as or for what?"

Desired Learning Outcomes

Outcomes are derived from and define the goals. Stated as the desired measurable or observable results, effects, or consequences of schooling, outcomes describe what students must know, be like, and be able to do to achieve the stated goals. Outcomes are broad enough to be interdisciplinary and to permit flexibility.

Standards

Based on and derived from the desired learning outcomes, standards specify the levels and types of knowledge or performance we expect from students. Standards describe the knowledge, characteristics, and levels of performance embedded in the outcomes.

A Framework for Curriculum and Assessment

The framework guides the development of curriculums in schools and classrooms and ensures that all students have the opportunity to achieve the outcomes adopted by the district. The framework comprises three main elements:

- *Curricular strands,* derived from the outcomes and standards adopted by the district, give direction to what is taught.
- *Benchmarks,* for selected age or grade levels, set targets for measuring students' progress toward meeting the standards.
- *Assessment and curriculum strategies* suggest appropriate methods for assessing students' performance within each strand. Teaching and curricular suggestions geared to helping students meet the benchmarks and standards are tied to assessments.

Standards for Professional Practice

These standards reflect a belief system for how children learn and the best of what we know about effective teaching. The standards set out the criteria for how professional roles and preferred practices are carried out by teachers, administrators, support staff, and others involved in the learning process.

Organizational Structures

These structures facilitate an organization plan for decision making, communication, and allocation of resources. The plan supports everyone in helping all students meet the desired goals and outcomes.

comes for students—and on determining standards and assessment strategies for those outcomes—before engaging in curricular design (see Martin-Kniep and Kniep 1992).

However, other questions are even more fundamental for us and for the communities we have been working with: How are decisions about valued educational outcomes made? Who makes those decisions? From our perspective, those outcomes—and the standards that define them—must proceed directly from goals set for students. Those goals, in turn, are based on a community's shared vision for its educational system. In Education 2000, *community* has included all educational stakeholders: teachers, administrative staff, parents, students, and community members.

We began this project nearly seven years ago because of the serious mismatch that we believe exists between schools and their programs and the realities of an increasingly interdependent, rapidly changing, and ever more diverse world (see Study Commission on Global Education 1987). In fact, the task of establishing educational systems that will equip students to function effectively in such a world and to contribute to society and the economy is one of the greatest challenges facing our nation today.

To meet the challenge, schools must change radically. The curriculum will play a major part in those radically different schools. As James Beane says in the introductory chapter of this volume, the curriculum must make "sense as a whole; and its parts are unified and connected by that sense of the whole." School-by-school restructuring efforts are unlikely to create such radically different schools. We need a new design that focuses, first of all, on the entire educational system.

Characteristics of the Design Process

By choosing to participate in Education 2000, administrators, teachers, parents, and community members commit themselves to a process driven by one central question: What kinds of schools and schooling will the children of our community need to prepare them for the 21st century? Three unique characteristics of the process distinguish it from most other restructuring and school improvement efforts in the United States: coherence around a worldview, systemic coherence, and coherence through consensus.

Coherence Around a Worldview. We explicitly designed the project to surface a worldview. That approach has two purposes:

• To engage the community in determining how rapid change, increasing interdependence, and cultural diversity are reflected within the community, and

• To engage the community in determining how schools should re-spond to those conditions to prepare students for the challenges of the future.

The goal of Education 2000 is to involve the entire community of stakeholders in shaping a vision of how students should be educated for a changing world. Our strategy is to organize community forums that both provide information and seek input. Typically, the forums have featured presentations and panel discussions on changing local, national, and global trends. In focused discussion groups following the forums, participants consider the implications of those trends for local education. Written records from the focused discussion groups are the raw material used in developing the vision for the educational system. Ultimately, those records are the basis for identifying goals, outcomes, and standards.

Practically, then, by explicitly engaging a community in considering the nature of the changing world, we place students and their needs squarely at the center of the design process. As a result, the design of the entire blueprint is based on and driven by desired student goals, outcomes, and standards that respond to the community's needs and perceptions.

By starting with students' needs in a changing world, we have con-fronted one of the first issues of coherence cited by Beane: creating and maintaining visible connections between purposes and everyday learning experiences. Ultimately, this approach to designing curriculums and pro-grams sets standards for what students should understand, be able to do, and value. Our starting point in setting those standards is not the subjects and disciplines that have traditionally defined the curriculum and contrib-uted, by separating subjects, to its inherent incoherence. Rather, our starting point is the student, and his or her needs, irrespective of subject.

This approach also ensures that we come closer to resolving Beane's second issue of curricular coherence: creating contexts that organize and connect the learning experience. In this design process, just as in confront-ing a real-life problem as described by Beane, we bring to bear whatever we need to know or do without regard for the source. Here the problem is to set standards based on the best collective estimates of what children will need to know or do. By starting with students and their needs, we set standards that naturally cut across subjects. These standards are inherently integrative because most will require us to draw on various disciplines as we help students to meet them. Knowledge and skill become organically integrated, more closely mirroring what happens in real life.

Setting outcomes and standards in that way renders irrelevant the arguments about subject-centered versus integrated and interdisciplinary curricular designs. By using student-centered, rather than subject-centered, standards, the onus is on the separate-subject argument to justify anything but an integrated design. In other words, there must be some justifiable reason for disaggregating the naturally occurring clusters that result from this approach. Not surprisingly, by constructing a curricular framework based on students' needs, we have not been led to a separate-subject structure.

Systemic Coherence. Education 2000 has generated a systemic, systemwide process of design. Rather than tinkering around the edges of the existing system or trying to make piecemeal changes in programs or schools, the process results in a systemwide infrastructure that ultimately enables us to redesign at the school and classroom level. The process draws heavily on the work of systems design theorists (e.g., Banathy 1991).

In practice, we have focused the design process on the entire system and the range of functions within it. The design process addresses three primary elements of the system:

• The substance and organization of programs and curriculums,

• The specifications for valued and effective professional practice, and

• How far the system's organization and its structures support effective programs and practice.

By taking that approach, we have aimed to achieve a systemic coherence that transcends curricular coherence. As we focus on the entire system, our goal is to achieve coherence among all its parts:

• In the curriculum that students will experience,

• In how learning experiences are organized and delivered, and

• Within an organizational culture created to effectively support and nurture effective programs and practice.

The basis for achieving that coherence is in the goals, outcomes, and standards generated through informed input from the community of stakeholders.

One important idea that has surfaced throughout the Education 2000 project illustrates how systemic coherence results from this approach: Each community we have worked with has placed great value on helping children develop a sense of the interdependence that characterizes today's world. That idea appears in the mission and goals of every Education 2000 community. Obviously, the opportunity to inquire about the many manifestations of interdependence in the world must be a prominent element in the curriculum. But teachers and students will both realize a fuller sense of coherence when learning experiences are organized so that students consistently encounter interdependence, rather than dependence or independence, and when an organizational culture is created that allows all those within the system to share in decision making interdependently.

Coherence Through Consensus. Our approach embodies a commitment to involve all the educational stakeholders in the local community, both in the decision to participate in Education 2000 and in the design process itself. From the outset, we knew that we would need the support and involvement of entire communities to successfully redesign educational systems.

How we plan and orchestrate the design process first shows that commitment. In each of the communities, a steering committee broadly representative of all stakeholders—teachers, administrators, parents, students, and representatives of the community-at-large—directs the project. Their charge is to develop and carry out a strategic plan that will involve the entire community in developing the educational blueprint.

How we put the various elements of the blueprint together further shows our commitment to the broadest possible community involvement. The community forums—the mechanism for developing the community's vision for the educational system—are open to all and are, by design, broadly representative. In subsequent steps of building the blueprint, task forces are formed to accomplish tasks such as generating goals, outcomes, and standards. Those task forces have mirrored the composition of the steering committee. To the extent possible, each task force involves a new segment of the community of stakeholders so that each task accomplished also results in expanded involvement and ownership.

Finally, the commitment to broad involvement is tied to a commitment to making decisions by consensus. To successfully redesign their educational systems, communities must avoid polarization and win-lose situations. In all the steering committees and task forces, that commitment to consensus has resulted in decisions and products that all the members can live with and support.

That commitment to broad involvement and consensus relates directly to Beane's observations about the politics of coherence. Our experience has demonstrated the power of involving the entire community's stakeholders, in all their diversity, in the conversation about the nature of the changing world, the needs of children in that world, and the role of schools in preparing children for that world. By focusing on those issues, we have transcended many of the petty differences that divide communities. We have achieved consensus on visions, goals, outcomes, and standards.

The Experience of Two Communities

The Yonkers Experience. One of the most successful communities in the project is Yonkers, New York, an increasingly diverse, urban community in the New York City metropolitan area. Because of its location, Yonkers has both the rich diversity and many of the problems of large cities. But because of its size (33 schools; 20,000 students), Yonkers has a scale and manageability that makes it an excellent laboratory for the redesign process in a large urban district.

In Yonkers, literally hundreds of people participated in community forums and other events focused on how the educational system might look if designed to fit the realities of a changing world. Their input resulted in a new vision for the educational system that is embodied in both the district's mission statement and five central goals in carrying out that mission. The new mission and goals have provided the foundation for developing the Yonkers blueprint (see Figures 9.2 and 9.3).

Figure 9.2
The Community's Vision: Yonkers Public Schools

The educational system is committed to taking the bold actions necessary for preparing students to competently adapt to change, think critically and creatively, model ethical integrity, and value democratic ideals.

Our students develop self-esteem, recognize the contributions of diverse groups, uphold the dignity and rights of others, and acknowledge the responsibility of each individual for the welfare of the whole.

All students become literate and numerate, are steeped in the arts and sciences, develop sophisticated skills, and possess a balanced perspective of humanity. They realize their full potential to become well-rounded individuals and contributing members of society.

The schools are responsive to the entire community and model their goals for students by engaging all educators and parents in shared decision making and problem solving, resulting in productive and inspiring learning environments.

All children have their basic needs—for safety, food, shelter, health, and self-esteem—met.

Students, parents, teachers, and administrators—along with government, business, health, community, and religious agencies—all consider themselves members of the learning community and take responsibility for the education of the community's children.

This educational system is designed to prepare all students to be lifelong learners who fulfill their potential to meet the challenges of today's world and the 21st century: living and thriving with diversity, interdependence, and accelerating change.

—Adapted from the Mission Statement of Yonkers Public Schools

---

Broad community involvement has continued to play a strong role in developing the subsequent parts of the blueprint. Task groups comprising staff members, students, parents, and community members worked from the five goals to develop student outcomes, exit standards, and performance assessment measures that can apply to all students. Figure 9.3, using the first goal and its first outcome as the example, demonstrates how we derived outcomes from central goals and standards from outcomes.

The design of the curriculum, based on those outcomes and standards, is now under way. In the first phase, a communitywide task force worked for several months developing recommendations for how to define and organize the knowledge base offered by the schools. After months of research, the committee generated a list of specifications, shaping them into guiding principles for designing the curriculum. In summary:

> *Principle 1*. Consistent with our goals, outcomes, and exit standards, the curriculum must be holistic and learner-centered.
>
> *Principle 2*. The curriculum should engage students in addressing universal questions: Who am I? What effect do I have on the world around me? How does change (and interdependence and diversity) affect me?
>
> *Principle 3*. The curriculum should be organized around themes that focus on unifying ideas and concepts that cut across subjects and disciplines—such as communication, change, systems, environment, diversity, choices, time, and space.
>
> *Principle 4*. Within the curriculum, skills should be embedded in all content areas rather than taught separately.
>
> *Principle 5*. The curriculum should provide a common core of learning for students, regardless of the school or program they are enrolled in. In each school, unique curriculums serving students' specific needs and the particular focus of school programs will enhance and supplement that common core.

In the second phase of curricular design, three pilot schools have taken over. Using those principles for curriculum design, along with the rest of the blueprint, they are designing and implementing the concrete models of curriculum. This strategy reflects the belief that while the entire community can own visions, goals, and standards, local schools and communities are in the best position to determine how to do so in their own context.

The pilot schools are now struggling with their own process of redesign. Each, with the broad involvement of stakeholders, has developed its own vision for how to accomplish the district's mission. Each has set its own benchmark standards for students based on the district goals, outcomes, and standards. And each is trying to find its own identity.

The elementary pilot school, for example, has adopted Howard Gardner's theory of multiple intelligences (1991) as a primary basis for organizing programs and instruction. The school is committed to parents' extended

Figure 9.3
Yonkers Goals, Outcomes, and Standards

GOALS	STUDENT OUTCOMES: GOAL 1	EXIT STANDARDS: GOAL 1, OUTCOME 1
1. Students completing their education in Yonkers Public Schools will be prepared to live in a world that is characterized by a variety of individual differences and great diversity in social and natural systems.	1. Understand, value, and act to preserve the great biological and physical diversity of the planet's ecosystems.	• Demonstrate an awareness of the concept of ecosystems.
2. Students completing their education in Yonkers Public Schools will be prepared to live with the challenges and opportunities of a world that is characterized by interdependence and a variety of interconnections.	2. Understand the historical contributions and contemporary roles of the variety of groups that make up their community, nation, and world.	• Be familiar with biological and physical characteristics of ecosystems.
	3. Understand that all societies and cultures adopt unique economic and political systems based on their own histories and circumstances.	• Have practical knowledge of how various forces can upset the balance of nature.
3. Students completing their education in Yonkers Public Schools will be prepared to live in a world that is characterized by accelerating change.	4. Appreciate that many diverse cultures have contributed to humankind through unique forms of artistic expression and their histories of ideas.	• Engage in ongoing ecological activities.
		• Know local, regional, and world topography.
4. Students completing their education in Yonkers Public Schools will achieve their full human potential as individuals and contributing members of society.	5. Interact effectively with a variety of people regardless of individual differences in heredity or culture.	• Be knowledgeable consumers.
	6. Respect and be open to the opinions of others in a free exchange of ideas.	• Be able to participate in the management of limited natural resources.
5. Students completing their education in Yonkers Public Schools will develop a love of learning and will be prepared and committed to be lifelong learners.	7. Understand the perspective of others and be able to negotiate and resolve conflicts.	• Actively contribute toward preserving and restoring the natural balance of the planet's ecosystems.
	8. Be aware of the differences in how they see themselves and how others see them.	

and meaningful involvement in all aspects of school life. They are working on a new curricular model, based on the adapted exit standards, that will have fewer strands and be more integrative than the traditional curriculum that has been in place.

At the high school, the faculty, students, parents, and community are working together to redesign their school. Their design will break the school into "houses" of no more than 400 students where teachers will relate to fewer students. This new school will reflect their commitment to curricular integration—in a thematic organization of core academic programs and in the relationship between core and magnet programs.

In the third and final phase, the Yonkers steering committee has assembled a districtwide task force to develop a curricular framework to guide curriculum development in the next generation of school-level implementation. Their charge is to work from the district exit standards and to draw from the experience of the pilot schools in developing their models.

As the pilot schools work on their design efforts, work on the system-wide design has continued:

• A task force has developed criteria for professional roles and practices in the district that will guide personnel policies and professional development activities.

• A task force on assessment has recommended using alternative assessment approaches for evaluating student achievement of the district's exit standards. Their plan tries to balance the need for individual schools and teachers to develop assessment strategies and systems for their own programs and contexts with the need for an overall districtwide assessment system that is valid, reliable, equitable, and manageable. Assessment design teams in each school and a district-level office will coordinate curriculum and assessment.

• In addition, the district will carry out an extensive staff development plan over the next several years.

District 146. Community Consolidated District 146 is an elementary (K–8) school district serving three villages in suburban Chicago. Its offices are in Tinley Park. In contrast to Yonkers, District 146 is a small district—serving about 2,500 children—with a relatively homogeneous student population from a stable middle-class community. As in Yonkers, the designers in District 146 have worked hard to involve the broad range of stakeholders in developing a new blueprint for their educational system. Hundreds of people from the community have participated in community forums, task forces, and other Education 2000 activities. Over 70 percent of the district's professional staff have participated in the design process.

District 146's new curricular framework has five strands. A curriculum and assessment task force developed those strands directly from the district's standards. The strands are as follows:

- Student development
- Communications
- Math, science, and technological processes
- American and global studies
- Humanities and fine arts

In the district's curriculum model, the communications strand is central (see Figure 9.4). Student development, which includes critical thinking, problem solving, and decision making about healthy lifestyles, is associated with all strands. The task force also developed outcomes and standards associated with the strands. Within each strand, the framework also includes:

Figure 9.4
Curricular Framework, District 146

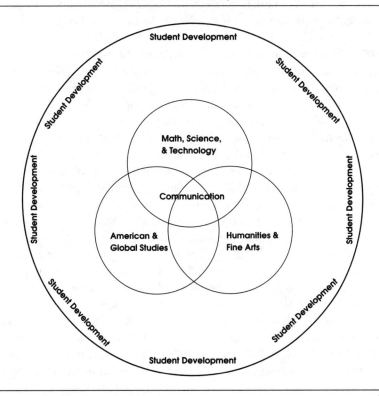

• Benchmarks for student knowledge and performance set at 2nd, 5th, and 8th grades;
• A description of possible strategies for assessing students' progress toward meeting those benchmarks; and
• Teaching and curricular suggestions tied to those assessments and geared to helping students meet the benchmarks and standards.

The two communities described here have followed a similar process in designing an educational blueprint for preparing their children for the 21st century. Each started by considering the needs of their students in a changing world to develop a new vision for their educational system. Each has worked from a commitment to broadly involve the entire community. Each has worked hard to achieve coherence, not only in curriculums, but in the system as a whole.

But the results of the process, in each case, reflect the needs and unique circumstances of the community, especially in curriculum development. Yonkers has taken a phased approach, moving from overarching principles, to design activities in individual schools, to the development of a districtwide framework. District 146 has moved directly from standards, to a districtwide curricular framework, to implementation in all its schools. In Yonkers, two separate task forces on parallel tracks have developed curriculums and designed an assessment system. In District 146, one task force undertook the design of curriculums and assessment.

It is too soon to know if one approach will result in greater curricular coherence than the other. We might speculate that District 146's approach, with its integrated process of curriculum and assessment development, will result in great coherence across the system. On the other hand, the Yonkers approach, emphasizing local development of curricular models, may result in many coherent models more appropriate for a large, complex district.

The work continues in these two communities. What they have already accomplished embodies the significant challenges facing those who try to design educational systems that will prepare children for a changing world. Among the most serious of those challenges is creating workable, coherent curricular frameworks that are holistic and learner-centered. We need not look too far to see that the subject-centered or discipline-focused teaching and learning models that are dominant in schools today are decontextualized, driven by curriculum objectives divorced from learner outcomes (see Fullan 1993, Goodlad 1984, Lortie 1975). As a result, most of us have difficulty imagining a curriculum that differs significantly from the one we have always had. The subject-centered curriculum we know is compartmentalized, not organized around universal questions or big ideas and themes. In practice, that curriculum seldom involves real or authentic tasks and challenges.

The designers in both communities are increasingly aware of the inconsistency of a subject-centered curricular framework, with educational outcomes derived from a vision of what students should know and be able to do to face the 21st century. That inconsistency is especially apparent when outcomes are defined in terms of using what is learned and when they are, in many cases, interdisciplinary. Unfortunately, few available models fit the new paradigm emerging from these design efforts. The most promising of those available are circumscribed to specific curricular areas or levels of education and have not been fully implemented (see Sizer 1992, American Association for the Advancement of Science 1989).

A curriculum that addresses universal questions is equally problematic. To develop curriculums that address universal questions and that foster affective connections between the learner and the material learned without sacrificing substance and integrity, we need a strong knowledge base and the ability to distill the relevant and universal from the remote and abstract. It is much easier, for example, to engage students in the study of families using popular television programs than it is to convey the universality of such a theme through the study of Shakespeare and other classics.

A related part of the challenge is specifying the knowledge components of the curriculum. When outcomes and standards are defined in terms of students' performance, it is often difficult to identify the specific knowledge that students need to have. Moreover, it seems easier to distill the curricular implications from a performance-based standard focusing on skills—for example, *organize, evaluate, and process data*—than from knowledge-based or value-laden outcomes—for example, *contributes to preserving the natural balance of the planet's ecosystems*.

Those difficulties in deriving curricular implications from different kinds of outcomes are exacerbated somewhat when individual teachers and schools have greater flexibility in defining specific content and developing local assessments. Although greater flexibility has the potential for increasing curricular coherence and relevance for students, it also presents the challenge of maintaining equal opportunity for all students. The challenge is to find ways to avoid the situation where some students will receive a better or more complete education than others.

The mixed messages coming to local communities from state and national levels have not made our task any easier. On the one hand, communities are encouraged to create "break-the-mold" schools that challenge commonly held assumptions about how and what students learn and the nature of schools and their governance. On the other hand, national goals have been created, based on the subject-centered curriculum; and massive resources are going toward developing "world-class" standards for the subjects framing that curriculum. The apparent message—"Create a new kind of school around an improved version of the subject-centered curriculum now in place"—is incompatible with local systemic design efforts based on students' needs and is frustrating to the development of new curricular models.[2]

Our experience with Education 2000 has demonstrated that, with support and under the right conditions, local communities can develop a vision and a blueprint for their educational systems quite different from the systems in place today. We have seen the possibilities and challenges of designing coherent curriculums to fit the goals, outcomes, and standards that communities set for students. What remains to be seen is if the blueprints can be implemented, and sustained over time, and if they will yield the kinds of educational outcomes that their designers envisioned.

References

American Association for the Advancement of Science. (1989). *Science for All Americans*. Washington, D.C.: Author.

Banathy, B. (1991). *Systems Design of Education: A Journey to Create the Future*. Englewood Cliffs, N.J.: Educational Technology Publications.

Fullan, M. (1993). *The New Meaning of Educational Change*. San Francisco: Jossey-Bass.

Gardner, H. (1991). *The Unschooled Mind: How Children Think and How Schools Should Teach*. New York: Basic Books.

Goodlad, J. (1984). *A Place Called School: Prospects for the Future*. New York: McGraw-Hill.

Goodlad, J. (1987). "A New Look at an Old Idea: Core Curriculum." In *Next Steps in Global Education: A Handbook for Curriculum* Development, edited by W. Kniep. New York: American Forum for Global Education.

Kniep, W. (1992). "From Image to Implementation: Some Results of Education 2000." Paper presented at the annual meeting of the American Educational Research Association, San Francisco.

Lortie, D. (1975). *Schoolteacher: A Sociological Study*. Chicago: University of Chicago Press.

Martin-Kniep, G., and W. Kniep. (Winter 1992). "Alternative Assessment: Essential, Not Sufficient, for Systemic Change." *Holistic Education Review* 5: 4–13.

Sizer, T. (1992). *Horace's School: Redesigning the American High School*. New York: Houghton Mifflin.

Study Commission on Global Education. (1987). *The United States Prepares for Its Future*. New York: American Forum for Global Education.

---

[2]Of course, that does not mean that such national content standards are of no value. Clearly, schools involved in redesign efforts like Education 2000 can benefit greatly from using such standards as resources to inform the local generation of outcomes, standards, curriculums, and assessment.

10

Curricular Coherence and Assessment: Making Sure That the Effect Matches the Intent

Grant Wiggins

For too long, we have acted on the implicit premise that assessment is what we design and do *after* curriculum writing, teaching, and learning are over—as an afterthought, in too many cases. We have reified that view in the separate divisions for curriculum and assessment in most educational organizations. Could a revolution be under way? The move in many places toward instructionally supportive assessment may yield a result more important than better testing: We are close to understanding that curriculums are not finished until they specify the kinds of assessment tasks that embody curricular goals. Only when we grasp the harm of stuck-on and one-shot indirect testing will we see how nonpurposeful (hence, incoherent) curriculums and student learning have unwittingly been until now.

This way of putting the matter does not do justice, however, to the changes in the air. Coherence is in the *learning*, not the teaching, and is possible only when worthy assessment tasks frame the curriculum. How does designing backwards from known assessment tasks make curriculums more coherent? Because with clarity about the intended performances and results, teachers will have a set of criteria for ordering content, reducing aimless "coverage," and adjusting instruction en route; and students will be able to grasp *their* priorities from day one.

What Is Curricular Coherence?

If we reflect on what we mean by coherence in a curriculum, we can see the vital link between assessment design and curriculum design. At its most basic, the word *coherence* implies a sensible and effective organiza-tion. *Coherence,* according to the *Oxford English Dictionary,* is "logical connexion or relation; congruity, consistency." A clear, rational relation of parts to the whole and of parts to each other should exist—an apparent unity. Coherence is "consistency in reasoning, or relating, so that one part of the discourse does not destroy or contradict the rest; harmonious connexion of the several parts, so that the whole hangs together."

Individual syllabuses and K–12 curriculums *should* move seamlessly and intelligently forward, based on clear—to students, not just teachers—principles. But they rarely do.

The work of Jacobs (1991) and others makes clear how more deliberate planning can avoid the redundancies, gaps, and missed opportunities at integration—the most basic signs of incoherence. Jacobs likes to tell the story of the suburban, relatively small district where four teachers in four grade levels were each unaware that the others were teaching *Charlotte's Web.* We can solve that kind of redundancy in the K–12 curriculum with better advance "curricular mapping" and collaboration across grades and school units, based on explicit and public goals. Such an approach will enable us to find our blind spots. Then, we might even argue that it is all right to use a book repeatedly, as long as we do so deliberately, or view different assignments of the same text, at different levels of sophistication, as a wise choice.

But incoherence is not just a problem of redundancy or gaps across courses. Incoherence exists within many courses: Too often, the lessons and units do not hang together or focus on an overarching purpose or goal. Thus, a "micro" and a "macro" problem of coherence exist. At the micro level, we ask: Does each course of study, as students experience it, provide a coherent set of work and learnings? At the macro level, we are asking: Is there a seamlessness and meaning to the K–12 experience? Do the students experience all their simultaneous and consecutive coursework as coherent?

Even when considering both macro and micro perspectives, we too often view the problem only in terms of written plans. But then we misunderstand the deeper problem of incoherence. A curriculum is not just a blueprint; it is a building code and contract, as well: Does the finished building—the products of classroom work—match the plans and "hang together in harmonious connexion"? Are the *effects* of our intentions coherent, even if the plans are coherent? From this vantage point, coher-ence concerns the realized curriculum, not just the idealized one.

In both micro and macro cases, I am arguing that learners' experiences will be coherent only if performance assessment requirements, agreed on beforehand, cause teachers and students to adjust their performance in the light of the required tasks, criteria, and standards. Implicit in that view are several assumptions about the performance requirements:

- That they are predominantly direct (i.e., complex and authentic performances vs. short-answer or multiple-choice),
- That all students know them in advance, and
- That they are sufficiently important to cause teachers to cease blind coverage of content so that the desired performance results can be most likely obtained.

Coherent to the Learners

To speak of coherence this way thus brings to the surface a key question that is too often ignored: Coherent from whose point of view? The answer: From the learners', not the designer's, perspective. We should be looking at the logic of the learnings, not at the intended teachings in judging coherence. Syllabuses and course sequences may well have an abstract rationale, but learners rarely sense that rationale as such. Typically, learners experience no clear purpose, hence consistency, in lesson plans—a unity that would be clear only if students saw how specific overarching objectives (framed as questions, criteria, and performance tasks) necessitate content choices and ordering. "Why are we doing this?" is a question students should rarely need to ask. The answer should be evident.[1]

Therefore, we cannot judge coherence apart from the meaning that learners experience and construct. Lessons, units, and courses should build toward understanding and meaning. And meaning is not "taught" but derived from integrative performance by learners. Such understanding can thus occur only when ongoing demands require that we wisely consider and use what we teach; when learners can *see* that knowledge has value and how seemingly isolated facts and skills do, in fact, cohere. Feedback through formal assessments ensures that courses end up achieving teacher intentions and giving students a coherent experience.

To my dismay, I have found that many teachers, including many veteran teachers deemed successful, still do not fully grasp that point of view. When I ask them to state their performance goals—the *results* they seek from their written curriculum—they describe for me what they intend to teach and what they intend for students to know: "I want them to read Salinger and understand what it's like to be an alienated adolescent," and

---

[1] I am not referring to students' implicit request for more relevant information. I mean the question in the sense of students seeing why this lesson or unit makes sense, given the overall syllabus and its purpose.

"I want them to solve problems of multiple variables." Or when I describe the kinds of performances that might anchor a course, they argue that "I can't do such intensive work because it takes time away from the content." But those answers reveal the teachers' misunderstanding of the role that assessment should play in teaching (and perhaps their job): I do not want to know what they intend students to learn, or what calendar suits *their* plans. I want to know what will count as compelling and valid evidence that students have understood what is to be learned, or that the teachers know that they should *change* their plans in the light of ongoing results. I want to know how they will ensure the best possible performance. Prior clarity about the most apt assessment tasks, scoring criteria, and justifiable standards—given the aims—can answer that question.

The failure to see that logic is what I call the *educator's egocentric fallacy*—the view summed up by the old chestnut "I taught it, so they must have learned it." The fallacy is based on a view of learning, held by many teachers, that falsely assumes that *teaching* causes learning, as opposed to the successive approximations that students take to accomplish the learning. Those successive approximations involve slowly mastering, sometimes by trial and error, the most worthy and demanding (assessment) performances where key content is required. Aiming for such mastery invariably takes a different logic than the linear march through "logically" organized content, covered once.

Back to Tyler—and Beyond

The illusion of thoroughness derived from considering only one's own lesson plans and not their impact means that teachers can go a lifetime without conducting a key ongoing experiment at the heart of pedagogy, summarized in these questions: How is performance optimized? What do my current results mean? How might they be improved? Which poor results were due to the incoherence of my design and methods, and which were due to the "givens" of my students? The staunch defenders of an overly didactic and unresponsive syllabus have typically never done the experiments that follow from the questions; they have usually rationalized their own habits—and blamed students for poor performance. "Coverage" as a habit is sustained as a consequence: By talking I maximize "teaching" while failing to consider whether my talk is maximizing learning; by assigning lots of pages and hoping for the best, I absolve myself of responsibility for results.

Thinking of curriculum as framed by measurable objectives is not new. Almost fifty years ago, Tyler most clearly and concisely formulated this view in *Basic Principles of Curriculum and Instruction* (1949). There he argues that a logical curriculum is possible only if clear, explicit purposes guide all choices of lessons, texts, and tests. But do not confuse mere teacher intentions with tangible purposes: He insists that curricular objectives need to be stated in terms of the learners' actions, not the teacher's: "Since the real purpose of education is not to have the instructor perform certain activities but to bring about significant changes in the students' patterns of behavior, it becomes important to recognize that any statement of the objectives . . . should be a statement of changes to take place in the student" (p. 44).

The Tyler position makes clear that a curriculum is coherent to the degree that lessons and units provide a unified, effective experience. Content and texts are means to some end, as visible in learner action. The ultimate unity of curriculums depends on the experienced curriculum, not just the planned curriculum. In students' actions and words, we learn whether or not the curriculum was coherent and effective.

The "coverer" forgets that any curriculum or syllabus is a sample of a much larger domain of subject matter. Our dilemmas as designers often come from forgetting that fact. Our "complete" course can seem sketchy and random to learners. When curriculums are textbook driven, the appearance of coherence is even greater: Texts are typically written to provide the illusion of thorough coverage of a subject, while in fact providing only breadth of coverage—and a sample at that. Textbook-driven courses also implicitly suggest that *everything* covered is important or it wouldn't have been selected and that students' only job is to learn what is in the text. (Robert Hutchins once said that you can identify good teachers by the number of important things they decline to teach.) If everything is important, then nothing is important: Students discover and verify importance through inquiry; they cannot understand importance through being told something is important.

To say that learners must experience the importance of ideas is to argue that users of curriculums have to organize the material to reveal *relative* importance. That depends on apt and focusing assessment tasks more than we realize: Usually, students can grasp relative importance or value only if the ideas, skills, or attitudes in question are ranked through performance challenges that demand and lead to perspective. Achieving coherence of learners' experiences thus requires sacrifices in coverage on the part of the curriculum writer. Performance is only effective and meaningful when work is reworked. That takes more than time and patience: It takes a curriculum sensitive to the need for repeated rehearsals and performance attempts; it takes a recursive, not a linear, curriculum.

Coherence thus depends on integrative tasks that all work points toward. The complex performances we eventually want mastered take precedence over our lesson plans, even as they are designed to require the key subject matter. For example, my vision of a Global Studies portfolio includes projects such as holding debates on U.S. aid to former U.S.S.R. republics, forming a model United Nations, and writing course materials for younger students.

Whatever delays, diversions, or following of student interests occurs, all parties know that students must master those tasks—and thus that the content required to master the tasks needs to be apt and wisely used; the tasks are designed that way. (Nothing in this plan precludes a change in direction, however, based on unanticipated interests and angles arising in the midst of teaching and inquiry. The tasks could be altered with adequate advance warning—and by mutual consent, if the teacher were so inclined.)

Any curriculum, therefore, should enable students to gain control of a *few* worthy tasks that both require and reveal deep understanding—"performance understandings," as David Perkins, Howard Gardner, and Vito Perrone describe them (see Gardner and Boix-Mansilla 1994, Perkins 1993). Otherwise, the (ultimately misguided) urge to cover subjects dominates curricular design and instruction. Depth becomes properly valued only when the coherence of learners' experiences becomes a primary criterion of success. According to Bruner, it is an "epistemological mystery why traditional education has so often emphasized extensiveness and coverage over intensiveness and depth" (1966/1973, p. 65). But when tests value mere breadth of knowledge and teachers are fooled into thinking that coverage maximizes learning, the mystery disappears.

Control over "performances for understanding" bears little relationship to doing well on traditional test questions. Performance is always intensive, synthetic, and recursive—thus *never* the sum of once-over-lightly coverage and neat-and-clean items that are the stock-in-trade of most courses. The defense of the dissertation is more than the sum of the subject-matter exams; successful doctoring and engineering is something more and different than the sum of the courses taken and passed. That's why more and more professional schools now anchor their teaching and assessment in simulations and apprenticeships (e.g., through the case method, internships, and problem-based learning situations in medical school).

Here I am not describing what some have called *measurement-driven instruction* or *mastery learning*. Those projects have been bedeviled by the very view of testing the assessment reform movement is fighting—that testing should efficiently determine whether students learned the elements taught. Such a view leads inevitably to teaching and measuring what is easy to measure—a bogus articulation of curriculum and assessment where teachers teach to unauthentic items instead of worthy performances. Worthy performance tasks are not merely derived from the atomized content many teachers *now* teach; they must be found and validated against performance obligations, contexts, and criteria found in the wider world. We want to know whether students can "do" history or science, not whether they merely know an incoherent bunch of historical or scientific facts, ideas, and subskills. We need to build curriculums on "messy" authentic tasks, validated against real-world challenges and contexts (see Wiggins 1993, Chapter 6).

I have made the previous points from a micro perspective, but they apply to students' concurrent and longitudinal experiences across courses, too. Faculties need to ensure that all work requirements, not the ideas to be covered, are framed in ways that maximize the coherence of learners' course of study. Adler (1982) provides one such structure in their distinction of didactic instruction from the seminar in the *Paideia Proposal*. The seminar was deliberately construed as a synthesizing experience; through discussion of a common set of experiences or texts, students could take stock of ideas and questions arising in their normal coursework and tutorials. Carroll's (1989) *Copernican Plan* casts the same idea in different form. His high school students, instead of taking five or six isolated courses, take one "macrocourse" for six weeks and a seminar devoted to topics of student interest. The experience is actually more coherent for students, though that solves only the problem of concurrent coherence, not sequential coherence: Students take only one major course instead of five.[2])

Regardless of how we describe or define these synthesizing courses, the purpose is clear: regularly scheduled "meta" courses that require students and teachers alike to reflect on and pull together their disparate efforts in the more didactic, traditional courses. As Bruner (1966/1973) says, we need coursework that enables students to "sense an emphasis upon ratiocination with a view toward redefining what has been encountered, reshaping it, reordering it" (Chapter 6). Put differently, coherence will be enhanced when depth, not breadth, is the primary criterion in curriculum design.

As important as such structures are, they aren't as likely to yield coherent learning if we don't face the assessment issue directly. One simple

---

[2]I taught a summer school that was one of the programs Carroll used to frame his views. I can vouch for the fact that students learned more in our intensive six-week course than they did in the same course taught over thirty weeks in a normal secondary school schedule (cf. Carroll 1989).

way to build such coherence from assessment requirements is too *demand* coherent learning: At Upper Arlington High School in Upper Arlington, Ohio, all graduating seniors must develop major projects, with the aid of an adviser, that cross at least three curricular boundaries.

Central Park East Secondary School, the extraordinary school founded by Deborah Meier in New York City, has taken the idea to the next level: The last two years of schooling are *defined* by the performance requirements; the school must adapt to learners, not the reverse. After two years of required courses, the students enter the Senior Institute, where the final performance requirements determine everything about their direction, schedule, and timetable. For example, graduation requirements include a postgraduate plan, school and community service, projects involving ethics and social issues, and demonstrations of higher-order thinking skills in various disciplines.

Note the following guidelines for the final portfolio:

> Portfolio items are evaluated for quality and demonstrated mastery using a grid that reflects five major criteria: *viewpoint* that encompasses wide knowledge and deep understanding; an ability to *draw connections* among information and ideas; appropriate use of *evidence;* an engaging *voice* and awareness of audience; and use of proper *conventions.*

Nor is such a flexible contract novel: The so-called Dalton Plan of eighty years ago proposed that students make a contract with their teacher concerning their performance obligations, thus giving them the freedom to tailor their schedules and in-class requirements to the performance requirements (Edwards 1991). At the least, all these ideas suggest that we need to consider whether or not students' obligations (not to be confused with students' interests) should take a primary role in organizing the student work and day.

Toward a Results Focus in Curriculum: Organized Adjustment

Calling our paper plans a *curriculum* means that we tacitly assume that learners and school life will have no impact on our plans. All learning involves unanticipated difficulties, detours, epiphanies, and emergent interests. Therefore, an effective curriculum must be fluid while being focused, built on feedback loops in relation to fixed operational goals—*where we are* versus *where we need to eventually be*. Learners' idiosyncratic and unpredictable responses to our teaching toward goals must cause the curriculum to adjust; learners' emerging performance and needs as performers ultimately determine how the curriculum unfolds; but the curriculum must enable students to meet our preestablished performance goals.

We will not solve the incoherence of curriculums by merely more and better planning. The curriculum is not incoherent because the paper plans made in August weren't intelligently organized. The curriculum inevitably *becomes* incoherent when we have no overarching performance objectives that keep all students and teachers focused. Learners' unanticipated responses alter what the curriculum ends up being, and the vagaries of school keeping cause all curricular plans to play out in unintended ways. Unforeseeable interruptions, serendipitous teachable moments, student mobility, and diverse learning rates dominate the work of curriculum *users*, but curriculums are written as if those problems didn't exist. As a result, too many courses are mere conglomerates of activities instead of coherent: The courses have no organizing thread. Overarching purpose, supplied by "essential questions" (Wiggins 1993) and final tasks, provides the thread, hence the criterion for how to adjust curriculums en route.

I often use an anecdote from my soccer-coaching experience to illustrate this point. When I was a junior varsity boys' soccer coach, during one season we were 0–6 halfway through the campaign. The curricular plans, no matter how well thought out or coherent in the abstract, were clearly not working. My carefully crafted August lesson plans suddenly looked foolish. So, what do I do as a coach? I adjust my own plans (and performance) in the light of the results and the feedback from student performance. Are we weak on corner kicks and offside traps, even though our logically organized syllabus covered them in sets of drills for two weeks? Then let's do lots more corner kick and offside drills than we had planned. I alter the curriculum to respond to evident need—need established by my aims (play the game well) and by student performance (weak this year in corner kicks and offside plays).

How frequently, however, have we seen an individual teacher think and act like an effective soccer coach *once the curriculum is under way?* (Special education and performance-based courses in the arts are notable exceptions.) When have we seen a syllabus altered en route, in other words, in the light of the effectiveness—or the ineffectiveness—of the planned syllabus? When have we heard at a staff meeting—"We're 0–6 in reading; let's completely rethink the rest of the syllabus"? The universal addiction to coverage—teaching *in spite of* results—can only sustain itself in a world where the curriculum designer's intent is viewed as more important than the results wanted from a syllabus. (Even the most successful programmatic adjustments in instruction such as Reading Recovery call for an external intervention in the form of an additional syllabus and teacher.)

A continuous focus on core performance requirements ensures that (inevitable) adjustments to the course of study en route don't cause us to lose sight of our aims. Performance requirements make our objectives tangible and keep them constantly in view. Thus, we ironically end up teaching more than by traditional means—if by *more* we are referring to the *aggregate core learnings* of all students, not the teacher's talk or the learnings of the few best students. Teaching for competence requires a curriculum that can stay focused on the hoped-for learner accomplishments. Otherwise, we risk the design of too many aimless and noneducative projects and activities.

Perhaps no one has made that point more clearly than Elbow (1986). In "Trying to Teach While Thinking About the End," Elbow sums up the benefits (and problems) in teaching toward known competencies embodied in performance tasks. In discussing why this teaching approach causes more, not less, to be effectively learned, he notes that teachers feel more obligated and able to help those students having difficulty. Why? Because student problems are now more understandable because they can be cast in tangible performance-deficit terms (as opposed to vaguer, more fatalistic views that tend toward analysis of intellect and character instead of performance deficiencies). As a result:

> The teachers that thrive in these programs often seem to have been bothered in the past by the large number of students who passed courses without really attaining the given knowledge or competence. They are exhilarated at finally having an approach which ensures that their students will learn. I talked to a whole range of teachers who were initially skeptical about a competence approach, but when they finally saw the results on the learning of their own students, they became enthusiastic supporters (Elbow 1986, p. 109).

A curriculum should contain criteria for making ongoing adjustments, not just a plan. The only way to stay on course is to know your destination and to have a compass and sextant—performance tasks and standards and troubleshooting guides. At present, teachers receive or work from only a list of sites to visit. Curriculum guides must become more like a compass and a sextant than an itinerary. We need more than a well-planned set of work requirements and supporting lesson ideas; we need clarity about how courses can help students attain objectives in the face of various "adventures" and "detours." That adjustment depends on knowing in advance the specific performance "destination": the tasks students should be able to perform, and to what standard, as a result of our teaching.

Therefore, we have an inevitable tension to resolve in the original curriculum design, and few writers are sensitive to it. We want students to learn and to learn to do certain things; however, they may or may not learn on our timetable or in response to our methods. We then have a stark choice: Either design a curriculum that can be responsive and flexible without losing sight of its goals, or continue teaching the "logical" curriculum as if nothing had happened. In most schools, the latter practice predominates. One reason for that tendency is that curriculums are rarely written backwards from the performance results the curriculum is meant to yield, no matter what the unexpected detours.

Let me give an example to illustrate how a performance logic can provide meaningful goals and thus overtake the logic of a textbook-driven syllabus when final tasks are specified up front. Consider a typical high school course in geometry. The curriculum is usually dictated by the textbook and its many, many topics and exercises. Though the course is organized by topics, it can't usually be said to have a purpose; it doesn't have a direction or end up anywhere in particular. We cannot say that it leads to a deepening understanding of what geometry is, what it *means*. But suppose students were required to keep a portfolio of geometry projects. The categories would establish priorities and goals for students and teachers alike. Portfolio categories I have designed for the National Council of Teachers of Mathematics standards on geometry include the following: real-world applications of the Pythagorean theorem, models of spacial relationships, and the use of technology to discover relationships within and between two dimensional figures—as well as a self-assessment of the portfolio as a whole.

With such projects, we see that the course goes somewhere: The students must take the fruits of the many specific skills and notions of the course to address more sweeping, substantive questions and challenges. An aimless following of the book through its chapters and end-of-chapter problems now becomes unwise and far less likely: Integrative tasks to be mastered require a logic of efficiency. The (known and required) portfolio tasks ensure that teachers and students keep them in view while in the midst of their studies; the curriculum now appears properly separate from the textbook's organization and its countless exercises. The teacher's job is to use that text—as a reference book, not a syllabus outline—to help students master the key complex tasks outlined in the portfolio categories. Coherence will improve because the teacher will not select seemingly apt but ultimately directionless problems from the end of the chapter when making up quizzes and tests.

This concern for felt coherence also implies a sweeping change in our view about how to audit and evaluate curriculums (see Kliebard 1992, Chapter 9). If incoherence is the inevitable result of failing to deliberately and wisely alter the curriculum en route, based on learners' actions and reactions, then we need to regularly monitor actual coherence. We need to see and anticipate what kinds of plans and interventions enable teaching to adjust or not adjust intelligently. That intelligent adjustment requires *ongoing*—not once-yearly—assessment and results analysis. What we usually call *program evaluation* doesn't do justice to the idea that curriculum writers and users must constantly adjust their work in the light of results.

We can now extend the point to the macro-level problem of coherence. Portfolio categories and the questions they imply should recur across courses. Ultimately, the power of assessment-driven curriculums comes from the fact that the teacher, not just the student, is usefully constrained by the already-fashioned formative and summative assessment tasks. Teacher and students alike can then better see that coverage or aimless activities will not ensure enablement; they can see that rehearsals and teaching on the basis of performance feedback should enter into planning and adjusting the curriculum; they then would easily see that adjustments—perhaps even negotiated adjustments—become central to an effective syllabus.

Toward a New Logic: Revisiting Dewey's Distinction Between the Logical and the Psychological Ordering of Subject Matter

Caswell, the inventor of the idea of *scope and sequence,* understood that phrase far differently than we do now. He saw the need to consider the clash of the expert's concerns and the learner's needs: While *scope* refers to "the major functions of social life," *sequence* refers to the "centers of interest" in students' lives; the proper ordering of topics—the logic of the syllabus—should thus derive from developmentally appropriate areas of focus.[3] That we have lost sight of his original meaning should further alert us to the incoherence that easily arises when we forget learners' needs as would-be intellectual performers in favor of abstract adult schemas.

---

[3]Kliebard wryly notes, however, that even here the idea of making curriculums interest-centered has been corrupted somewhat from the more radical approach intended by the "activity curriculum" proponents like Kliebard. To him, it appears "open to question" whether the proposed sequence of topics "actually represented interests of children" or a more benign but still arbitrary adult conception of how to order topics (see Kliebard 1987, pp. 223–224).

Coherence concerns the logic of things. But *which* logic is the question we now must consider. That seems like an odd question until we realize that the logic of almost all courses derives from the logic of completed knowledge analyzed into its logical parts. But such a logic is not necessarily the ordering that suits learners; it certainly isn't the logic or direction followed by the producer of the knowledge. What logic supports learners' attempts to understand—that is, perform effectively with knowledge? That logic is *"Backwards Design,"* from performance requirements and questions that inform every other choice of selection and ordering. We might then solve a key problem of long standing: thinking that students need to learn all the logical parts and theoretical assumptions of a subject before learning to "do" the subject. That view is false, as any examination of performance-based work reveals.

To understand the complaint in simpler terms, consider how difficult mastering baseball would be if we had to learn the game through a syllabus based on the logic of the rules codified in the rule book, by a methodical study of the box scores of past important games in chronological order, and by a logic of drill that went from offense to defense and simple to complex hitting, catching, and throwing—without ever actually playing the game. Mastery works differently: constant involvement in the target performance, successive approximations, a movement in and out of performance for coaching, and drill through feedback loops. We *never* front-load all possible information about the subject and performance requirements.

Dewey (1933) has provided the classic formulation of the problem: The logic required to master inquiry differs from the logic of a textbook; the logic of efficient learning differs quite a bit from the logic of completed knowledge. A manual or textbook is orderly in the same way the dictionary or encyclopedia is orderly: It analyzes a complex subject into its elements. It doesn't follow, however, that we should teach the dictionary or encyclopedia from start to finish, page by page—even if coherence exists within the text as organized alphabetically, analytically, or chronologically.

What we want is an efficient order related to unfolding performance or inquiry needs. But our habits run too deep. We teach the textbook instead of treating the text as a reference book for performance problems, and we pay the price:

> There is a strong temptation to assume that presenting subject matter in its perfected form provides a royal road to learning (Dewey 1916, p. 220).

The sad outcome:

> is written large in the history of education. . . . Technical concepts, with their definitions, are introduced at the outset. Laws are introduced at a very

early stage. . . . The necessary consequence is an isolation [of the work and its unfolding] from significant experience (Dewey 1916, p. 220).

Dewey's arguments still stand and suggest that we need a different logic for the organization of material, one where "specific properties" are only taught, in turn, as an outgrowth of a logic of problems arising in encountered or fashioned experience. Coverage is less, but "what the pupil learns he at least understands." From such a critique comes the demand for a responsive and recursive logic to curriculum design, as opposed to a linear logic of coverage.

Overarching questions and worthwhile tasks must make texts and exercises clear means to performance ends. We need problems that cause students to *use* (and want to use) texts to conduct inquiry, fashion arguments, and develop quality products (Dewey 1933).

In areas like skiing and computer use (where clarity about the ultimate challenges exist), curricular designers made that leap quickly. Ski classes no longer require the learner to learn snowplows, stem christies, and other overly abstract analytical approaches to building up performance; you learn to parallel ski quickly, using short skis. Similarly, software manufacturers now provide tutorials and usage hints in separate manuals along with the complete reference manual organized analytically.

This view has also given birth to the whole-language movement (with its encouragement, for example, of naive spelling amid constant writing). But just such movements foster a strong backlash because most laypeople (and many educators) have difficulty imagining a successful strategy that enables the novice to practice and mimic eventual performance while we tolerate inevitable performance mistakes along the way. What critics do not see is that performance is never just the sum of drill or mastery of analytic elements. Who in fact really learns anything this way, when not in school? Who learns software, for example, by reading through the manual page by page? The adult easily forgets, it seems—a more subtle form of the egocentric fallacy—that teaching logically organized theorems or even chronologically organized history does not necessarily help the novice gain control and understanding of a subject.

Science and mathematics textbooks still universally make the mistake of organizing their content around the analytic logic of completed results. The textbooks rarely revisit postulates, axioms, and theorems in the light of later understandings; no overarching questions and problems inform the choice of subject matter and student work. Instead of helping teachers use the elements to frame performance objectives, questions and tasks that would make the content useful, the text presents definitions, principles, postulates, and elementary theorems first and more complex laws and theorems later—with exercises in between. I believe that approach to text (hence, the actual syllabus) design is a major cause of our failure to get more students to understand and appreciate the sciences. With no over-arching and clear performance task requirements akin to "fluency in software use" or "mature skiing ability" (i.e., agreement on what "doing" science and mathematics means), we fall back on organizing the *knowledge*—as opposed to organizing the work by the strategies and criteria that produce knowledge and reveal its meaning—so that students think that science is a catechism of fixed results.

This is an ironic problem. We still teach physics as metaphysics. We can say confidently, I think, that no matter how precise and well-ordered the proposed lessons and exercises, a student *cannot be said to understand* the importance or nature of geometry postulates or physics laws without grasping their justification, their problematic nature, and their history—how they were needed and derived to enable geometers and physicists to prove what they wanted to prove. A curriculum *for understanding* thus requires that we regularly revisit the postulates and laws—the spiral—through ever-complex problems and counterintuitive results to see that they are neither arbitrary nor unproblematic givens. Can we say that students understand geometry or physics without their doing work and encountering problems that make their understanding clear? I do not believe so. Most students come away from a course in geometry with the idea that somehow the postulates are God-given and self-evident.

Nor is that a new lament. Mathematicians and philosophers have complained about this problem in pedagogy for centuries. The father of modern analytic geometry, Descartes, was one of many to argue that learning geometry from the systematic results (the "synthetic" treatment, in his terms) impedes understanding. Such an approach hides the fact that the results were derived by completely different (analytic) methods—ones far simpler to use than is suggested by studying the resultant theorems in logical order, which led Descartes (1961) to a cynical conclusion:

> Indeed, I could readily believe that this mathematics was suppressed by [the Greek mathematicians] with a certain pernicious craftiness, just as we know many inventors have suppressed their discoveries, being very much afraid that to publish their method, since it is quite easy and simple, would make it seem worthless. And I believe they preferred to show us in its place, as the product of their art, certain barren truths which they cleverly demonstrate deductively so that we should admire them (p. 160).

It takes one to know one, by the way: Descartes was guilty of the same crime in his analytic geometry, as history shows and his own writings reveal.

The philosopher Hegel, a clear influence on Dewey, also protested the inertness and alienation from genuine thinking inherent in studying geometry in its logical form: When students "blindly obey" instructions to draw certain lines, they do not see the "necessity of construction" and are left with "rigid, dead propositions . . . without any necessary connection arising through the nature of the thing itself" (Hegel 1807/1977, pp. 25–26).

More recently, Piaget (1972/1973) has argued the same point. According to him, to understand is to *invent*, not merely to discover what someone else knows. Inquiry must precede and establish the value of formal proof. Students must verify key truths encountered, not just receive them unthinkingly: "The teacher is often tempted to present far too early notions and operations in a framework that is already too formal." Piaget encouraged intuition, with formal proof kept "for a later moment . . . in its own time and not because it is forced by premature constraints" (p. 732).

That insight was at the heart of the fine work by Papert and Judah Schwartz with the LOGO and the Geometric Supposer computer programs, but few textbook authors have taken the point seriously enough to rethink how to order texts to honor the needs of inquiry (even if they include more inductive work). Few curriculum designers have asked what questions and tasks "naturally" lead from novice to expert insight into a subject.

Bruner, of course, thought that way. With his stark postulate that "any subject can be taught effectively in some intellectually honest form to any child at any stage of development," Bruner has popularized the idea of the curriculum as a spiral of continuous discovery and refinement (1960, p. 33). Essential to a field, he claims, is its "way of thinking—the forms of connection, the attitudes, hopes, jokes, and frustrations that go with it." From the outset and all along the way, the "young learner should be given the chance to solve problems, to conjecture, to quarrel, as these are done at the heart of a discipline" (1966, p. 60). Thus, we can say that the ultimate coherence of curriculums depends on students having repeated opportunities to directly experience not just adult work but the context of that work: the challenges, messes, and dilemmas at the heart of a profession—knowledge in use (see Brown, Collins, and Duguid 1989; Wiggins 1993).

Though Bruner gets credit for popularizing the idea of the spiral curriculum, Dewey has, in fact, used the metaphor to describe how to organize subject matter to move naturally from performance problem to problem. Understanding increases as tasks are taken on and as attempts at mastery give rise to new questions. Facts and ideas "become the ground for further experiences in which new problems are presented. The process is a continual spiral" (Dewey 1938, p. 79). Otherwise, knowledge is inert and meaningless, perpetually "isolated from the needs and purposes of the learner. . . . Only in education, never in the life of farmer, sailor, merchant, physician, or scientist does knowledge mean primarily a store of information" (Dewey 1916, p. 184).

The teacher's task is to construct a genuinely "educative experience" out of problems as they arise in context—the ultimate result being, as it is for the scholar, "the production of new ideas." Dewey believes that a modern curriculum, one fit for a democracy, demands that we master the past learnings of others (systematized as "knowledge") as the means for our *own* intellectual performance, not as the aim of a curriculum. In other words, students should perform with knowledge in the same way that the professional performs—where the aim is the *production, criticism, and extension* of knowledge.

Whether or not we agree with him about the purpose of schooling, Dewey presents us with a challenge that remains unanswered: how to organize the learnings so that students, even novices, are never puzzled by what is to happen next. The unfolding of a curriculum should appear logical to the *students*. The simplest way to do that is to adapt lessons to performance problems and queries as they arise in the attempts to master worthy tasks—as all coaches do. That approach is truly "in students' interest" (as opposed to what they may like or think they need).

We can summarize what whole language, constructivist theories of instruction, philosophic critiques of theorem systems as a model for truth and pedagogy, and recent past trends like discovery learning all imply about coherent ordering of learning: They all seek a logic to curriculums based on movement through *successive approximations of masterful performances* by students to understand ideas, problems, questions, and tasks. Content is a means; it solves a problem or provides an answer. What, then, is the sequence of (recurring and logically prior) intellectual problems that content should be ordered around? Such a logic implies that we should search for the most efficient movement from a necessarily crude grasp of the whole of a subject matter to a sophisticated, systematic view of the whole of a subject matter. That is feasible only if we identify key questions and performance understandings that represent the "doing" of a subject (such as we find in writing, where the same genres recur at all grade levels).

This has profound ramifications for assessment as well as curriculum. We will need far more longitudinal assessment of performance over time than we now have. We will want to chart novices' performance gains on a continuum that ends in expert performance—as we find in the foreign-language proficiency guidelines of the American Council on the Teaching of Foreign Languages and as the British have recently done in all subjects (see Wiggins 1993, Chapter 5). Curriculums would then always be designed backwards from expert, fluent performances and genres that we want novices to master, influencing even the work of curriculum design in the earliest grades. We would then seek what yields the most likely progress on the continuum, designing in the earlier grades and courses "milepost" performance requirements that are simplified "scaffolded" versions of final performances—as opposed to overly simplistic, decontextualized lessons.

There should be no mystery here, really: The Little Leaguer gets to play baseball right from the beginning. So do the beginning musician, dancer, and actor get to do their fields of activity right away. What, then, is the equivalent in chemistry, history, and mathematics? What are the core performance challenges in each subject? How *do* we begin to teach calculus to 1st graders, if the ability to use derivatives and integrals in problem solving is an aim? What challenges do working scientists and historians actually face, and how can curriculums be more like apprenticeships and assessment like authentic simulations? Learning to do the subject, not merely learning about the *results* of the doing of others, is what is at stake in making curriculums more coherent and effective.

Conclusion

Ultimately, the ubiquitous mistakes of unrelenting coverage and curriculums impervious to students are only possible if teachers misunderstand their jobs. Too many teachers still act as if their job is to teach what they know or what is in the text, regardless of results. On the contrary, their job is to cause apt learnings and performance masteries to occur, using worthy and publicly known and validated performance tasks. If teachers determine that their syllabus is not working to cause the desired results, they should continue to adjust it and their teaching strategies—possible only when assessment against specific desired understandings and exemplars is ongoing. (Another clue that we fail to understand the job: We still study *teacher* behaviors in appraisal systems, not *learner* performance on worthy tasks.)

Then, teachers would need a curriculum that also provided performance troubleshooting tips and texts: "Here is what to try when students do not grasp how to divide fractions." But troubleshooting guides are not enough. We must have clarity about and design criteria for the ultimate performances we consider worthy of mastery. Only by building units and lessons backwards from worthy assessment tasks requiring the use of core content will we make students more likely to learn and teachers more likely to receive praise (and blame) for their accomplishments instead of their intentions and plans.

References

Adler, Mortimer, for the Paideia Group. (1982). *The Paideia Proposal: An Educational Manifesto*. New York: Macmillan.

Brown, John S., Allan Collins, and Paul Duguid. (January/February 1989). "Situated Cognition and the Culture of Learning." *Educational Researcher* 18, 1: 32–42.

Bruner, Jerome. (1960). *The Process of Education*. Cambridge, Mass.: Harvard University Press.

Bruner, Jerome. (1966/1973) "Growth of Mind." In *The Relevance of Education*. New York: Norton.

Carroll, Joseph. (1989). *The Copernican Plan: Restructuring the American High School*. Andover, Mass.: Regional Laboratory for Educational Improvement of the Northeast and the Islands.

Descartes, Rene. (1961). "Rules for the Direction of the Mind." In *Philosophical Essays*, translated by L. LaFleur. Indianapolis, Ind.: Bobbs-Merrill.

Dewey, John. (1916). *Democracy and Education*. New York: Macmillan.

Dewey, John. (1933). *How We Think: A Restatement of the Relation of Reflective Thinking to the Educative Process*. Lexington, Mass.: Heath.

Dewey, John. (1938). *Experience and Education*. New York: Collier-Macmillan.

Edwards, June. (January 1991). "To Teach Responsibility, Bring Back the Dalton Plan." *Phi Delta Kappan* 72: 398–401.

Elbow, Peter. (1986). "Trying to Teach While Thinking about the End." In *Embracing Contraries: Explorations in Learning and Teaching*. New York: Oxford University Press.

Gardner, Howard, and Veronica Boix-Mansilla. (February 1994). "Teaching for Understanding—Within and Across Disciplines." *Educational Leadership* 51: 5.

Hegel, G.W.F. (1807/1977). *Phenomenology of Spirit*, translated by A.V. Miller (1977). New York: Oxford University Press.

Jacobs, Heidi Hayes. (October 1991). "Planning for Curriculum Integration." *Educational Leadership* 48: 10.

Kliebard, Herbert. (1987). *The Struggle for the American Curriculum, 1893–1958*. New York: Routledge and Kegan Paul.

Perkins, Dave. (Fall 1993). "Teaching for Understanding." *American Educator* 17: 3.

Piaget, Jean. (1973). "Comments on Mathematical Education." In *The Essential Piaget: An Interpretive Reference and Guide*, edited by H.E. Gruber and J.J. Voneche. New York: Basic Books.

Tyler, Ralph. (1949). *Basic Principles of Curriculum and Instruction*. Chicago: University of Chicago Press.

Wiggins, Grant. (1993). *Assessing Student Performance: Exploring the Purpose and Limits of Testing*. San Francisco: Jossey-Bass.

11

An Outcome-Based Systems Perspective on Establishing Curricular Coherence

Kathleen A. Fitzpatrick

> A shared vision is the answer to the question, "What do we want to create?" Just as personal visions are pictures or images people carry in their heads and hearts, so too are shared visions pictures that people throughout an organization carry. They create a sense of commonality that permeates the organization and gives coherence to diverse activities [emphasis added].
>
> —Peter Senge (1990), *The Fifth Discipline: The Art and Practice of the Learning Organization*

The shared vision of the well-educated graduate serves as the basis of the coherence of the curriculum in an outcome-based system of teaching. Decisions about the instructional process are aligned with the knowledge and skills expected of the successful graduate. Specifically, the instructional functions of developing curriculum, designing instructional strategies, and assessing student learning are guided by the vision of the well-educated graduate. The answer that schools develop to respond to the question, "What do we want our students to know and be able to do?" gives coherence to each function and ensures that the curriculum is a coherent instructional system, not a series of diverse and fragmented activities. This chapter describes a systems perspective for establishing curricular coherence that is grounded in the operational principles of outcome-based education.

The Operational Principles of Outcome-Based Education

Over the past decade, four key defining features, or operational principles, of outcome-based education have emerged from the work of schools and districts that have been actively involved in developing and implementing comprehensive outcome-based systems for teaching and learning. These principles include the following features: clarity of focus, beginning with the end in mind, high expectations for all students, and expanded opportunities for student success.

Establishing Clarity of Focus. Clarity of focus requires defining the intended learning outcomes that students are expected to achieve and aligning the curriculum design, instructional delivery system, and assessment procedures with the outcomes.

Beginning with the End in Mind. This principle calls for defining the exit outcomes of significance—that is, what graduates of our schools should know and be able to do to lead fulfilling and productive lives in the 21st century. Once this vision of the successful graduate is clearly defined in terms of learning outcomes, the vision becomes the key element for planning each instructional unit that students receive throughout the K–12 program. Consequently, the curriculum is designed to ensure that all students will be able to demonstrate these essential outcomes on completion of their studies.

Maintaining High Expectations for All Students. The principle of high expectations is based on a fundamental belief of outcome-based education: All students can learn. Applying this principle means not only establishing high expectations for student achievement but also underscoring the importance of defining the standards for learning. These standards must be clearly articulated and shared with students prior to instruction. Predetermined achievement standards, not predetermined distribution of achievement (i.e., the normal curve), drive the instructional process.

Expanding Opportunities for Student Learning Success. In providing expanded opportunities, teachers may need to vary instructional time and support to enable all students to achieve the essential learning outcomes. Implementing this principle contrasts with the prevailing practice of schools' organizing time as a fixed constant and achievement as a variable. The expanded-opportunity principle reverses this relationship: Achievement of the essential learning outcomes is a constant, and time is a variable.

These four principles of outcome-based education call for establishing a coherent curriculum through developing the curriculum as well as designing instructional strategies and assessments of student learning. The *clarity-of-focus* principle establishes coherence by articulating a vision of the well-educated student and then using that vision to define the learnings of significance that should be made coherent throughout the instructional process. This principle challenges schools to determine what students will need to know and be able to do, regardless of whether they pursue higher education or enter the work force immediately following their high school graduation. The clarity-of-focus principle helps ensure that the curriculum is not designed coherently for the sake of establishing coherence alone, since it is indeed possible to develop a curriculum around insignificant or even inappropriate learnings in a coherent fashion. Instead, this principle requires that the basis for establishing coherence is the pursuit of learnings of significance that all students can achieve.

The clarity-of-focus principle is related to a chief distinction between leadership and management posited by Warren Bennis and Burt Nanus (1985). Based on their extensive study of the work of several prominent leaders in a variety of fields, Bennis and Nanus have offered the following observation: "Managers are people who do things right and leaders are people who do the right thing." The clarity-of-focus principle challenges schools and districts to dedicate their energy and resources to accomplishing the "right thing" (i.e., implementing the vision of the well-educated student). Further, they need to firmly establish that vision as the focus of the instructional process, rather than simply hope that the vision will be achieved as a consequence of doing things right. One can apply the finest curriculum development and pedagogical skills and yet fail in helping students meet the learning challenges that lie ahead if the application of those skills is not focused on the outcomes that hold the greatest promise of enabling young people to grow and thrive in their learning.

The principle of *beginning with the end in mind* also calls for establishing coherence by using the vision of the well-educated graduate as the basis for designing the K–12 curriculum. By beginning with the end in mind, rather than providing students with a fragmented series of lessons that may or may not relate to each other across grade levels or content areas, an outcome-based system connects instructional experiences from kindergarten through the 12th grade. The curriculum is designed to enable students to achieve meaningful learning outcomes.

The principle of *high expectations* demands that standards for high-quality performance serve as the target for instruction. Both the learning outcomes and the established levels of student achievement reflect the challenging standards. Consequently, in applying Beane's metaphor described in Chapter 1 of this yearbook, the picture on the jigsaw puzzle, which serves as the basis for designing a coherent curriculum, is a picture that is worthy of pursuit by students.

The fourth operational principle, *expanding opportunities* for student learning success, ensures that curricular coherence is supported through instructional strategies and assessment procedures. Student achievement of the learning outcomes is a constant. The amount of time and instructional resources to support student learning varies depending on the results of ongoing assessments. The expanded-opportunity principle requires a feedback system that integrates the instructional strategies and assessment procedures. Such a system ensures that assessment does not become the end point in the instructional sequence. Instead, the evaluation of assessment data is factored into the instructional decision-making process. Consequently, decisions concerning the amount of instructional time and the types of instructional strategies and resources to employ depend on student achievement of the learning outcomes and the performance standards that students are expected to demonstrate. Focusing the decisions that pertain to developing the curriculum and designing and integrating instructional strategies and assessment measures on the essential learning outcomes strengthens coherence of the curriculum.

Establishing Coherence Across, Between, and Within the Curriculum

An outcome-based instructional system establishes connections *across, between, and within* the curriculum to provide students with greater opportunities to achieve outcomes of significance. A prime example of current efforts to establish coherence *across* the curriculum is evident in the work of school districts and colleges that have been active in the Expanded Assessment Consortium sponsored by ASCD from 1991 to 1994. Among the participants are the Edmonton Public Schools (Alberta), Frederick County Public Schools (Maryland), Littleton Public Schools (Colorado), Township High School District 214 (Illinois), and Alverno College (Wisconsin). These institutions have each identified a set of transdisciplinary outcomes or abilities that they expect their graduates to demonstrate. Examples include effective problem-solving, communication, and decision-making skills. These school systems have incorporated such learning outcomes throughout the instructional program. For instance, teaching problem-solving skills is not the sole responsibility of the mathematics and science teachers, nor are communication skills only addressed by the English department faculty. Instead, each department or division shares the responsibility for these learning outcomes. Consequently, these transdisciplinary learning outcomes give coherence to the work of teachers across every department and grade level.

Establishing curricular coherence calls for building connections *between* curricular areas by designing interdisciplinary approaches to learning. However, it may be helpful to note a word of caution in light of the current increased emphasis on developing integrated or interdisciplinary approaches to the curriculum. Clearly, fragmentation of knowledge and skills, which can result from overreliance on traditional discipline-based curricular designs, should be avoided. But we should not overcompensate by imposing an interdisciplinary approach just for the sake of having an interdisciplinary curriculum. Within an outcome-based system, depending on the particular set of outcomes to be achieved, a discipline-based system may not only be the most practical and manageable way to organize the curriculum, but it may also be the most effective. Here again, in designing an approach to the curriculum, the shared vision of the learning outcomes of significance is the deciding factor in an outcome-based system.

One dilemma that will continue to challenge instructional leaders is how to take into account the recommendations proposed by each independent national standards panels in each discipline within a coherent and meaningful K–12 curriculum. In an outcome-based system, the process of translating these lists of discrete knowledge and skills within the context of larger sets of learning outcomes of significance, such as effective problem-solving and communication skills, can help solve this dilemma. Consequently, meaningful connections can be established between curricular areas to help break down artificial boundaries that sometimes restrict true understanding. At the same time, the contributions of the disciplines can be honored. Further, an analysis of the commonalities among the recommended knowledge and skills in each discipline can lead to identifying learning outcomes that can best be achieved within an interdisciplinary or integrated approach.

Designing a coherent curriculum within an outcome-based framework also involves making connections *within* a particular course of study, regardless of whether the course reflects an interdisciplinary or a discipline-based design. In an outcome-based system, connections across the lessons and units of instruction that are within the course of study are established to enhance students' achievement of the essential outcomes of the course. Unfortunately, however, one of the prime instructional resources that many teachers rely on in presenting the curriculum for a particular course is the course textbook; and these textbooks are not always a useful resource because of their fragmented and incoherent design. In many cases, textbook publishers, attempting to please textbook-selection committees gathered from Portland, Maine, to Portland, Oregon, have packed their textbooks with anything and everything they believe that a selection committee might be interested in seeing featured.

Dempster's (1993) review of current curricular practices within a given course or program of study has led him to make the following observation:

> What one sees and hears in the classroom is a torrent of disconnected facts, procedures, lists, and dates. When an imaginative teacher suggests the deletion of material, the voices raised in protest have usually won out. Indeed, research suggests that teachers, curriculum planners, and administrators are much more eager to add topics and supporting material to the existing curriculum than they are to remove them. . . . *For reform efforts to be successful, difficult choices will have to be made about what students ought to learn.* Research provides guidelines for identifying elaborations and for distinguishing between effective and ineffective ones, but it says little about the range of topics or the specific concepts and skills within each topic that should remain. Supporting material must be distinguished from key educational objectives; only then can time-consuming elaborations that do not serve their purpose be weeded out (p. 434, emphasis added).

As Dempster's argument suggests, if we hope to establish a coherent curriculum, we will have to make difficult choices about what students should learn. The learning outcomes essential for student success must serve as the basis for distinguishing what is truly important from what is an elaboration; for establishing meaningful and relevant connections; and for building coherence across, between, and within the curriculum.

Establishing Coherence Across Instructional Functions

The goal of designing a coherent curriculum and ensuring that coherence is evident across, between, and within each area of the curriculum is clearly an important goal for curriculum designers. Realizing it, however, may be jeopardized unless instructional strategies and assessment measures are aligned with the outcomes that serve as the basis of the coherence. If such an alignment does not occur, it is highly probable that the curriculum will remain only a paper document that never achieves its intended purpose.

As Cuban (1993) has argued, there are multiple curriculums, not one curriculum, evident in most schools. The "official" curriculum—that is, the curriculum that is documented by those responsible for curriculum development—is often not the curriculum that is taught. Nor is it the curriculum that students learn:

> Most policymakers engaged in curriculum reform since the turn of the century assumed that the official, taught, learned, and tested curricula were one in the same. By the 1970s, however, it was clear that the official and taught curricula differed. In the 1980s and 1990s, there is far more attention paid to the official and tested curricula than to the curriculum that teachers teach after they close their classroom doors (p. 183)

A sharp contrast to this phenomenon of multiple curriculums and resulting fragmentation is the coherence that can be established within an outcome-based framework. Coherence is established not only within the design of the curriculum but also within the design of the instructional delivery and assessment systems. The learning outcomes that serve as the basis of the coherence also serve as the decision screen for selecting the instructional strategies and resources that hold the greatest promise in helping students achieve the intended learning outcomes. The design of the assessment measures focuses on assessing what is valued (i.e., essential learning outcomes), rather than on testing students on what may be easy to test but unrelated to either the scope or the rigor of the essential learning outcomes. Consequently, the tested, taught, and learned curriculums are aligned with the intended learning outcomes. And, perhaps most important, the responsibilities for developing curriculum, designing instruction, and administering assessments are fulfilled within a collaborative effort based on a shared vision of the well-educated student.

Challenges

There are four challenges that can perhaps make the greatest difference in the success of schools' efforts to establish a coherent curriculum through an outcome-based system. The first is *forging consensus around a shared vision of the well-educated student.* Building a community of learners, including those who have a stake in the success of our schools (i.e., parents, teachers, administrators, support staff, students, alumni, church and civic leaders, and representatives of the business and higher education communities)—and involving these stakeholders in a collaborative study of the future to help establish their commitment to a shared vision of the well-educated student for the 21st century—is critical to the development of a coherent, outcome-based curriculum. In this effort, the politics of school reform cannot be ignored, nor can its impact be underestimated if the goal is to foster genuine commitment to a shared vision for student learning, rather than settling with compromised responses to the question "What should students know and be able to do?"

We must also remember that pursuing a shared vision is labor intensive and time consuming—we should not take shortcuts. The adage that one needs to occasionally go slow to go fast aptly describes the relationship between achieving a shared vision and developing a coherent curriculum. Once the shared vision is articulated, developing a coherent curriculum can move more expeditiously.

It is also important to keep in mind that developing a shared vision is an ongoing journey that leads to a never-ending trail of working drafts. Because we live in an era of knowledge explosion and the information highway, the best we can hope to achieve is an accurate picture of what students will need to know and be able to do, based on what is known today. That picture will most certainly be challenged tomorrow in light of new understandings that have been gained about the nature of the learning challenges that students will need to conquer, as well as new insights about the potential of young people as learners. Consequently, school districts must make a commitment to continually renew and refine their vision of the successful graduate.

The second challenge of developing a coherent curriculum is demon-strating a *willingness to employ organized abandonment*—applying the "less is more" principle that members of the Coalition of Essential Schools (Sizer 1984) and others support. The "overstuffed and undernourished" mathematics and science curriculums critiqued in the Project 2061 Task Force Report (1989) are a clear example of how the abdication of leadership in curriculum reform has led to an unwieldy amount of material being packed into curriculums that many teachers feel obligated to teach for "exposure."

An outcome-based system requires making tough decisions about learning outcomes that are truly essential. School systems must clearly distinguish these outcomes from the information that students have re-ceived superficial exposure to in the past. Neither the unspoken mandate to "cover the book" nor adherence to tradition can be used as an excuse for avoiding decisions on what learning outcomes are essential and what does and does not belong in the curriculum.

The third challenge is *capacity building* that focuses on both individual and organizational development. In designing professional development programs for those responsible for instruction, instructional leaders should address the technical skills needed to develop and implement an outcome-based instructional system and establish a coherent curriculum. Likewise, the organizational development skills required to support systemic change need to become "standard operating procedures" to move from a traditional educational system to one that emphasizes coherence and the achievement of outcomes of significance.

The fourth and perhaps the most fundamental and challenging requirement for establishing a coherent, outcome-based system is *a commitment to a systems perspective.* As Senge (1990) notes:

> Today, systems thinking is needed more than ever because we are becoming overwhelmed by complexity. Perhaps for the first time in history, humankind has the capacity to create far more information than anyone can absorb, to foster far greater interdependency than anyone can manage, and to accelerate change far faster than anyone's ability to keep pace. . . . Systems thinking is a discipline for seeing wholes. It is a framework for seeing interrelationships rather than things, for seeing patterns of change rather than static "snapshots." And systems thinking is a sensibility—for the subtle interconnectedness that gives living systems their unique character (p. 27).

The outcome-based systems perspective offered in this chapter has attempted to present a model of how the interconnectedness of essential knowledge and skills can be more fully realized by developing a coherent curriculum based on a shared vision of a well-educated student, and how the interrelationships among the functions of developing curriculum, designing instruction, and assessing student learning can be more fully developed within a coherent instructional system designed to enable students to achieve outcomes of significance. Applying the "discipline for seeing wholes," or systems thinking, to developing a coherent curriculum can transform the diverse array of curriculum reform puzzle pieces into a picture of the successful graduate. Although the challenges outlined— building a shared vision, employing organized abandonment, capacity building, and commitment to a systems perspective—require a tremendous investment of time and energy, the return on that investment can yield significant dividends for student learning.

References

American Association for the Advancement of Science. (1989). *Project 2061: Science for All Americans*. Washington, D.C.: Author.

Bennis, W., and B. Nanus. (1985). *Leaders*. New York: Harper and Row.

Cuban, L. (October 1993). "The Lure of Curricular Reform and Its Pitiful History." *Phi Delta Kappan* 75: 182–185.

Dempster, F. (February 1993). "Exposing Our Students to Less Should Help Them Learn More." *Phi Delta Kappan* 74: 432–437.

Senge, P. (1990). *The Fifth Discipline: The Art and Practice of the Learning Organization*. New York: Doubleday.

Sizer, T. (1984). *Horace's Compromise: The Dilemma of the American High School*. Boston: Houghton Mifflin.

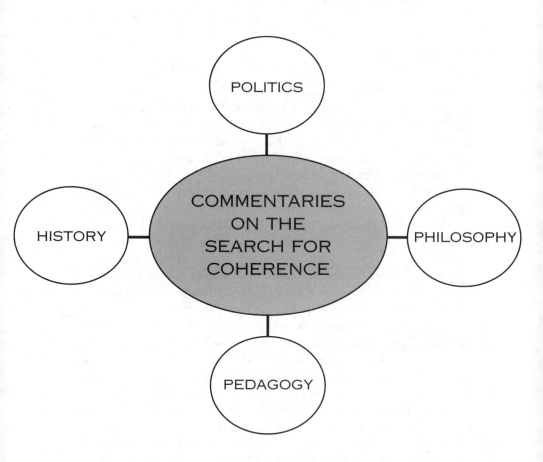

POLITICS

HISTORY

COMMENTARIES
ON THE
SEARCH FOR
COHERENCE

PHILOSOPHY

PEDAGOGY

12

Facing Reality

Michael W. Apple

Doing curriculum work is like plowing in a field that was the site of an old battle. The labor that the women and men put into planting and harvesting may lead to bountiful crops. Yet there is always a danger that the activity will unearth a hidden bomb or land mine. It can be fruitful and dangerous at the same time.

Why should this be the case? One of the major reasons is that whether we like it or not, curriculum planning is deeply involved in what might best be called "cultural politics." The curriculum—and our ways of organizing it and connecting its elements together and giving it coherence—is never simply a neutral object, somehow appearing in our texts and classrooms. It is always part of a *selective tradition*, someone's selection, someone's vision of the knowledge that needs to be taught to everyone. As such, it is produced out of conflicts and compromises that sometimes leave those land mines buried beneath the surface. As I argue in *Ideology and Curriculum* (Apple 1990) and *Official Knowledge* (Apple 1993), the decision to define some groups' knowledge as the most important—as "official Knowledge"—while other groups' knowledge hardly sees the light of day, says something extremely important about who has power in society.

Think of social studies textbooks that continue to speak of "The Dark Ages" rather than the historically more accurate and perhaps less racist phrase "The Age of African and Asian Ascendancy." Or think of books in our classrooms that treat Rosa Parks as merely a relatively naive African American women who was simply too tired to go to the back of the bus, rather than discussing her training in organized civil disobedience at the Highlander Folk School. Or finally, think of the creation/evolution controversies and the recent battles in California over deleting questions based on short stories by Alice Walker from state tests because the stories might be anti-religious or "anti-meat-eating."

Each of us could add many more examples of our own to this list of conflicts, depending on our political, cultural, and religious leanings (see, e.g., Delfattore 1992). The fact that the list could grow documents my argument. Concerns about the curriculum are often involved in deeply held beliefs about the nature of this society, about the patterns of inequality that organize it, and about fundamental values that we cherish. This is the stuff of land mines. Ignoring these issues by treating the choice of knowledge and values in too simplistic a way or by attempting to sweep these political and moral conflicts and economic realities under a rug might make for a few days of seemingly tranquil plowing. But it won't make the buried dangers any less apt to be hit by our plows. One of the tests of the depth and seriousness of treatments of curriculum and of attempts at bringing coherence to it is the extent of these treatments' recognition of such conflicts and realities. This is one of the issues I shall raise about the various chapters included in this book. We can call it the "reality test."

The authors of this yearbook do not speak with one voice. This makes the task of the commentator even more difficult. Though many chapters have the capacity to teach us a good deal about what is possible in bringing about serious and thoughtful changes in our fragmented and disconnected curriculums in schools, some of them are less useful or sometimes seem to largely misconstrue the depth of our problems and what may be necessary to honestly face them. Because of this, I shall speak relatively broadly here. I want to remind us of the economic and educational realities we face and of some of the irreducible principles in establishing the conditions for coherence in these troubling times.

I apologize if at times a little of my impatience shows; but I have spent a goodly portion of my life working in schools and trying to step back and critically analyze why so many of our best intentioned "reforms" go awry. My tolerance for rhetorical reforms is at a low point. And even though I myself have toiled in the fields of curriculum theory and research for years, I must admit to a bit of impatience with (perhaps unconscious) recapitulations of theoretical talk that we have heard before in more sophisticated ways. Thus, some of the more theoretical contributions here are being done without ever connecting themselves to, for example, Dwayne Huebner's (1966) and Maxine Greene's (1988) work on multiple realities and the personal in curriculum. Other chapters are unconnected to the immense debates over how and whether we should reorganize the curriculum around the disciplines of knowledge that were found in the work of Phenix (1964) and Macdonald (1966). This is a tragedy. Why do we have to reinvent all of this de novo?

Finally, although it is crucial to step back from our daily realities and critically reflect on them, I must admit to some impatience with those who do not connect their abstractions to the gritty inequalities of this society and to the immense amount of work that teachers, administrators, community activists, and others are currently engaged in to deal with them. Theory *does* count, because *all* of our activity in schools is guided by conscious or unconscious assumptions—when it is organically connected to these social and educational realities. Yet some of the theories and organizational and curricular reforms proposed here—whose words sound so democratic—seem to ignore a number of important social and educational trends. Thus, for example, some reformers do not seem to realize that we are well on our way to a national curriculum and national testing (Apple 1993b). They assume that curriculum models with more of a "systems" approach (such as outcome-based systems) will connect to these national movements—but this connection might occur in ways not intended by their proponents. More tests, of more *things*, will likely be the result. And these tests will be driven *not* by local needs but by national agendas that will insist that local schools should be integrated into these goals and tests that are not usually democratically arrived at.

Forgetting Our History

A major difficulty we educators face in dealing with the difficult problem of establishing coherence is that the field as a whole has nearly lost the ability to justify what it does. As educators have turned more and more to procedural models, to a focus on "how tos," we have paid much less attention to *what* we should teach and *why* we should teach it. This is not an inconsequential problem. It goes to the very heart of the daily practices of our lives in classrooms. Because we have paid considerably less attention than we should to how we justify what we teach, to actually trying to answer Spencer's historically important question of "What [and whose] knowledge is of most worth?" (see Kliebard 1986), we are not prepared to face challenges to what we are doing now.

Let me give an example. Some neoconservative spokespersons have vehemently argued that we must teach "traditional values" and the "facts" that would make us all "culturally literate" (Bennett 1988; Hirsch, E.D., Jr. 1986). As the material that is pouring from E.D. Hirsh's pen or keyboard indicates, it is now possible to purchase the exact content that "children need to know" for each grade level from the lists of facts that commercial publishers are now putting out for use by teachers and parents. I believe that the idea of a curriculum based on identifiable lists of names, dates, places, and things is quite limiting and does not provide a wise foundation for serious educational activity. But that is not my point. The very fact that powerful groups are taking seriously the idea that what we should teach should be the central focus of curriculum debate gives them immense power in the public arena. They are listened to, even by people who may not initially agree with their position, in part *because* they attempt to answer that question. Even such elaborate procedural models as outcome-based education fail in this regard. They are so totally concerned with process that their proponents are apt to falter when asked by critics to answer what this means for specific content in schools. (The fact that such outcome-based proposals assume consensus and—as I mentioned—will probably lead to even more test-based curriculums, with teachers feeling even more locked in to a "grand plan," is important, but is not the point here.) Thus, those groups who are so certain that they possess a lock on reality and on what we all must learn—think of some fundamentalist activists and those who produce lists for reductive fact-based curriculums—will impose their specific policies on schools unless we begin *now* to have more adequate answers to what we should teach and why.

For this reason, the chapters of this yearbook that try to specify what we should teach to make our curriculum more coherent are interesting. Yet, as James Beane reminds us in his introduction, there is a long history of doing this. Several authors, but not enough, consciously link their work to this valuable historical tradition. Thus, for instance, Grant Wiggins connects his own interesting efforts at reforming curriculums by reforming assessment to John Dewey's arguments about the nature of educational activity. This was a welcome sight, for just as I argued that we have partly lost our ability to justify what we teach, it is also the case that we have nearly lost our collective memory of prior attempts to deal with the issue of coherence. In the past, thousands of practicing teachers and administrators—to say nothing of scores of authors—spent their entire professional lives trying to build more integrated curriculums and trying to give more coherence to a disjointed school experience. We have much to gain by reconnecting with their successes and with the difficulties they faced and may have sometimes overcome, by seeing how they dealt with the realities they confronted (and perhaps we still confront).

Ignoring Reality

Though I find many of the chapters included here to be quite interesting, for some there is an air of unreality about them in another way. It is as if schools and the curriculum and teaching that goes on within them sit isolated from the daily events of the larger society and of these schools themselves. Thus, aside from a few references, one looks in vain for a recognition of the gritty realities of life in, say, our inner-city and rural schools. For many chronically poor school districts, the fiscal crisis is so severe that textbooks are used until they literally fall apart. Some schools have to share textbooks because there is not enough money to pay for texts for each student (Kozol 1991). Basements, closets, gymnasiums, and any available space are used for instruction. Teachers are being laid off, as are counselors and support staff. Art, music, and foreign-language programs are being dropped. Extracurricular activities—from athletics to those more socially and academically oriented—are being severely cut back. In some towns and cities, the economic problems are so severe that it will be impossible for schools to remain open for the full academic year.

The draconian cuts that many states and local districts have had to make because of the fiscal crisis have created another crisis in their wake. Many school systems have been unable to even keep up with their mandated programs, such as classes for children with special needs or who speak languages other than English. Many schools will find it nearly impossible to comply with, say, health and desegregation programs rightly mandated by state and federal governments, to say nothing of other needs.

At the same time, the levels of poverty and despair that our children face in these same areas have reached the stage that words have nearly lost their ability to describe what is happening to the lives and hopes of these children. These are the social realities that teachers, administrators, parents, and students face every day. A few chapters of this book do take these realities as a backdrop for their concerns. Yet these social issues should not merely provide the unstated backdrop for how we might transform the curriculum. They should provide the central focus for a much more serious examination of the depth of our problems and should provide the central focus of curriculum in schools in the affected geographical areas (see, e.g., Ladson-Billings, in press). In fact, these very social problems can be powerful generators of coherence and can assist students in understanding and acting on them.

At the same time that the realities of many schools seem much too distant in some of these chapters, there is another lack. Many of the proposals—some of which I agree with, by the way—have a picture of the lives of teachers and administrators that is more than a little romanticized, that makes it seem as if with a little bit of tinkering, or through some grand new administrative design, or by thinking some deep thoughts, then curriculum reform will naturally arise. I wholeheartedly agree with proposals that seek to empower local actors, such as teachers, in curriculum deliberation from the outset, rather than continuing our lamentable history of producing teacher-proof material as we did in the discipline-centered curriculum plans or in the infamous teachers' guides in standardized textbooks that tell the teacher what she or he should know, say, and do at every step. This was and is demeaning.

On the other hand, one of the most obvious aspects of teachers' work right now is what I have called *intensification*. There is more and more to do—more tests, more mandated content, more paperwork, more meetings, and more social problems dumped on the school to solve with insufficient resources to do it. Thus, there is more responsibility and less time and access to human, material, and financial resources to deal with it (Apple 1988, 1993a). Because of this intensification, we must ask how the ideas advanced in this book relate not only to fiscal and social crises, but with the daily realities of a teaching force that is already immensely overburdened, that is already blamed for social and economic dislocations that are very hard for educators to solve, and that is often apt to see new "reforms" toward coherence (or anything else) as one more burden that may soon be just another example of past attempts that litter the landscape of education. This is not to say that the proposals that are articulated in the chapters here should be ignored. A number of them are indeed thoughtful. But I ask that we squarely face reality, recognizing that even our best intentions will falter unless we take these realities as seriously as they deserve.

This very sense of unreality concerns me in another way, for some of the chapters here seem to be in flight from the political and educational realities I have mentioned. Aside from Beverly Cross's articulate picture of Malcolm X Academy, the description of detailed attempts at actually linking the curriculum to the concrete lives of students—many of whom will be in schools and neighborhoods deeply scarred by the inequalities of this society—is largely muted. I shall return to this point in a moment.

Yet I don't want to be overly critical here. Reality does find its way into the chapters in important ways. For example, several chapters recognize one of the most important facts about the curriculum in the United States and in many other nations. Whether we like it or not, the curriculum in many schools is the standardized, grade-level-specific textbook. Thus, it is not unusual for someone to ask a teacher or curriculum coordinator of a local district to talk about their "curriculum" and to get the name of the textbook that they employ as a response. "Our curriculum is the Ginn reading series" (or Scott-Foresman, or Macmillan, or another textbook). The use of such texts has a long, complex history, some positive and some negative (Apple 1988, 1993a). The most important point here, however, is that the *tool* to teach content has become the entire curriculum. The principles of coherence are determined by what will sell in states such as Texas and California, the two most powerful state-textbook-adoption states. In essence, most publishers will print *only* material that will gain approval by these states, simply because of the economics of publishing. Between 20 and 30 percent of all textbooks are sold to such textbook-adoption states. A large commercial publisher would be acting irrationally if it did not aim its texts at the educational practices and policies of these states (Apple and Christian-Smith 1991). One publisher actually made *national* news when it decided not to accept the changes in its health textbook demanded by Texas.

I want to stress this point because any attempt to make the curriculum more coherent or to change the underlying principles of coherence that now exist (or in many cases don't exist) must begin with the conditions that determine coherence *now*. If we do not understand the existing power of texts and tests, and do not understand how the curriculums and teaching of so many schools are organized around them, our proposals will once more founder on the shoals of reality. Thus, as I mentioned earlier, we are moving toward both a national curriculum and a national set of achievement tests (Apple 1993b). Large publishing firms will write their textbooks specifically for these tests and texts. It will be even harder for non-textbook-dominated ideas of coherence to make an impact as these movements pick up steam. If we do not take into account these larger movements to coordinate local, state, and national curriculums and standards together into one increasingly centralized (and ostensibly coherent) system, our proposals for coherence in the curriculum will probably remain at the rhetorical level.

Once again, my point is not to say that we should ignore the ideas that stand behind some of the chapters in this book. It is to remind us that reality will not be willed away by simply ignoring it.

Connecting with Our Students

One other "reality" needs to take center stage in our deliberations—one about which James Beane is eloquent, in this yearbook and elsewhere (Beane 1993). I refer to the need to connect with students. Too often we treat students as simply one more "input" in a larger equation; yet as Dewey reminded us, our curriculums always end in an act of personal knowing (see Kliebard 1986). Eliminate the personal, eliminate the connections between the concrete student and the school experience, and curriculums and teaching quickly lose both their vitality and their legitimacy in the eyes of students. Then we are left with what Linda McNeil (1986) has clearly documented in her research on students and teachers—a cynical bargain in which students who sense no connection between the world of the school and their own individual and collective lives do the bare minimum to get by and resist any teacher who expects more. Or they simply turn off and ultimately drop out.

This is not a question of developing "gimmicks" to maintain student attention. It speaks to what I believe is the irreducible principle for the foundation of coherence: the connection between knowledge and both the lived reality of students and the communities from which they come. Beverly Cross's chapter clearly describes one instance of this connection. Yet other powerful examples of such connections can be found in the Rindge School of Technical Arts in the Boston area and its integration of the vocational and the academic, which focuses on studying and solving real community problems. Other examples occur at the Fratney Street School in Milwaukee, where a two-way bilingual program has been established and where the curriculum is expressly connected to the cultures, histories, and needs of its multiethnic clientele. Other instances abound (Apple and Beane, in press; Ladson-Billings, in press). Where success occurs, especially in those areas where children are economically and culturally dispossessed, it occurs precisely *because* this fundamental principle of coherence has been taken seriously.

Conclusion

In this commentary, I have urged those of us who are deeply committed to transforming the curriculums in our schools to treat the problems involved in doing this work with the seriousness and the historical sensitivity that they deserve. I have suggested that we should not be satisfied with simple solutions to complicated problems. We should be cautious of technical solutions to political problems. We should be cautious about fine-sounding words that may not take account of the daily lives of the people who work in these institutions. Any attempt at bringing coherence to the curriculum that does not begin with the role of the school in the larger society and the deepening financial crisis schools and communities face should make us a bit nervous. And any suggestion for transforming curriculums that is not grounded in a recognition of the texts and tests that *now* provide the hidden principles of coherence for schools—and that have their own hidden biases and social effects—should make us equally nervous.

My arguments here have not been aimed at casting stones at theory; after all, I've written a considerable amount of curriculum theory myself. Nor do I want to suggest that the efforts represented by the authors in this book are not valuable. Rather, let us not pretend that schools are simple places. Let us not forget that people as smart and dedicated as we are have labored mightily in the past on exactly these issues. Let us not ignore the growing economic disparities in this country. Let us not turn away from the growing racial structuring of these disparities and the effects of them on schools. Finally, let us look the realities of the economics and politics of the curriculum and the daily lives of the people who now work in our schools squarely in the eye and not flinch. With this will undoubtedly come the realization that action on the curriculum and in schools will not be enough. But this recognition must not become an excuse for *not* creating a coherent curriculum in an incoherent and unequal world. In fact, a coherent curriculum might enable students to better understand, and act on, the causes of these inequalities. The futures of our children demand no less.

References

Apple, M.W. (1988). *Teachers and Texts: A Political Economy of Class and Gender Relations in Education*. New York and London: Routledge.

Apple, M.W. (1990). *Ideology and Curriculum*. 2nd ed. New York and London: Routledge.

Apple, M.W. (1993a). *Official Knowledge: Democratic Education in a Conservative Age*. New York and London: Routledge.

Apple, M.W. (Winter 1993b). "The Politics of Official Knowledge: Does a National Curriculum Make Sense?" *Teachers College Record* 95: 222–241.

Apple, M.W., and J. Beane (in press). *Democratic Schools*. Alexandria, Va.: Association for Supervision and Curriculum Development.

Apple, M.W., and L. Christian-Smith, eds. (1991). *The Politics of the Textbook*. New York and London: Routledge.

Beane, J. (1993). *A Middle School Curriculum*. 2nd ed. Columbus, Ohio: National Middle School Association.

Bennett, W. (1988). *Our Children and Our Country*. New York: Simon and Schuster.

Delfattore, J. (1992). *What Johnny Shouldn't Read*. New Haven: Yale University Press.

Greene, M. (1988). *The Dialectic of Freedom*. New York: Teachers College Press.

Hirsch, E.D., Jr. (1986). *Cultural Literacy*. New York: Houghton Mifflin.

Huebner, D. (1966). "Curricular Language and Classroom Meanings." In *Language and Meaning*, edited by J. Macdonald and R. Leeper. Washington, D.C.: Association for Supervision and Curriculum Development.

Kliebard, H. (1986). *The Struggle for the American Curriculum*. New York and London: Routledge.

Kozol, J. (1991). *Savage Inequalities*. New York: Crown.

Ladson-Billings, G. (in press). "Making Math Meaningful in Cultural Contexts." In *New Directions in Equity for Mathematics Education*, edited by W. Secada, E. Fennema, and L. Byrd. New York and London: Cambridge University Press.

Macdonald, J. (1966). "The Person in the Curriculum." In *Precedents and Promise in the Curriculum Field*, edited by H. Robison. New York: Teachers College Press.

McNeil, L. (1986). *Contradictions of Control*. New York and London: Routledge.

Phenix, P. (1964). *Realms of Meaning: The Philosophy of the Curriculum for General Education*. New York: McGraw-Hill.

13

Notes on the Search for Coherence

Maxine Greene

I write as a teacher educator who does philosophy with relation to American culture, education, and the arts. Doing philosophy involves posing particular kinds of questions about the experiences in human beings' lives. They are questions having to do with meaning and with different ways of seeing and describing the landscapes people inhabit.

Like Richard Rorty (1979), I reject the vision of philosophy as a "mirror of nature" or a privileged insight into an objective essence of the totality of things. Clifford Geertz is persuasive when he points to "an enormous multiplicity" as "the hallmark of modern consciousness" (1983, p. 161). It follows that the attainment of any general orientation or coherence is unlikely. For Geertz, the best we can expect is that those who belong to different worlds (cultures, disciplines, discourse communities) will begin having a reciprocal effect on one another. "If it is true," Geertz writes, "that insofar as there is a general consciousness, it consists of the interplay of a disorderly crowd of not wholly commensurable visions, then the vitality of that consciousness depends upon creating the conditions under which such interplay can occur" (p. 161).

When devising curriculum today, we may need to consciously create conditions that stir learners to reach out from their own vantage points into spaces where they can attain some reciprocity. Paying heed to other voices, learners may begin to reflect on such incommensurable visions, even as they strive to make patterns and achieve integrations in their thinking and imagining. Educators must create the kinds of situations in which dialogue is encouraged, in which individuals, despite their differences, can open themselves to what Cynthia Ozick calls "imagining the familiar hearts of strangers" (1989, p. 283).

Whenever I recall John Dewey's conception of philosophy as "thinking what the known demands of us—what responsive attitude it exacts," I am always stirred by his relating it to "an idea of what is possible, not a record of accomplished fact" (1916, p. 381). As we devise curriculum and work on curriculum frameworks, it seems important to hold in mind the prospective, the possible. This means encouraging the kind of learning that has to do with becoming different, that reaches toward an open future—toward what might be or what ought to be.

I find many of the same themes in some of the existential phenomenologists I read. Merleau-Ponty writes, for example, that "because we are in the world, we are condemned to meaning" (1967, p. xix). The very notion of being "in the world" as a perceiving, imagining, thinking being is quite at odds with an abstract, objective view. Interestingly enough, it is very close to the feminist conception of relational and situated thinking and knowing (Benhabib 1992). Feminists and existential phenomenologists are much like Dewey in that they object to universalism and objectivism. They take issue with those who depend on a "God's Eye View of the Universe as One Closed System" (Putnam 1985, p. 27) and build curriculum with such a view in mind. The alternative is a vision of women and men, girls and boys as living, incomplete beings embedded in life situations that are always to some extent distinctive and never stay quite the same. The alternative is a vision of consciousnesses thrusting into the world, grasping its appearances through multiple *acts* of consciousness—perceiving, imagining, believing, judging, remembering, thinking, intuiting. These acts take place in an intersubjective domain where networks of relationship are woven, where people sometimes "make music together" (Schutz 1964, p. 159ff.) Communication, according to Schutz, presupposes "a mutual tuning-in relationship" between the one who communicates and the one who attends. This relationship is established by "the reciprocal sharing of the Other's flux of experiences in inner time, by living through a vivid present together, by experiencing this togetherness as a 'We' " (p. 177). Within such experiences, human conduct becomes meaningful to those who are "tuned in" and recognize the connection between experiences in inner time and experiences in the outer world.

Whatever we comprehend by coherence, then, involves dimensions of inner and outer time in face-to-face relationships like those between teachers and learners, and those between co-learners and one another. It depends also on the experiences of freedom that, for both Deweyans and existentialists, must be achieved in the course of time. Spaces must be opened over and over for choice and action and (not incidentally) for choosing to learn. Determinism, conditioning, or what Rorty (borrowing from the poet Philip Larkin) calls the "blind impress/ All our behavings bear" (1989, pp. 23–24) must be understood and resisted. If not, what we think of as coherence will give way to the rigid uniformity of belief imposed by some authoritarian kind of training. Teaching, after all, as opposed to training, presumes a voluntariness, a willingness to dissent as well as consent on the part of those choosing to learn.

There must be a loose coupling among concepts, values, and beliefs, even those structured by means of traditional disciplines. We must, as well, pay attention to the role of imagination in sense-making, in "tuning in." Imagination is the capacity to look at things as if they could be otherwise, to break through the limits of the actual and the taken-for-granted, to bring "as if" universes into being (as in the realms of the arts). A live imagination, as Mary Warnock writes, brings with it a sense that "there is always *more* to experience, and *more in* what we experience than we can predict. Without some such sense, even at the quite human level of there being something that deeply absorbs our interest, human life becomes perhaps not actually futile or pointless, but experienced as if it were" (1978, pp. 202–203). It is understandable that Warnock believes boredom and a sense of futility are among the worst enemies of education. At a time of diminishing opportunity in so many lives, at a time when upward mobility cannot be guaranteed, feelings of futility are widespread.

This is partially due, of course, to the association of becoming different and being successful with consumerism and material possession, with the priority of "having" rather than "being." The rendering of the American dream in *The Great Gatsby* becomes increasingly recognizable, even for those who feel themselves among the disinherited. This is the description of James Gatz, who changed his name to Gatsby when he was 17:

> His parents were shiftless and unsuccessful farm people—his imagination had never really accepted them as his parents at all. The truth was that Jay Gatsby of West Egg, Long Island, sprang from his Platonic conception of himself. He was a son of God—a phrase which, if it means anything, means just that—and he must be about His Father's business, the service of a vast, vulgar, and meretricious beauty (Fitzgerald 1954, p. 96).

The narrator says this was exactly the sort of Gatsby a 17-year-old boy would invent, and that he remained faithful to the conception until the end. The radiance of it, the extravagance of it do not reduce the fixity and pathos of it; and it may be that one of the obligations of those who devise curriculum is to make it possible for the young to perceive ranges of alternatives that are significant "possibles" for themselves.

One of the great arguments for making the arts central in the curriculum is that informed encounters with them may indeed open vistas on alternative possibilities for being in the world. *The Adventures of Huckleberry Finn* and *The Invisible Man* offer no existential directives for charting a way through the cruelties of American society or achieving personal visibility. Grace Paley's stories, Toni Morrison's *Beloved*, and Isabel Allende's *Eva Luna* show their readers many things but cannot instruct them on how to pursue liberation, salvation, or success. If attentively read, however, and imaginatively realized, they can tap domains of experience ordinarily obscured or ignored. Each one, as Jean-Paul Sartre puts it, may be seen as "an act of confidence in the freedom" of those who come to it. "A writer," he says, discloses a world and offers it "as a task to the generosity of the reader"; the writer's work may be defined "as an imaginary presentation of the world insofar as it demands human freedom" (1949, p. 63). To demand human freedom is to be contingent on the choices human beings can make, on the actions they can undertake, on the degree to which (conscious of deficiencies) they are ready to repair. Again, it takes imagination to engage with literature and other art forms—aesthetic imagination and social imagination. If *King Lear, Medea, Schindler's List, Howard's End, The Color Purple*, and *A Streetcar Named Desire* present—each in its own fashion—a "task," it is to call on us to be present to ourselves and to others, to pose questions even where there are no answers.

Encounters of this sort (obviously adjusted to ages and capacities) push back the boundaries of which James Beane speaks: They locate learners in a wider world, even as they bring them in closer touch with their own actualities. They make more likely the activity of mind viewed, as Dewey wrote, as a verb rather than a noun: "It denotes all the ways in which we deal consciously and expressly with the situations in which we find ourselves" (1934, p. 263). Viewed in this manner, the fragmentation against which Beane warns is far less likely. The point of curriculum making is to order experiences in such a fashion as to move diverse persons to mindfulness and to care.

Where purposes are concerned, we must go beyond the Gatsbyan illusion, even as we widen the commitments of the public school rather than narrow them. Of course, the workplace makes its demands, but this does not require that schools concentrate their attention on preparation for work in the technological society. We are aware of the speed of change where technologies are concerned; we are only now becoming acquainted with the range of open capacities, as well as skills, needed for adequate participation in a society changing at every moment. We are only beginning to act on our awareness of the special needs of newcomers from countries all over the world. We are being asked to take responsibility for a diversification of what we think of as our heritage—to extend the substance of what we teach to include texts and voices rarely attended to in our past. At once, we are challenged to devise new ways of engaging persons as participants in a community that is always in the making, as members of a reflective and articulate public aware of what freedom signifies, and justice, and equality. In part, it is a matter (as Beane makes clear) of discovering how young people make sense of their worlds and going on to effect connections between their sense-making and the constructions of social reality that characterize our ways of being together.

Part of our work involves enabling students to enter what Alfred Schutz calls "provinces of meaning," each with its own cognitive style (1967, p. 231ff). Schutz found his inspiration in William James' view that to call something real means that "this thing stands in a certain relation to ourselves" (Schutz 1967, p. 208). Then Schutz goes on to say that meaning is "the result of an interpretation of a past experience looked at from the present Now with a reflective attitude" (p. 210). He compares this idea of meaning with various "subjectively meaningful experiences of spontaneity" (p. 211), referred to as conduct and not reflected on when they occur. When conduct is planned in advance, however, when it is based on a preconceived project, it becomes action. That suggests an awareness of embarking on a beginning, of taking an initiative. It differs from conduct because it responds to an intention to bring about a projected state of affair. When this happens, says Schutz, the preconceived project becomes an aim, and the project becomes a purpose.

If, say, I desire to find out some of the long-obscured truth about the landings on Omaha Beach on D-Day in 1944, the action I undertake may be seen as a process of projected thinking—an effort to solve a historical puzzle through various kinds of questioning, decoding, interpreting and reinterpreting, comparing, reasoning, and imagining. I will draw from meanings in my already lived experience: what I have come to know about wars, censorship, fascism, military authority, poetry about the deaths of young men, personal losses, memory. That entails looking through various lenses or perspectives. It entails using the schemata or the patternings made available by the social sciences, literature, the media, critical theories, and subjectively lived life. But it means using them for the sake of clearing up something that goes beyond mere information for me. It has to do with my values, my commitments, with where I have been in the past and where I stand today.

For Dewey, experience becomes conscious "only when meanings enter it that are derived from prior experience. Imagination is the only gateway through which these meanings can find their way into a present interaction. . . . But the experience enacted is human and conscious only as that which is given here and now is extended by meanings and values drawn from what is absent in fact and present only imaginatively" (1934, p. 272). And he makes the point that, because of the gap between present and past, "all conscious perception is a venture into the unknown," whereas when past and present fit exactly into one another,"there is only recurrence, complete uniformity; the resulting experience is routine and mechanical; it does not come to consciousness in perception." Schutz uses the term "wide-awakeness" when he speaks of projects and purposes; Dewey, always concerned about the prospective, about what might or should come to be, talks of the concentration and enlargement of immediate experience.

What is significant is the possibility of connection between diversely lived experiences and an increasingly meaningful world. The meanings are funded—or sedimented, some would say—on the lived landscapes of those who learn; questioning, patterning, futuring, we render them landscapes of possibility. The coherence is to be found in the rhythm and vitality of the process itself, the willingness to turn outward, to enter into dialogues, to continue to create provisional relationships, to reach beyond. What is significant as well—deeply significant in what strikes so many as a chaotic world—is the weaving of wider and wider webs of relationship, what may become a common world. Hannah Arendt has said:

> Education is the point at which we decide whether we love the world enough to assume responsibility for it and by the same token save it from that ruin which, except for renewal, except for the coming of the new and the young, would be inevitable. And education, too, is where we decide whether we love our children enough not to expel them from our world and leave them to their own devices, nor to strike from their hands their chance of undertaking something new, something unforeseen by us, but to prepare them in advance for the task of renewing a common world (1961, p. 196).

That may be where coherence is fulfilled—in the making of a common world.

References

Arendt, H. (1961). *Between Past and Future.* New York: The Viking Press.
Benhabib, S. (1992). *Situating the Self: Gender, Community and Postmodernism in Contemporary Ethics.* New York: Routledge.
Dewey, J. (1916) *Democracy and Education.* New York: The Macmillan Company.
Dewey, J. (1934). *Art as Experience.* New York: Minton, Balch, & Co.
Fitzgerald, F.S. (1954). *The Great Gatsby.* Philadelphia: Franklin Mint.
Geertz, C. (1983). *Local Knowledge.* New York: Basic Books.
Merleau-Ponty, M. (1967). *Phenomenology of Perception.* London: Routledge and Kegan Paul.
Ozick, C. (1989). *Metaphor and Memory.* New York: Alfred A. Knopf.
Putnam, H. (1985). "After Empiricism." In *Post-Analytic Philosophy,* edited by J. Rajchman and C. West (pp. 20–30). New York: Columbia University Press.
Rorty, R. (1979). *Philosophy and the Mirror of Nature.* Princeton, N.J.: Princeton University.

Rorty, R. (1989). *Contingency, Irony, and Solidarity*. New York: Cambridge University Press.

Sartre, J-P. (1949). *Literature and Existentialism*. New York: The Citadel Press.

Schutz, A. (1964). *Collected Papers II. Studies in Social Theory*. The Hague: Martinus Nijhoff.

Schutz, A. (1967). *Collected Papers I. The Problem of Social Reality*. The Hague: Martinus Nijhoff.

Warnock, M. (1978). *Imagination*. Berkeley: University of California Press.

14

Toward Lives Worth Living and Sharing: Historical Perspective on Curriculum Coherence

William H. Schubert

What is worth knowing and experiencing? Why? What good does it do? Who benefits? Does it hurt anyone? How should this knowledge and experience be gained, and who should decide? Such questions probe deeply into basic human questions: What makes a life worth living? What makes it worth sharing? Those are the questions that call me to learn, teach, and do curriculum work (see Schubert 1986, 1990; Schubert and Ayers 1992; Schubert and Lopez 1993). They raise many other questions, both practical and theoretical.

What is fundamentally curricular and what is fundamentally human are of the same fabric. We see this theme—and the questions it provokes—in the history of curriculum development, from Dewey's (1902, 1916, 1938) emphasis on students' interests and concerns; to Ulich's (1947) work, *Three Thousand Years of Educational Wisdom*; through landmark works such as *The Elementary School* by Herrick, Goodlad, Estvan, and Eberman (1956); and on to modern (and not-so-modern) ideas about interdisciplinary and integrated curriculums (Kilpatrick 1918, Jacobs 1989, Drake 1993). One such question is, "What makes a curriculum fit together—what makes it cohere?" Another is, "How do we capture people's penetrating interest in creating a life worth living?"

Finding the answers to these questions is a quest that in itself is the destination. Put another way, "the medium is the message" (or "massage"—see McLuhan and Fiore 1967). As Huebner (1966) pointed out, thinking of students as just *learners* isn't enough; we are all questors. This chapter records a personal quest of mine for coherence in the curriculum, from a historical perspective. It leads, in the end, back to my original question: "What makes a life worth living, a life worth sharing?"

Key aspects of the history of curriculum thought speak powerfully to educators as we address this question—and hope for curriculum coherence. In this chapter, I highlight a chronology of characters and events in the past century and a half that have helped me keep the hope alive.

Coherence in the 19th Century

When I think back to the mid-19th century for influences on coherence, I think of Johann Friedrich Herbart (1776–1841), Johann Heinrich Pestalozzi (1746–1827), and Friedrich Froebel (1782–1852). All three had worldwide influence. Lesser known is their influence on novelist Leo Tolstoy (1828–1910), who founded "progressive" schools in his Russian estate of Yasnaya Polyana in the 1850s (Tolstoy 1967) that seemed to be a precursor to the education advocated by Dewey and his followers in the 20th century.

From Herbart, I have gleaned the idea of *apperceptive mass,* or repertoire of experience and knowledge in every person. That is what gives us our own perspective on the world—what educational processes consciously reconstruct as we create a life.

Froebel's doctrine of *unity* (e.g., seeing the child as a unity within many other wider concentric unities, from family, to world, to universe) provides an overarching faith in the possibility of coherence. Play as a force of unity was also prominent in Froebel's founding of the kindergarten. My work with my own children and with elementary school students has pointed to the coherence possible in play, acting, make-believe, and story. Today, Kieran Egan (1986) is a strong advocate of story and imagination in pedagogy.

In Pestalozzi, I found rudiments of the last kind of coherence: the *integration of diversity,* particularly of the rich and poor. Such an awareness helps to forge a new response to the central curriculum question that Herbert Spencer (1820–1903) raised in 1861: "What knowledge is of most worth?" A careful look at Spencer's book, however, quickly reveals his social Darwinism—his emphasis on self-preservation and survival of the fittest in social situations. Pestalozzi's message, however, provides a different answer to the Spencerian query; not mere self-preservation, but a care and concern for self, others, and the world. As I am learning from my experience in the urban setting, where inequality is not erased from view, a life worth living is a life worth sharing. While sharing clearly means considering what you have that helps another, it also entails realizing that any other might have something worth sharing with you.

In the late 19th century, other prominent educators advocated perspectives that enriched my idea of coherence. An agronomist named Lester Frank Ward countered Spencer's social Darwinist ideas by offering a position that Herbert Kliebard (1986) has called *social meliorist*. On another front, followers of Herbart—Frank McMurry, Charles McMurry, and Charles De Garmo—developed systems for what they call *concentration* and *correlation*. Those systems are partially based on Herbart's idea that each developing person recapitulates the development of the human race. If, for instance, we consider 10-year-olds at a stage of development equivalent to an era of human history when daily life focused on survival through hunting and gathering, the story of Robinson Crusoe might be an appropriate organizing center.

The height of the Herbartian movement in America (circa 1895–1905) saw more mechanized approaches and less attention to the idea of apperceptive mass. Francis Parker (1835–1909)—a self-fashioned leader in curriculum, method, and teacher education of the late 19th century who aligned with the Herbartians—kept alive Herbart's notion of apperceptive mass and minimized the emphasis on recapitulation, correlation, and concentration of subject matter. In retrospect, some thirty years after the prime of Herbartian practice in America, Frank McMurry wrote:

> As I look back on it now, he [Francis Parker] was searching for the problem or project of work, where you find your starting point for both curriculum and method within the child rather than within some branch of knowledge. In that tendency he was a long way in advance of the rest of us (1927, p. 331).

Today's prominent calls for coherence, usually under the titles of *interdisciplinary* or *integrated studies*, are often more subject oriented than child or community centered. They, too, fail to realize Parker's insight. Like William Torrey Harris, 1835–1909), whose powerful leadership in debates that opposed Parker in shaping the renowned reports of the National Education Association Committee of Ten (1893) and Committee of Fifteen (1895), many of today's advocates of interdisciplinary studies offer a more subject-oriented approach. Though a proponent of subjects of traditional liberal education, Harris (the staunch Hegelian) sought synthesis as a means to coherence. His phrase "the five windows on the soul"—mathematics, biology, art and literature, grammar (including philosophy and logic), and history—ties subjects together. He claimed that their essence provides perspective on the soul. That view is not unlike Mortimer Adler's contemporary call in the *Paideia Proposal* (1982) and in many earlier works (including his work with Robert M. Hutchins that developed the Britannica Great Books). Adler's notion of great ideas—truth, beauty, goodness, liberty, equality, and justice—is another intellectual traditionalist approach to seeking coherence (1981).

20th Century Coherence

The 20th century effort to provide coherence in the curriculum that has influenced me most is the work of John Dewey (1859–1952). His advocacy started with the interests and concerns of learners, moved through interaction and shared concerns, probed to deeper human interests, and drew on personal and public knowledge to develop projects that help resolve real-world problems. That perspective clearly involves a science of problem solving and critical thinking (Dewey 1910), tempered with acutely refined aesthetic perception (1934a); and it engages the individual integrally in participatory democracy (1916, 1927). For good reason, therefore, Dewey is associated with the phrase *educating the whole child.* His theory connected work and play, school and home, interest and effort, personal concerns and extant knowledge, knowledge and values, and much more. Moreover, Dewey saw the artificial separation of subject matter areas as a prime culprit in education that is divorced from life (1931).

Dewey's progressive followers (e.g., William H. Kilpatrick, Harold Rugg, George S. Counts, Caroline Pratt, Boyd H. Bode, L. Thomas Hopkins, and Harold and Elise Alberty) pushed toward an image of coherence that helps me think about creating a life worth sharing. Kilpatrick's interpretation of Deweyan pedagogy (1918) shows teachers how to develop projects from children's common interests and how to relate an array of school subjects to any interests studied.

Also in 1918, the NEA's Commission on the Reorganization of Secondary Education sought coherence by identifying seven "cardinal principles" for education:

- Health,
- Command of fundamental processes,
- Worthy home membership,
- Vocational preparation,
- Citizenship,
- Worthy use of leisure time, and
- Ethical character.

The idea was to make a substantial move from a curriculum that found coherence in subjects of academic life to a curriculum based on principles necessary for functioning in life generally. Historian Lawrence Cremin (1955, p. 307) said of the report, "Most of the important and influential movements in the field have been footnotes to the classic itself."

In the same year the NEA report was published, Franklin Bobbitt (1918) argued for a different kind of coherence that stems from a *social efficiency* or *social behaviorist* stance. He proposed that curriculum should cohere around the prominent activities of successful adult life. By studying what successful adults spend their time doing and by translating those activities into behavioral objectives, Bobbitt (1918, 1924) inaugurated "scientific curriculum making," which he claimed was based on contemporary social life. W. W. Charters, a student of Dewey's, refined the process by emphasizing core ideals of society, rather than the more debatable activities of "success" as a basis for determining objectives in a social efficiency mode (1923). Ideals, then, are the avenue to establish coherence. The need is to induct the young into society's ideals.

Rugg and Counts each differed considerably in their emphasis on perpetuating society. Drawing on the most radical strain of the progressive legacy, both were more interested in reconstructing society than in merely perpetuating its dominant values.

Rugg and Shumaker argued for a child-centered school that built on child interests (1928). In numerous works, Rugg encouraged educators to reflectively question the social purposes of education. Taking the questioning to students directly, Rugg developed a series of social studies textbooks with Ginn and Company under the title *Man and His Changing Society*; over the 1929–1939 decade, the series sold about 1.3 million texts and 2.7 million workbooks. Public criticism of anticapitalist questions raised in the series contributed to its decline (see Kliebard 1986, pp. 200–208). Rugg later defended the series in *That Men May Understand* (1941). Clearly, he pushed hard for coherence around the issue of social reconstruction.

Augmenting that effort, Counts devoted a career to reconstruction. In his best-known book, *Dare the School Build a New Social Order* (1932), he contended that the world needs to change quickly from its self-destructive course. Some saw that position as a marked departure from the child-centered practitioners who focused more on individual growth and less on societal reconstruction. Bode called eloquently for a compromise, or more precisely for moving to a deeper level than that of seeing child and society as polar opposites that we must choose between (1938). Dewey, in numerous writings, also pointed to the correlative or reciprocal benefit of the child and society. If one is truly enhanced, Bode and Dewey argued at different times, so is the other. Nevertheless, the progressive education movement floundered and declined because of its inability to find a center of coherence that brought the child and societal focus together as Dewey and Bode had hoped.

In fact, we could view the history of curriculum and the search for curriculum coherence as a debate over which of three competing factors to give primacy:

- The individual (child),
- The society, and
- The subject matter.

Dewey and Rugg, as well as Tyler in his landmark summary of curriculum questions (1949), identified the need for balance among those factors as a perennial curriculum problem.

Tyler drew much of his insight from practical work as evaluation director of the Eight Year Study, a work that too few are aware of today. Organized by Wilford Aikin, and growing out of the efforts of the Progressive Education Association, the project researchers sought empirical evidence for the value of progressive education over traditional education. Aikin's first volume, *The Story of the Eight Year Study* (1942), in the five-volume set published by Harper and Brothers, is an excellent overview. Aikin recounted how researchers carefully studied 1,475 matched pairs of students (one educated progressively and the other traditionally), following them through high school and college and comparing them on a host of measures—academic, social, emotional, and more. The results favored those educated progressively. However, because the study was published during World War II, it did not receive the attention it was due. Nevertheless, the details of the study—the accounts of curriculum development, evaluation, workshops for teachers, and stories from the schools—are a rich resource for those today seeking to develop integrated curriculums that derive coherence from students' interests and concerns.

Many of those influenced by the Eight Year Study and the early progressives, especially Dewey, refined responses to the question of coherence in the 1930s, '40s, and '50s. For example, L. Thomas Hopkins developed a major statement on integration, showing that expertise in disciplinary inquiry necessitates interdisciplinary inquiry (1937). He further argued that integration cannot reach its potential unless it is embedded in interactive democratic processes (1941). His last book integrated various sources from psychology, biology, philosophy, and practical experience to make a case for the emerging self as the source of curricular coherence (1954). Thus, creating the self in an organic social context is the job of home, school, individual, and society. Hopkins (1976) referred to that conscious creating of self as the "*is* curriculum," contrasting it with the "*was* curriculum," which he saw as mere accumulation of lifeless, irrelevant knowledge.

In his last major address (which I vividly recall introducing at the 1980 meeting of the Society for the Study of Curriculum History) Hopkins, at age 90, sketched the development of those ideas in his early life—in interactions with his mother and in his early high school teaching experience in Truro, Massachusetts, beginning in 1904. Hopkins pointed out that students who explained how the history he taught had no meaning to the concerns of their lives actually taught him to be a good teacher (1983). With their help, he was able to teach history that used their own histories as the starting points for actively creating their lives. Thus, Hopkins's students found coherence in the educational experience that refined their own lives. For me, Hopkins is one of the two or three most influential educational writers of the first half of the 20th century, and his work is too much neglected today. (For a thorough review of Hopkins's contributions, see Wojcik 1991.)

The push given by Hopkins, Dewey, Bode, Rugg, and others to find coherence in the project of creating a life worth living found its way into the literature on coherence of the 1940s and '50s. Caroline Pratt (1948) poignantly reminded readers that to help young children create their lives, teachers must listen and genuinely learn from children. Harold Alberty (1947, 1953, and 1962 with Elise Alberty) usefully classified several types of coherence under the rubric of approaches to *core curriculum*, a term that came into prominence at mid-century (see Smith, Stanley, and Shores 1950, Faunce and Bossing 1951). Although some versions of core curriculum were satisfied with mere combinations of subjects around themes or projects, the most sophisticated visions focused on larger social problems of creating a life. Today, we need to rekindle interest in the latter; the most popular strivings for coherence under integrated or interdisciplinary curriculums remain at the level of finding themes to connect subject matter. Witness the plethora of workshops on integration today that do not emphasize potential coherence in creating a life worth living and sharing.

In the late 1960s, Louise Berman offered an insightful means toward this effort by calling for new curriculum priorities—perceiving, communicating, loving, knowing, decision making, patterning, creating, and valuing (1968). Those processes could be considered a new set of subjects, or they could be seen as great strands of human interest that come alive in any authentic project. As a stepping-stone to these formidable strides toward coherence, Berman suggested a matrix where conventional subject matters could be listed across the top and the new priority processes down the side. Interactions would show the presence of the processes in every subject area.

Contemporary Coherence

It is difficult to know where to conclude a brief history of ideas that can give coherence or integrative power to curriculum. When does historical perspective become contemporary discourse? Although that question has no definitive answer, several developments are important. The subtitle of James Beane's recent book, *Affect in the Curriculum*, captures three important dimensions of such developments: *Democracy, Dignity, and Diversity* (1990). The Deweyan progressive legacy clearly emphasizes democracy, which was a major feature of the open-education reincarnation of progressivism. The 1960s appeal to humanistic psychologists like Carl Rogers and Abraham Maslow brought an emphasis on dignity, though a subtle part of progressivism, to the fore. The 1962 ASCD Yearbook—*Perceiving, Behaving, Becoming*—an Association best-seller for many years, epitomized that focus. The ideals of democracy and dignity gave coherence to the popular first-person accounts of such teachers as A. S. Neill, John Holt, Jonathan Kozol, Sylvia Ashton-Warner, and Herb Kohl. (Schubert and Ayers 1992, Chapter 9, cite many of those authors' works and others in the same vein on teaching.) Few books on education have reached as many teachers as those by these authors. In fact, William Van Til has collected excerpts from some under the label of *relevance.* Implicit in his *Curriculum: Quest for Relevance* (1971) is the idea that this quest is not merely the explorations of curriculum specialists and educational policymakers. Instead, it is the search for whatever gives meaning and coherence to teachers, students, and parents as they try to shape their lives together.

Beane's use of diversity raises a perspective on the search for coherence that I see as both a main contribution of the curriculum field since 1970 and as a still-neglected area. Pinar, Reynolds, Slattery, and Taubman (in press) maintain that the curriculum field has been reconceptualized. The broad range of reconceptualist writing has pointed to the need for coherence through diversity (see Pinar 1988). It may seem strange that diversity could bring a kind of coherence. However, the awareness of the diverse cultures, norms, ways of knowing, and ways of being in the world augments repertoires of possibility and enriches our capacity for creating lives worth living and worth sharing. Many writers since 1970, too numerous to name here, have enabled us to see a diverse range of possibilities in discourses on race, class, gender, aesthetics, health, ableness, place, and more.

In much the same way, my life as an urban educator helped me to appreciate diversity, even to *affirm diversity,* as Nieto (1992) compellingly puts it. Other key writers have opened my vision. That vision has helped me to conclude that creating a life worth living is profoundly creating a life worth sharing. Freire (1970) helped me see the need for sharing between oppressed and oppressor as they pose problems anew and rename their worlds. Apple (1979) and Giroux (1979) helped me ask, "Who benefits from what is taught and learned?" Because of my exposure to many subsequent works by Freire, Apple, and Giroux, and by those influenced by them, I have continued to ask who gets hurt in the process—and many do (see Kozol 1992). So, the obvious question is how to share so that we overcome the hurt. Hellison has spent a career helping urban youths learn to overcome hurtfulness by sharing greater social responsibility (see Georgiadis 1992, Hellison 1990).

To create lives worth sharing requires a special perspective on diversity, one possible only through increased sharing. The curriculum field, for instance, has suffered from a dominance of white male scholars, as beneficial as our contributions may be in some ways. The field itself, as well as students and teachers, must become multiculturally literate (see Simonson and Walker 1988). Although W.E.B. DuBois was a contemporary of Dewey's and both were founding members of the NAACP, DuBois's writings on education are seldom noted in the curriculum literature. Many women progressives of the 1920s and '30s wrote of their work as teachers, but most of their writings have been neglected. Cuban liberationist José Martí wrote extensively on education (1979), but he is rarely cited or even thought of as an educator. Carter G. Woodson wrote *The Mis-Education of the Negro* (1933), but this title and even his name are virtually unknown among white educators. Such sources raise questions of knowledge and power that William Watkins (1994) persuasively argues lie at the center of what multicultural education can coherently become.

These few examples illustrate a lack of sharing, even among those who promote the vast sharing necessary for democracy. Chris Pellikan, a Native American adjunct faculty member at my university, recently said to me that we all *are* what others have shared with us. I add that we are also what we share with others. Although that message may also come from the literature, it is brought into bold relief for me by the complexity of urban life. In her study of the possibility of coherent experience from progressive curriculums in three urban contexts, Ann Lopez concludes, "Urban [settings] are . . . places of value, diversity, freedom, possibility, and complexity rather than barren wastelands of filth, corruption, decay, and vice to be condemned, feared, and distrusted" (1993, p. 3). To realize that potential requires great effort to keep alive a Deweyan faith in the good intentions of humanity and the possibility of authentic democracy (Dewey 1934b).

* * *

Let's go back to the question I asked at the beginning—and ask students and educators alike to consciously address it: "How can I make myself into a life worth living, a life worth sharing?"

References

Adler, M.J. (1981). *Six Great Ideas*. New York: Macmillan.

Adler, M.J. (1982). *The Paideia Proposal: An Educational Manifesto*. New York: Macmillan.

Aikin, W. (1942). *The Story of the Eight Year Study*. New York: Harper and Brothers.

Alberty, H.B., and E.J. Alberty. (1962). *Reorganizing the High School Curriculum*. New York: Macmillan (previous editions 1947 and 1953, authored by H. Alberty).

Apple, M.W. (1979). *Ideology and Curriculum*. London: Routledge.

ASCD Yearbook Committee and W.W. Combs, Chair, eds. (1962). *Perceiving, Behaving, Becoming*. Washington, D.C.: Association for Supervision and Curriculum Development.

Beane, J. (1990). *Affect in the Curriculum: Toward Democracy, Dignity, and Diversity*. New York: Teachers College Press.

Berman, L.M. (1968). *New Priorities in the Curriculum*. Columbus, Ohio: Merrill.

Bobbitt, F. (1918). *The Curriculum*. Boston: Houghton Mifflin.

Bobbitt, F. (1924). *How to Make a Curriculum*. Boston: Houghton Mifflin.

Bode, B. H. (1938). *Progressive Education at the Crossroads*. New York: Newson.

Charters, W.W. (1923). *Curriculum Construction*. New York: Macmillan.

Commission on the Reorganization of Secondary Education of the National Education Association. (1918). *Cardinal Principles of Secondary Education*. Washington, D.C.: U.S. Government Printing Office.

Counts, G.S. (1932). *Dare the School Build a New Social Order?* New York: John Day.

Cremin, L. A. (March 1955). "The Revolution in American Secondary Education." *Teachers College Record* 56: 295–307.

Dewey, J. (1902). *The Child and the Curriculum*. Chicago: University of Chicago Press.

Dewey, J. (1910). *How We Think*. New York: D.C. Heath.

Dewey, J. (1916). *Democracy and Education*. New York: Macmillan.

Dewey, J. (1927). *The Public and Its Problems*. New York: Henry Holt.

Dewey, J. (1931). *The Way Out of Educational Confusion*. Cambridge, Mass.: Harvard University Press.

Dewey, J. (1934a). *Art as Experience*. New York: Minton, Balch.

Dewey, J. (1934b). *A Common Faith*. New Haven, Conn.: Yale University Press.

Dewey, J. (1938). *Experience and Education*. New York: Macmillan.

Drake, S.M. (1993). *Planning the Integrated Curriculum*. Alexandria, Va.: Association of Supervision and Curriculum Development.

Egan, K. (1986). *Teaching as Storytelling*. Chicago: University of Chicago Press.

Faunce, R.C., and N.L. Bossing. (1951). *Developing the Core Curriculum*. New York: Prentice-Hall.

Freire, P. (1970). *Pedagogy of the Oppressed*, translated by M.B. Ramos. New York: Seabury.

Georgiadis, N. (1992). "Practical Inquiry in Physical Education: The Case of Donald Hellison." Doctoral diss., University of Illinois at Chicago.

Giroux, H.A. (1979). "Toward a New Sociology of Curriculum." *Educational Leadership* 37, 10: 248–253.

Hellison, D. (August 1990). "Making a Difference—Reflections on Teaching Urban At-Risk Youth." *Journal of Physical Education, Recreation, and Dance* 61: 44–45.

Herrick, V., J.I. Goodlad, F.J. Estvan, and P.W. Eberman. (1956). *The Elementary School*. Englewood Cliffs, N.J.: Prentice-Hall.

Hopkins, L.T., ed. (1937). *Integration, Its Meaning and Application*. New York: Appleton-Century.

Hopkins, L.T. (1941). *Interaction: The Democratic Process*. Boston: D.C. Heath.

Hopkins, L.T. (1954). *The Emerging Self in School and Home*. New York: Harper and Brothers (also see 1970 reprint by Greenwood Press of Westport, Conn.).

Hopkins, L.T. (1976). "The *Is* vs. the *Was* Curriculum." *Educational Leadership* 34, 3: 211–216.

Hopkins, L.T. (1983). "My First Voyage." In *Papers of the Society for the Study of Curriculum History,* edited by M.R. Nelson. DeKalb: Northern Illinois University.

Huebner, D. (1966). "Curricular Language and Classroom Meanings." In *Language and Meaning,* edited by J.B. Macdonald and R. Leeper. Washington, D.C.: Association for Supervision and Curriculum Development.

Jacobs, H.H., ed. (1989). *Interdisciplinary Curriculum: Design and Implementation*. Alexandria, Va.: Association for Supervision and Curriculum Development.

Kilpatrick, W.H. (1918). "The Project Method." *Teachers College Record* 19, 4: 319–335.

Kliebard, H.M. (1986). *The Struggle for the American Curriculum: 1893–1958*. Boston: Routledge and Kegan Paul.

Kozol, J. (1992). *Savage Inequalities*. New York: Crown.

Lopez, A.L. (1993). "Exploring Possibilities for Progressive Curriculum and Teaching in Three Urban Contexts." Unpublished dissertation, University of Illinois at Chicago.

Martí, J. (1979). *On Education,* translated by Elinor Randall and edited by Philip S. Foner. New York and London: Monthly Review Press.

McLuhan, M., and Q. Fiore. (1967). *The Medium Is the Message*. New York: Bantam.

McMurry, F.M. (1927). "Some Recollections of the Past Forty Years of Education." *Peabody Journal of Education* 4, 325–332.

NEA Committee of Ten on Secondary School Studies, chaired by C. Eliot. (1893). *Report*. Washington, D.C.: National Education Association.

NEA Committee of Fifteen, chaired by W.T. Harris. (1895). *Report*. Washington, D.C.: National Education Association.

Nieto, S. (1992). *Affirming Diversity*. New York: Longman.

Pinar, W.F., ed. (1988). *Contemporary Curriculum Discourses*. Scottsdale, Ariz.: Gorscuh Scarisbrick.

Pinar, W.F., W.M. Reynolds, P. Slattery, and P.M. Taubman. (In press). *Understanding Curriculum: An Introduction to the Study of Historical and Contemporary Curriculum Discourses*. New York: Peter Lang.

Pratt, C. (1948). *I Learn from Children*. New York: Simon and Schuster.

Rugg, H.O. (1941). *That Men May Understand*. New York: Doubleday, Doran.

Rugg, H.O., and A. Shumaker. (1928). *The Child-Centered School*. Yonkers, N.Y.: World Book.

Schubert, W.H. (1986). *Curriculum: Perspective, Paradigm, and Possibility*. New York: Macmillan.

Schubert, W.H. (1989). "Thoughts on the Future SSCH." In *Curriculum History,* edited by C. Kridel. Lanham, Md.: University Press of America.

Schubert, W.H. (1990). "The Question of Worth as Central to Curriculum Empowerment." In *Teaching and Thinking About Curriculum,* edited by J.T. Sears and J.D. Marshall. New York: Teachers College Press.

Schubert, W.H., and W.C. Ayers, eds. (1992). *Teacher Lore: Learning from Our Own Experience*. New York: Longman.

Schubert, W.H., and A.L. Lopez. (1993). "Teacher Lore as a Basis for Inservice Education." *Teaching and Teachers' Work* 1, 4: 1–8.

Simonson, R., and S. Walker, eds. (1988). *Multicultural Literacy*. Saint Paul, Minn.: Graywolf Press.

Smith, B.O., W.O. Stanley, and J.H. Shores. (1950). *Fundamentals of Curriculum Development*. Yonkers-on-Hudson, N.Y.: World Book.

Spencer, H. (1861). *Education: Intellectual, Moral and Physical*. New York: Appleton.

Tolstoy, L. (1967). *Tolstoy on Education*, translated by L. Weiner. Chicago: University of Chicago Press.

Tyler, R.W. (1949). *Basic Principles of Curriculum and Instruction*. Chicago: University of Chicago Press.

Ulich, R., ed. (1947). *Three Thousand Years of Educational Wisdom*. Cambridge, Mass.: Harvard University Press.

Van Til, W., ed. (1971). *Curriculum: Quest for Relevance*. Boston: Houghton Mifflin.

Watkins, W.H. (1994). "Multicultural Education: Toward Historical and Political Inquiry." *Educational Theory* 44, 1: 99–117.

Wojcik, J.T. (1991). "The Life and Contribution of L. Thomas Hopkins." Unpublished dissertation, University of Illinois at Chicago.

Woodson, C.G. (1933). *The Mis-Education of the Negro*. Washington, D.C.: Associated Publishers (also 1990 reprint by Africa World Press).

15

A Coherent Curriculum in an Incoherent Society? Pedagogical Perspectives on Curriculum Reform

Gloria Ladson-Billings

On a recent morning commute, I heard something on the car radio that caught my attention. The program host was talking with a woman (a photographer, I believe) who had received a grant that allowed her to purchase video cameras to be loaned to urban youths so they could "photograph their lives." The photographer described an African American teenage boy who was having a marvelous time with the video camera. He took video footage of all his relatives, plus his friends, the men at the neighborhood barbershop, and people from his church. When he went into his school, however, he turned the camera off. When asked why he did that, the young man replied, "You asked me to take pictures about my life. School is not about my life!"

This student's comments accurately reflect the sense of alienation found among too many of U.S. students (Fine 1986). They also help me pose questions about schooling in general, about curriculum coherence, and about the limitations of curriculum reform, as well as to advocate for more attention to issues of pedagogy.

What Is the Point of Curriculum Coherence?

If you were to ask people whether they favored coherence (of anything) over incoherence, the response most likely would be affirmative. So the argument over curriculum coherence may be moot. The real discussion is over what is meant by curriculum coherence and what objectives are served by a particular vision of coherence.

In his introductory chapter, Beane suggests that coherence equals integration. He poses questions central to his argument for curriculum coherence without critically examining the ways in which current curriculum arrangements are coherent, given our current social, economic, and political hierarchy.

More intriguing is Boyer's position, who, rather than asking what we can do to "fix" the current curriculum, asks what kind of person, citizen, and society we want to produce. Although these questions might seem too philosophical and detached from the real world of classroom teachers, they are precisely the kinds of questions that should drive our curricular and pedagogical decisions. Reflecting on past constructions of curriculum coherence makes this clear.

Gerald Graff (1992) argues that the incoherence of the university curriculum is not a recent phenomenon. He suggests that curriculum incoherence was the result of universities' switching from a classical education to the liberal arts. Thus, studying Greek, Latin, religion, and rhetoric was a coherent approach to the curriculum. Though I don't think this type of coherence is what the authors of this volume are advocating, it is illustrative of the wide-ranging views of curriculum coherence.

Eisner and Vallance (1974) present a framework for five differing conceptions of the curriculum—academic rationalism, cognitive processes, self-actualization, social reconstruction/social adaptation, and curriculum as technology.[1] More important than a full explication of these positions is the point that they are produced by their fundamental ideological grounding. Thus, any approach to curriculum change or reformation must address the basic beliefs or ideologies that shape them.

The classical university curriculum mentioned previously is an *academic rationalist* conception, grounded in a belief that the mark of an educated person is the ability to converse with the "great ideas" promulgated by "great minds." The question of who defines this greatness may be unanswered, but this position supposes that it can be answered. Many of the current curriculum standards efforts are premised on this perspective.[2] Some leaders in the standards-setting efforts argue that because we do know what ought to be taught in specific disciplines, all we need to do is specify the order in which it should be taught and at what level of profi-

---

[1]I don't mean to suggest that these are the only extant curriculum conceptions. Curriculum theorists such as Kliebard, Tyler, Broudy, Schwab, and others have proposed alternative conceptions.

[2]Currently, school reform at the federal level is based on notions of systemic reform, which includes the formulation of subject matter "standards."

ciency. Some of this thinking is reflected in some of the subject-specific chapters in this book.

The second position, *cognitive processes*, argues that the "what" of the curriculum is not nearly as significant as the "how." Rather than outline a specific content to be mastered, this approach is based on the belief that because knowledge is growing at an exponential rate, schools must equip students with the skills to handle all kinds of content.

The third position, *self-actualization*, suggests that the role of the curriculum is to help students become their best selves, with curricular choices grounded in specific contexts and individuals. Students are expected to decide for themselves (presumably with teacher input and guidance) which curriculums best meet their intellectual needs.

The fourth position, *social adaptation/social reconstruction*—opposite sides of the same ideological coin—argues that schools function either to socialize students into the existing social order (adaptation) or to help them challenge and reconstruct that order.

And the fifth position, *curriculum as technology*, posits that we can regularize and regiment curriculum to the point that teachers only need to present students with "learning packets or systems" and monitor their progress through those systems. But it doesn't refer merely to technological equipment (computers, laser discs, etc.). Indeed, the programmed reading approaches popular in the 1970s (used without any machinery) are also an example of this curricular approach.

Although Eisner and Vallance's rubrics are not the only ways to conceptualize the curriculum, without addressing the underlying ideological perspectives of the curriculum, we remain like dogs chasing our tails, asking the question, "Curriculum coherence for what?"

Curriculum Coherence and Integration

I want to argue for a disentangling of the notions of coherence and integration.[3] A curriculum can be integrated and coherent, integrated and incoherent, nonintegrated and incoherent, or nonintegrated and coherent (see Figure 15.1).

---

[3]I use the term *integrated* in this paper to refer to generic, nonseparate, subject approaches, rather than the more socially conscious, reconstructionist position Beane takes in this volume.

Figure 15.1
Curriculum Coherence and Integration

Integrated/Coherent	Integrated/Incoherent
Nonintegrated/Coherent	Nonintegrated/Incoherent

For the sake of brevity, I am assuming that integrated/ coherent and nonintegrated/incoherent are understood conceptions. The following are examples of what may seem to be oxymorons: nonintegrated/coherent and integrated/incoherent curriculums.

> **Example 1**: Ms. Wilkins' classroom is widely regarded by parents and students as orderly and well-managed, where students are challenged intellectually and treated with respect.
>
> Despite the fact that her predominantly African American 6th graders come from low-income families and have previously experienced little academic success, Wilkins insists on teaching curriculum content that rivals an elite private school across town. Her students read a range of literature, including works by Mark Twain, Langston Hughes, Edgar Allen Poe, and Alice Walker. The central topic of study in mathematics is algebra. Students study the Eastern Hemisphere in social studies and participate in science units in physical and life sciences. Wilkins' students study art, music, and physical education.
>
> In general, Wilkins teaches these areas as separate, discrete subjects. She argues that her students must have access to challenging curriculum to compete with more privileged peers when they reach the high school level.

> **Example 2**: Ms. Lester teaches 1st grade in the same school as Ms. Wilkins. A number of students have come to her class without having had a kindergarten experience.
>
> Her students are participating in an integrated, thematic study of bears. Ms. Lester brings in teddy bears and encourages the students to do the same. Less than half of the children comply. They read stories about bears, use gummy bears and Teddy Grahams as counters in mathematics, study about bears as endangered animals, sing songs about bears, draw pictures of bears, and make ceramic bears.

I describe Ms. Wilkins' class as nonintegrated/coherent. Despite the fact that students experience separate course offerings, Wilkins' establishes coherence based on the subordinate positioning of her students *vis a vis* the white, middle-class students they will encounter in high school. The "coherence" resides in Wilkins' ideological belief that her students are as intellectually capable as more privileged students and must experience similar academic challenges. What holds the curriculum together is her understanding that her students are not operating on a level playing field and will be considered unprepared and placed in lower ability tracks with little or no opportunity to enter college if they arrive at high school without the similar prerequisites as the middle-class students.

On the other hand, Ms. Lester's class is integrated/incoherent. Despite the surface coherence of the "bear" theme, its relevance to the students' lives is tangential. Lester contends that she is doing it because there are "so many neat activities" she and the students can do with the theme. However, when compared to the curriculum experienced by middle-class students, this curriculum may be regarded as watered down or lacking intellectual rigor. For Lester, coherence is the result of what she chose to study—bears. For Wilkins, coherence is the result of her rationale.

If we look carefully at schools where students are achieving, we see a fair amount of consistency (or coherence) between students' school lives and their home lives (Au and Jordan 1981, Cazden and Legett 1981, Erickson and Mohatt 1982). Where students experience a disjuncture between home and school, they tend not to be academically successful (Irvine 1990). It would seem, then, that we would want a coherent curriculum to help reduce the distance between home and school experiences to ensure academic success.

Ms. Wilkins' seemingly incoherent academic approach might be facilitated by her ability to make appropriate home-school connections. She may choose literature with which her students' parents are familiar, or the students may have opportunities to develop algebra problems and equations from their home and cultural experiences. Or, she may merely make frequent references to norms, values, and mores that coincide with those of the community.

On the other hand, Ms. Lester's teddy bears might seem innovative and appealing, but if her students don't have teddy bears at home, or if they regard teddy bears as babyish, the activities are just that—activities, disjointed and disconnected from students' lives. Like the student videographer, these students may feel that school, which may be pleasant enough, is simply not "a part of their lives."

Neither curriculum approach is inherently right or wrong. Indeed, without a coherent pedagogic approach, the curriculum lacks the power to transform and empower students to be active, critically aware participants in a democratic and highly technological society. The problem faced by both Wilkins and Lester is that their attempts at coherence are being superimposed over an incoherent, chaotic society. According to the Children's Defense Fund (Edelman 1986), black children are two to four times more likely than white children to:

• die before adulthood because of inadequate prenatal or postnatal health care conditions, abuse, or murder;

• live in a single-parent household because of parental death, separation, divorce, or no marriage;

• live in foster care or the custody of a child welfare agency; and

• be poor, living in substandard housing with an unemployed teenage mother.

In addition to these socioeconomic factors, educational inequities persist. The College Board (1985) and the *Carnegie Quarterly* (Carnegie 1984/1985) suggest that even when blacks attend school with whites, they receive a different and inferior education. For instance:

• Black students, particularly black male students, are three times as likely as white students to be in a class for the educable mentally retarded, but only half as likely to be in a class for the gifted and talented.

• Black students are more likely than white students to be enrolled in general and vocational tracks and to take fewer academically rigorous courses.

• Even when course titles are similar for black and white students, the content varies.

• Black students are more likely than white students to be enrolled in business or general math and less likely to be in algebra, geometry, trigonometry, or calculus.

These examples represent some of the social disorganization and injustice teachers and students confront. Therefore, solutions for curriculum coherence must recognize the monumental task of dealing with students' overwhelming social needs in an era of shrinking resources and growing resentment and apathy toward the poor and disenfranchised. The pedagogic task remains—not just to learn teaching strategies or methods, but to consider fundamental social change and use school as a vehicle of personal/individual empowerment and social transformation. For this type of pedagogical action, I suggest a culturally relevant pedagogy.

Culturally Relevant Pedagogy as Coherent Instruction

For the past five years, I've been investigating what I call "culturally relevant pedagogy" (Ladson-Billings 1990a, 1990b, 1992). I've spent several years in classrooms with teachers deemed successful with African American students. Early on, I was frustrated by what I saw as "incoherence" among the eight teachers with whom I was working. Some of the teachers used "traditional" approaches. Others seemed to be more "progressive." In some instances, teachers taught very separate and distinct skills and subject areas. Others used varying degrees of "thematic" or "integrated" instruction. Several principals required teachers to closely follow state- and district-mandated curriculum. Others gave teachers a lot of freedom to experiment with curricular innovations. Yet, despite their differences, I discovered that these teachers held some common, fundamental beliefs that informed their "culturally relevant" pedagogy.

I have deduced from their pedagogy and thinking three criteria for a culturally relevant pedagogy. First, students must be achieving academically. Second, students must be able to maintain or develop a sense of cultural competence in their home culture. Third, students must develop a critical consciousness that allows them to analyze and critique their sociocultural and political context.

These criteria and their arrangement as a set are not unique. In the 1960s, people dedicated to the freedom and justice of African Americans in the South developed what came to be known as the Mississippi Freedom Schools to improve literacy *and* political consciousness (Chilcoat and Ligon 1994, Lauter and Perlstein 1991). A similar kind of pedagogy was encouraged by Myles Horton, Septima Clark, and Esau Jenkins at the Highlander Folk School (Morris 1984). This kind of pedagogy, however, is rare in public schools serving African American and Latino youngsters.

In addition to these three criteria, the teachers I observed based their work on three broad conceptions of pedagogy. These conceptions were about themselves and others, how to structure social relations, and knowledge. The following is a brief sketch of these conceptions and how they were actualized in the teachers' thinking and pedagogy.

Conceptions of Self and Others. The literature on the sociology of teaching suggests that, despite the increasing professionalization of teaching (Strike 1993), the status of teaching as a profession continues to decline. The feeling of low status is exacerbated when teachers work with what they perceive to be low-status students (i.e., poor and minority group members) (Foster 1986). The teachers in my study challenged this perception. They:

- believe all students are capable of academic success;
- view their pedagogy as art—unpredictable, always in the process of becoming;
- view themselves as members of the community;

• view teaching as a way to "give back" to the community; and

• believe in Paulo Freire's (1973) notion of "teaching as mining" or pulling knowledge out of students.

Conceptions of Social Relations. The relationships between and among students and their teachers are so important that, in 1954, the landmark case *Brown vs. Topeka Board of Education* affirmed the need for different social relations to exist between white and African American students. The U.S. Supreme Court's thinking was that if black children attended school with white children, equal opportunity would prevail, and the social landscape could be transformed.

Despite the failure of *Brown* to realize its full promise, the structuring of social relations continues to be an important aspect of classroom life. In culturally relevant classrooms:

• social relations are fluid, are humanely equitable, and extend to interactions beyond the classroom and into the community;

• teachers demonstrate a "connectedness" with all students;

• teachers encourage a community of learners as a priority; and

• teachers encourage students to learn collaboratively and to teach each other and be responsible for each other.

Conceptions of Knowledge. Although the social construction of knowledge is commonly understood in the academy, "school knowledge" is often considered "objective truth." Students are asked to read, listen to, memorize, recite, and recall a wide array of facts, algorithms, and formulas. Even when asked to engage in critical thinking, what students are asked to think critically about is sometimes undeserving of serious analysis and critique. Culturally relevant pedagogy requires that teachers function as "transformative intellectuals" (Giroux 1988) and challenge the content of the curriculum. Culturally relevant teachers' conceptions of knowledge reflect:

• a belief that knowledge is continuously recreated, recycled, and shared by teachers and students, rather than static and unchanging;

• a commitment to view the content of the curriculum critically;

• a passionate involvement with the curriculum; they care about what they teach;

• an understanding that they must help students develop prerequisite knowledge and skills or construct "scaffolding" to support student learning; and

• an understanding that intellectual excellence is complex and affected by student diversity.

These three broad conceptions make a point about school reform: Changes in the curriculum alone cannot ensure school improvement.

According to Shujaa (1993), one urban school district attempted to mandate curricular change by infusing African and African American history and culture into the curriculum. Teachers were paid to participate in a series of professional development sessions that provided the information needed to infuse the curriculum. Although the teachers rated the quality of the presentations "high," many were unable to infuse the curriculum. The two primary reasons for their difficulty were ideological and pedagogical. Some teachers didn't believe in the infusion, seeing it as a political concession to African American parents' complaints. Others believed that the purpose of the infusion was simply to "improve the 'poor' self-esteem of black children." Still others didn't know how to modify their instruction to accommodate the new curriculum.

I offer this example not as an indictment against this particular school district, but because I believe the district's experience sits at the heart of thinking about curriculum coherence. On the macro level, we ask, What will a coherent curriculum mean in the context of an admittedly incoherent society? At the micro level, we ask, What is the point of curriculum coherence without pedagogical excellence?

So What Are We To Do?

I have raised questions about this book's call for curriculum coherence and pointed out that the notion of coherence is so fundamentally righteous that it would be difficult to argue against it. I have tried to make this concept somewhat problematic by asking how coherence is being constructed, providing examples of alternative constructions of "coherence," and insisting that without concurrent attention to the pedagogical implications of curricular change, coherence will not occur.

My critique is not intended to dissuade curriculum theorists, researchers, and educators from working toward improving the curriculum as a part of systemic reform. However, it has become increasingly clear that some of the best constructors of coherent curriculums are teachers who have the opportunity to function as professionals. The work of principals Deborah Meier at Central Park East Secondary School and Lottie Taylor at A. Philip Randolph Campus High School, both in New York City, exemplify two different styles of leadership that produce outstanding student achievement by capitalizing on the professional expertise of teachers.

Central Park East Secondary School. At Central Park East Secondary School (CPESS), a diverse group of students traditionally underserved by public schooling have high test scores, high attendance rates, low dropout rates, and high college attendance rates. One of the things that contributes to their successes is the faculty's autonomy and collegiality when creating a vision of the kind of graduate (and citizen) it wanted to produce.

CPESS has a "less is more" curriculum (Wood 1992) based on the cultivation of particular "habits of mind." The five habits of mind were determined through faculty consensus as teachers brought their best thinking and professional judgment to bear. Displayed in each classroom, the habits of mind are:

> 1. *Evidence*. How do we know what we know? What kind of evidence do we consider "good" enough?
> 2. *Viewpoint*. What viewpoint are we hearing, seeing, reading? Who is the author, where is he/she standing, what are her/his intentions?
> 3. *Connections*. How are things connected to each other? How does "it" fit in? Where have we heard or seen this before?
> 4. *Conjecture*. What if . . . ? Supposing that . . . ? Can we imagine alternatives?
> 5. *Relevance*. What difference does it make? Who cares? (Wood 1992, p. 172).

A requirement for graduation from CPESS is the development of an individual portfolio showing that each student has attained competency in fourteen areas (including postgraduate plan, autobiographical essay, school/community service, ethics and philosophy, fine arts and aesthetics, practical skills, math, history, literature, physical challenge). Each portfolio must include a final project showing special expertise and depth of understanding in one of the areas (Wood 1992, p. 170).

A. Philip Randolph Campus High School. At the A. Philip Randolph Campus High School (Randolph)[4], Principal Lottie Taylor takes what may seem a more conventional approach to administration by allowing teachers the "space" and support to make their own professional decisions. Rather than developing a single curriculum vision, teachers work in the more conventional departmental structure. The vision of the school emphasizes "excellence," which includes student achievement, positive community participation, and cultural integrity. Very different from Central Park East, Randolph gets similar results in student achievement, school attendance, low dropout rates, and high college admission rates. Each school has developed its own sense of "curriculum coherence."

---

[4]I initially learned of the work at Randolph through a television broadcast of *A Tale of Two Schools: Against the Odds*, produced by Channel 9 in New York City.

Standards in the Curriculum. By contrast, various curriculum content "standards" efforts are aimed at bringing about curriculum coherence by deciding what ought to be taught/learned at various grade levels in specific subjects. However, consensus about what is most important to learn has not been reached. In the area of social studies, for example, there are at least four separate standards projects— history, geography, civics, and social studies. Though the task may be somewhat simpler at the high school level where a teacher might teach only history, what will these myriad standards mean for the elementary teacher who must make sense of the standards written by all four projects? And this same elementary teacher will receive standards in mathematics, science, language arts, fine arts, health, and physical education. They may end up being coherent (internally), but will they be do-able?

Several years ago, I sat at a PTA meeting at the middle school my son was attending. The main item on the agenda was something called "curriculum articulation." For several of the educators at the meeting, this call for articulation represented a move toward a more coherent curriculum. Various speakers addressed the group, explaining that a district committee was working to integrate the various aspects of the curriculum. One teacher talked about the way that the English and social studies departments were working together to use literature that reflected the periods and events being studied in the social studies classroom. The parents seemed accepting of what was being said until one parent rose to express what I believe was on the minds of many. "When you said 'curriculum articulation,' I thought you were talking about telling us clearly and distinctly what you taught. I'm not sure I understand or agree with you about this integrated stuff. I just want to know what you're doing and why." Perhaps that is the "coherence" most of us are seeking.

References

Apple, M. (1988). *Teachers and Texts*. New York: Routledge.

Au, K., and C. Jordan. (1981). "Teaching Reading to Hawaiian Children: Finding a Culturally Appropriate Solution." In *Culture and the Bilingual Classroom: Studies in Classroom Ethnography*, edited by H. Trueba, G. Guthrie, and K. Au. Rowley, Mass.: Newbury House.

Carnegie Corporation of New York. (1984/85). "Renegotiating Society's Contract with the Public Schools." *Carnegie Quarterly* 29/30: 1–4, 6–11.

Cazden, C., and E. Leggett. (1981). "Culturally Responsive Education: Recommendations for Achieving *Lau* Remedies II." In *Culture and the Bilingual Classroom: Studies in Classroom Ethnography*, edited by H. Trueba, G. Guthrie, and K. Au. Rowley, Mass.: Newbury House.

Chilcoat, G.W., and J.A. Ligon. (1994). "Developing democratic Citizens: The Mississippi Freedom Schools as a Model for Social Studies Instruction." *Theory and Research in Social Education* 22: 128–175.

The College Board. (1985). *Equality and Excellence: The Educational Status of Black Americans*. New York: The College Board.

Edelman, M.W. (1986). "Save the Children." *Ebony* 41: 53–58.

Eisner, E., and E. Vallance. (Eds.). (1974). *Conflicting Conceptions of the Curriculum*. Berkeley, Calif.: McCutcheon.

Erickson, F., and G. Mohatt. (1982). "Cultural Organization and Participation Structures in Two Classrooms of Indian Students." In *Doing the Ethnography of Schooling*, edited by G. Spindler. New York: Holt, Rinehart, & Winston.

Fine, M. (1986). "Why Urban Adolescents Drop Into and Out of High School." *Teachers' College Record* 87, 393–409.

Foster, H. (1986). *Ribbin', Jivin' and Playin' the Dozens*. Cambridge, Mass.: Ballinger Publishing.

Freire, P. (1973). *Education for Critical Consciousness*. New York: Seabury Press.

Graff, G. (1992). *Beyond the Culture Wars: How Teaching the Conflicts Can Revitalize American Education*. New York: W.W. Norton & Co.

Giroux, H. (1988). *Teachers as Intellectuals: Toward a Critical Pedagogy of Learning*. Granby, Mass.: Bergin & Garvey.

Harding, V. (1970). *Beyond Chaos: Black History and the Search for a New Land*. Black Paper No. 2. Atlanta: Institute of the Black World.

Irvine, J. (1990). *Black Students and School Failure*. Westport, Conn.: Greenwood Press.

Ladson-Billings, G. (Summer 1990a). "Culturally Relevant Teaching: Effective Instruction for Black Students." *The College Board Review* 155: 20–25.

Ladson-Billings, G. (1990b). "Like Lightning in a Bottle: Attempting to Capture the Pedagogical Excellence of Successful Teachers of Black Students." *International Journal of Qualitative Studies in Education* 3: 335–344.

Ladson-Billings, G. (1992). "Liberatory Consequences of Literacy: A Case of Culturally Relevant Instruction for African American Students." *Journal of Negro Education* 61: 378–391.

Lauter, D., and D. Perlstein. (1991). "Mississippi Freedom Schools: Introduction." *The Radical Teacher* 40: 2–5.

Morris, A. (1984). *The Origins of the Civil Rights Movement: Black Communities Organizing for Change*. New York: The Free Press.

Shujaa, M. (February 1993). "What Teachers Teach When They Think They Are Teaching African and African American History and Culture." Talk given in the Visiting Minority Scholar's Series. Wisconsin Center for Educational Research, Madison, Wisconsin.

Strike, K. (1993). "Professionalism, Democracy, and Discursive Communities: Normative Reflections on Restructuring." *American Educational Research Journal* 30: 255–275.

Wood, G. (1992). *Schools That Work: America's Most Innovative Public Education Programs*. New York: Dutton.

16

Conclusion: Toward a Coherent Curriculum

James A. Beane

We come now to the last chapter in our search for coherence in the curriculum. As the contributors to this yearbook have emphasized, an education of value is not merely the accumulation and "banking" of bits and pieces of information and skills. Rather, it is an education that helps us develop broader and deeper understandings of ourselves and our world, to make sense of our experiences, and to come to terms with large and significant ideas. In this yearbook, we have tried to consider some "big" ideas that might hold the curriculum together, how they might aid in organizing the planned curriculum, and how we might help young people make sense of them. These are among the fundamental issues in considering how the curriculum might become more coherent.

Although there is clear agreement that what now passes for a curriculum is largely incoherent, there are many opinions about what we should do to create coherence. As a result, we are left with many questions, including some of those we began with.

Where should we focus our efforts to create coherence?

In asking how we can create a coherent curriculum, we have not heretofore attempted to define what we mean by "curriculum." Various definitions of curriculum generally follow two directions. In the first, "curriculum" refers to the organized intentions, plans, and programs for what students are expected to learn. The second approach refers to "curriculum" as (1) the experiences young people have under the school's guidance, (2) what students make of those experiences, and (3) in a sense, what they take away from their time in school. Starting from one or the other definition makes all the difference in deciding what will make for coherence in the curriculum.

Coherence is, ultimately, a matter of whether the individual makes some unified and integrated sense of experience. But the experiences we are talking about here are not simply tied to situations that young people encounter in the course of life affairs. These are, instead, experiences encountered under the intervention of a socially constructed institution— the school—and whatever it offers by way of educational intentions and organized transactions. In other words, these experiences are the direct result of the planned curriculum of the school. Thus, the idea of a coherent curriculum involves a two-way transaction: the individual making sense of what the school offers and the school offering something that can be made sense of and in a way that making sense is possible. Taken this way, coherence is a dialectic, a discourse, *a conversation between young people and the planned curriculum and whoever plans it.*

We must place our efforts toward a coherent curriculum in the context of *both* definitions of curriculum. We must see the curriculum as a planned activity and imagine what kinds of curriculum transactions—programs, activities, approaches—will support young people in their search for meaning. In the other, the curriculum that students experience, we must do more to find out what young people are trying to understand and how they construct meanings and organize them into large, coherent schemes.

How might we create coherence in the planned curriculum?

We do not grasp concepts and understandings in their full breadth in a single moment. This does not mean that there is no moment of "Aha!" but that such moments come in relation to activity—thinking and doing. Life in school must, therefore, involve a wide range of activities and experiences. If these are to be coherent, they must be unified in some way. There must be some "glue" that holds the activity of the planned curriculum together. As the authors of this yearbook suggest, that glue might come from several sources:

• *"Big" ideas* such as the aspects of the "educated person" suggested by Boyer.

• *Large themes* such as "reality" in the case of Brady, global education in that of Kniep, or connecting concepts such as those proposed by Palmer.

• *Culture* as suggested by Cross—not only culture in the sense of a conceptualized phenomenon in material resources, but culture as a lived experience of people participating in the schools.

• *Re-unifying the subtopics of particular disciplines* as in the descriptions by Tchudi and Ahlgren and Kesidou.

• *Broad, integrating outcomes or goals* as Fitzpatrick suggests.

• Activities such as the *authentic assessment tasks* that are described by Wiggins.

• The *questions and concerns of young people* described in the integrative curriculum proposed by Pate, McGinnis, and Homestead.

This array of sources suggests multiple possibilities that might be used singly or in combination to help create coherence.

In general, though, the kind of curriculum we need is one that is organized around large, explicit ideas *and* opens the many doors needed to accommodate the array of experiential lenses through which young people view their world. Thus, we must begin to speak of many coherences rather than one universal coherence.

What I propose is a broadly planned curriculum that has many points of access. I am not proposing a different planned curriculum for each young person, nor simply a clever reorganization of the present collection of courses, subjects, and skill areas under a new set of titles. Such reforms in the past led to their own kind of incoherence. For this reason, we must pay careful attention to Ladson-Billings' warning that some kinds of integration do little to create coherence, whereas the search for deeper understandings like "culturally relevant pedagogy" may offer more promising possibilities.

How can we promote coherence in the experienced curriculum?

What is so problematic about learning is that we actually do not know for sure how it happens. Many theories purport to explain how learning occurs, yet they only describe the varieties of its appearance and are, at best, personal or vicarious descriptions constructed through the values and experiences of the theorizer.

Because the schools deal with large numbers of young people and because educators are assigned to teach them, the search goes on for a single metatheory that would explain how learning occurs for all people. But, so far, we are denied such a metatheory and likely will be in the future. We do know that experience is a wonderful teacher, but the fact that people repeat mistakes also tells us that not everyone learns from experience; "doing," by itself, does not alone make a complete educative experience. Some people also seem to "learn" without direct experience; for example, when they hear or read the stories of others. But *what* is learned by either method: a process, some content, both? And does either method hold for everyone and for all kinds of learnings? The exceptions to the "rules" would suggest not.

Such ambiguity explains something very important about this book. Though all the authors imply views of learning design, their larger focus is on what might be learned and how it might be organized around "big ideas." They seek to name "the thread that runs so true" in a significant curriculum. This is, after all, what a coherent curriculum is really about: elevating the curriculum from accumulation of disconnected bits of information and skill to a level where it offers a unified sense of meaning and significance.

We must remember, however, that new ideas are most accessible when they are connected to previous experiences that give context and meaning—coherence—to what is learned. This concept is important because the ideas presented in this yearbook are interpretations of coherence constructed by adults based on their life experiences. The young have not had those experiences; although any of the proposals made in this book may provide effective contexts and may lead toward coherent meanings, we cannot be sure that they will.

Because experiences are personal and diverse, no externally defined version of coherence can be presumed to hold universally for all young people. Coherence, in a planned, institutional sense, *must* be somewhat ambiguous and messy. We may try to understand and use the experiences and perceptions of young people in our curriculum planning, but we cannot fully "know" them because they are not our own. Nor will the old adage "We were young once" do, because we were not young at the same time, in the same places, or as part of the same cultures as today's young people. And to the extent that there is variety among the young people in any one classroom, we can only imagine the scale across geography, race, class, gender, ethnicity, and other dimensions of difference.

But it is exactly this diversity in our complex world that is at the center of the human search for coherence. When viewed this way, diversity is not an excuse for fragmentation, specialization, and incoherence in the curriculum or for selectively excluding certain ideas, people, cultures, or histories. Rather, it is an invitation to imagine how all of the pieces in our complex world might fit together and take on richer meaning. This is, after all, just what so many young people are trying to do.

These questions bring us yet others: How might coherence be enhanced by more closely connecting the planned curriculum and the experienced curriculum? How might the gap between adult educational desires and the concerns of young people be bridged and the tension between them at least partly relieved? Although many efforts at curriculum reform argue for widening the participation of various adult constituencies in planning, it is clear that the voices of young people themselves need to be heard.

The idea of involving young people in planning their curriculum has a long and encouraging history. The fact that it has never been widely practiced is as much a cause of curriculum incoherence as a result of the nearly exclusive dominance of adult desires in historically popular curriculum designs. Some people believe that collaborative planning is done to reduce alienation and rebellion. This is simply a positive result. The real reasons we plan with young people are, first, because we live in a democracy and, second, because we need to know what experiences and concerns they bring to their school education. In the present context, the issue seems almost too obvious: If coherence finally comes down to making unified and integrated meaning out of educational experiences, how can we expect to have a coherent curriculum without finding out what questions and concerns young people have?

We might do this in many ways. For example, we might ask young people what questions they have related to Boyer's dimensions of the "educated person." Or we might follow Brady's lead by asking young people how they might begin to answer his "reality" questions. Or we might use Cross' idea of culturally influenced coherence to ask young people how their own cultures could more fully be a part of the curriculum. Or we might directly replicate the personalized writing experiences described by Tchudi or the collaboratively planned integrative curriculum of Pate, McGinnis, and Homestead. Or we might ask young people to name outcomes they are seeking as part of Fitzpatrick's scheme or to make recommendations for the kinds of assessments that Wiggins advocates.

The point is, again, that these ways may help us come closer to creating a coherent curriculum because they allow us to hear what meanings young people are trying to construct, as well as what they believe might be done. Obvious as this may be, creating such space in our curriculum plans is not easy because doing so means touching on issues of power and personal academic interest. It also requires us to face the fact that young people's concerns and aspirations may be different from our own. Unless we do this, though, it is hard to imagine how we will ever approach a really coherent curriculum, particularly one that engages Schubert's notion of "a life worth living and sharing" or Greene's invitation to imagine coherence "in the making of a common world . . . funded . . . on the lived landscapes of those who learn."

Is it possible to reach consensus on the ideas, concepts, or goals that might hold the planned curriculum together?

The fate of outcome-based efforts in many states and school districts and the negotiation over standards are but two examples of the struggle among many interest groups to have their way about what is taught in our schools. Because the concepts, ideas, or goals that might hold the planned curriculum together are expressions of value, it is worth asking whether it is possible to reach any kind of reasonable consensus regarding possibilities for coherence. This question is especially important in light of the current cultural politics of which Apple reminds us in his commentary.

The answer to this question hinges on three matters. The first is our understanding of "consensus." Consensus means *widespread* agreement, not universal agreement, which on any given topic is unlikely.

The second matter concerns who will participate in defining the sources of coherence and how they will participate. Certainly, the larger community—parents, especially—have a say in what is taught to young people. On the other hand, public schools are not maintained strictly for the particular interests of parents or localized interest groups. If this were the case, racial segregation and exclusion of the disabled would likely still be legally permitted. The fact is that schools are also intended to serve the interests of the "state" and, more elusively, the "common good." Such interests are not simply a matter of popular will at any given moment, but are founded on the intention that educational ideas allow for the extension of rights and responsibilities associated with democracy, dignity, justice, equity, and other moral principles.

Thus, reaching a consensus on "big" ideas—goals, outcomes, themes, and so on—finally hinges on a third critical matter: our capacity to articulate and continuously refine fundamental principles so they serve the widespread interests of a broad constituency. While several authors in this yearbook do exactly this, we may also draw some optimism from efforts in Baltimore County and other places in reaching broad public and professional consensus regarding values schools ought to promote. This kind of principled discourse is necessary to reach the kind of consensus that coherence requires. Limiting our conversations about coherence only to such matters as learning theory or a standardized system will simply not do, because the numerous exceptions to the "rules" are too easily raised and defended.

The crucial issue in coherence is not simply psychological or organizational; it is not simply about naming and exercising a theory of learning or streamlining the efficiency of school operations. The real issue is philosophical. What is it that we want young people to learn? What is of significance? Is it fragments or is it larger schemes? And what is the "glue"?

* * *

If there is any one message that clearly emerges from this yearbook, it is this: In moving toward coherence in the curriculum, there is no cook-book, no recipe, no packaged program. We can listen carefully to ideas and stories from many sources; but in the end, we all face the same questions faced by those who worked on this book. How might we create coherence in the planned curriculum? How might we promote coherence in the experienced curriculum? How might we build a new consensus around ideas that contribute to a coherent curriculum? It is these questions that can form the basis for the curriculum conversations we so desperately need to move toward a more powerful, more significant, more meaningful, and, in these ways, more coherent curriculum.

About the Authors

James A. Beane, editor of the 1995 ASCD Yearbook, is Professor in the National College of Education, National-Louis University, Evanston, Illinois. Address correspondence to Dr. Beane at 928 West Shore Drive, Madison, WI 53715.

Andrew Ahlgren is Associate Director, Project 2061, American Association for the Advancement of Science, 1333 H Street, N.W., Washington, DC 20005.

Michael W. Apple is John Bascom Professor of Curriculum and Instruction and Educational Policy Studies, University of Wisconsin, 225 N. Mills Street, Madison, WI 53706.

Ernest Boyer is President, Carnegie Foundation for the Advancement of Teaching, 5 Ivy Lane, Princeton, NJ 08540.

Marion Brady is an education writer and consultant, 4285 N. Indian River Drive, Cocoa, FL 32927 (phone 407/636-3448, Fax 407/632-8327).

Beverly E. Cross is Assistant Professor, Department of Curriculum and Instruction, Enderis Hall, Room 339, University of Wisconsin-Milwaukee, P.O. Box 413, Milwaukee, WI 53201.

Kathleen Fitzpatrick is Executive Director, National Study of School Evaluation, 1699 E. Woodfield Road, Suite 406, Schrumburg, IL 60173.

Maxine Greene is Professor Emeritus, Division of Philosophy, the Social Sciences, and Education, Teachers College, Columbia University, New York, NY 10027.

Elaine Homestead is Classroom Teacher, Duluth Middle School, 3057 Peachtree Street, Duluth, GA 30136.

Sofia Kesidou is Research Associate, Project 2061, American Association for the Advancement of Science, 1333 H Street, N.W., Washington, DC 20005.

Willard M. Kniep is Vice President for Research and Development, the American Forum for Global Education, 120 Wall Street, Suite 2600, New York, NY 10005. The founder of EDUCATION 2000, he now serves as the project's National Director.

Gloria Ladson-Billings is Assistant Professsor, Department of Curriculum and Instruction, University of Wisconsin-Madison, 225 N. Mills Street, Madison, WI 53706-1795.

Giselle O. Martin-Kniep is Assistant Professor, School of Education, Adelphi University, Garden City, New York. She is also the Director of Research for EDUCATION 2000.

Karen McGinnis is Classroom Teacher, Duluth Middle School, 3057 Peachtree Street, Duluth, GA 30136.

Joan M. Palmer is Deputy State Superintendent, School Improvement Services, Maryland State Department of Education, 200 W. Baltimore Street, Baltimore, MD 21201.

Elizabeth Pate is Assistant Professor, Department of Elementary Education, University of Georgia, 427 Aderhold Hall, Athens, GA 30602-7122.

William H. Schubert is Professor of Education and Coordinator of Graduate Curriculum Studies, College of Education, University of Illinois-Chicago, 1040 W. Harrison, Chicago, IL 60607.

Stephen Tchudi is Professor of Rhetoric and Composition, Department of English, Fransden Hall, University of Nevada, Reno, NV 89557-0031.

Grant Wiggins is Director of Educational Research and Development at the Center on Learning, Assessment, and School Structure (CLASS), 648 The Great Road, Princeton, NJ 08540.

ASCD 1994–95 Board of Directors

Elected Members as of November 1, 1994

Executive Council

President: Arthur Steller, Deputy Superintendent, Boston Public Schools, Boston, Massachusetts

President-Elect: Charles Patterson, Superintendent, Killeen Independent School District, Killeen, Texas

Past President: Barbara Talbert Jackson, Executive Director, Grants Development Branch, District of Columbia Public Schools, Washington, D.C.

Jan Adkisson, Staff Development/Early Childhood Supervisor, Arlington County Public Schools, Arlington, Virginia

Brenda Benson-Burrell, Assistant Professor, Secondary Education, Rowan College, Glassboro, New Jersey

Thomas Budnik, Planning Coordinator, Heartland Area Education Agency #11, Johnston, Iowa

Robert Clark, Principal, Mountain Park Elementary School, Lilburn, Georgia

Ramón Claudio-Tirado, Professor of Education, Inter American University of Puerto Rico, San Juan, Puerto Rico

Edward Hall, Assistant Superintendent, Instruction, Curriculum, and Staff Development, Talladega County Board of Education, Talladega, Alabama

Frances Jones, Executive Director, Piedmont Triad Horizons Educational Consortium, University of North Carolina, School of Education, Greensboro, North Carolina

Margret Montgomery, President, Professional Research Institute, Austin, Texas

David Rainey, Director, Arkansas Math/Science School, Hot Springs, Arkansas

Charles Schwahn, Leadership, Management and Organization Development Consultant, Custer, South Dakota

Isa Kaftal Zimmerman, Superintendent, Acton-Boxborough Public Schools, Acton, Massachusetts

Review Council

Chair: Art Costa, Kalaheo, Kauai, Hawaii

Maryann Johnson, Assistant Superintendent for Curriculum and Instruction, South Kitsap School District, Port Orchard, Washington

Marcia Knoll, Assistant Superintendent, Valley Stream Central High School District, Valley Stream, New York

Phil Robinson, Detroit, Michigan

Sandra Gray Wegner, Professor, Southwest Missouri State University, Springfield, Missouri

Elected Members-at-Large

Bonnie Benesh, Newton Community School District, Newton, Iowa
Marguerite Bloch, Oak Brook, Illinois
Sharon Bovell, Drew Elementary School, Washington, D.C.
Sandra Braithwait, Clinton School District, Clinton, Missouri
Marguerite Cox, Glenbard High School District #87, Glen Ellyn, Illinois
Gwen Dupree, Assistant Superintendent, Secondary Programs & Athletics, Kent
    School District, Kent, Washington
Mary Francis, Petersburg City School District, Petersburg, Alaska
Joanna Kalbus, Assistant Superintendent, San CLASS Regional School District, San
    Bernadino County Schools, San Bernadino, California
Sharon Lease, Western Heights School District, Oklahoma City, Oklahoma
Leon Levesque, Superintendent of Schools, M.S.A.D. #16, Hallowell, Maine
Francine Mayfield, Principal, Clark County School District, Whitney Elementary
    School, Las Vegas, Nevada
Lynn Murray, Principal, Williston Central School, Williston, Vermont
Annemarie Romagnoli, Little Tor Elementary School, New City, New York
Joseph Taylor, Jr., New Orleans Public Schools, New Orleans, Louisiana
Nancy Vance, Essex School Board Office, Tappahannock, Virginia
Robert Watson, Principal, Campbell County School District, Wright Junior-Senior
    High School, Wright, Wyoming
Fran Winfrey, Dade County Public Schools, Miami, Florida
Ellen Wolf, Superintendent, Walla-Walla School District, Walla-Walla, Washington
P.C. Wu, Professor of Educational Leadership, University of West Florida, College of
    Education, Pensacola, Florida
Donald Young, CRDG College of Education, University of Hawaii, Honolulu, Hawaii

Affiliate Presidents

Alabama: Catherine Moore, Assistant Superintendent for Elementary Curriculum
    and Instruction, Russell County Schools, Phenix City
Alaska: Mary Rubadeau, Assistant Superintendent, Juneau City and Borough
    School District, Juneau
Alberta, Canada: Peter Prest, Assistant Principal, John G. Diefenbaker High
    School, Calgary
Arkansas: Janie Russell, Director of Instruction, Lake Hamilton Public Schools,
    Pearcy
Arizona: Nancy Fiandach, Career Ladder Specialist, Mesa Public Schools, Mesa
British Columbia, Canada: Norm Bradley, Vice-Principal, Springvalley Secondary
    School, Kelowna
California: Joanna Kalbus, Assistant Superintendent, San Bernardino County Of-
    fice on Education, San Bernardino
Colorado: Beverly Bjork, Director of Curriculum and Instruction, Colorado Springs
    School District 11, Colorado Springs
Connecticut: Richard Nabel, Principal, Naugatuck High School, Naugatuck
Curaçao, Netherlands Antilles: Lucien R. D. Larmonie, Fundashon Material pa
    Skol
Delaware: David Campbell, Superintendent, Colonial School District, New Castle
District of Columbia: Lynne Long, Assistant Principal, Martin Luther King Ele-
    mentary School

Florida: Michael Walker, General Director, Academic Programs for Instruction, Duval County Schools, Jacksonville

Georgia: Ed Pajak, Professor, Department of Educational Leadership, University of Georgia, Athens

Germany: Linda McCauley, Principal, DoDDS-Augsburg Elementary School, Augsburg

Hawaii: Marian Holokai, Principal, Waimanalo School, Waimanalo

Idaho: Gary Delka, Associate Professor, University of Idaho, Lewiston

Illinois: Fred Schroeder, Assistant Superintendent for Curriculum, Schaumburg School District 54, Schaumburg

Indiana: Nancylee Buckley, Director of Curriculum, Carmel Clay Schools, Carmel

Iowa: Gordon Cook, Superintendent, Mid-Prairie Community School District, Wellman

Japan: Judy Beneventi, Assistant Principal, American School in Japan, Tokyo

Kansas: Dan Lumley, Associate Superintendent, Unified School District #230, Spring Hill

Kentucky: William Reiley, Assistant Superintendent, Dayton Independent Schools, Dayton

Louisiana: Linda Fortenberry, Assistant Superintendent, New Orleans Public Schools, New Orleans

Maine: Mary Dunderdale, Curriculum Coordinator, Maine School Administrative District #40, Waldoboro

Maryland: Evelyn Chatmon, Assistant Superintendent, Baltimore County Public Schools, Towson

Massachusetts: Caroline Tripp, Assistant Superintendent, Shrewsbury Public Schools, Shrewsbury

Michigan: Marion Ginopolis, Superintendent, Oxford Area Community Schools, Oxford

Minnesota: Maxine Strege, Director of Curriculum and Instruction, Little Falls Community Schools, Little Falls

Mississippi: Doris Smith, Superintendent, Winona Public Schools, Winona

Missouri: Larry Reed, Superintendent, Cole County R-II Schools, Jefferson City

Montana: Ed Courtney, Assistant Superintendent (retired), Missoula Elementary School District #1, Missoula

Nebraska: Dan Brosz, Assistant Superintendent, Grand Island Schools, Grand Island

The Netherlands/Flanders: Atse Spoor, Violenschool, Hilversum

Nevada: Teddy Brewer, Principal, Nate Mack Elementary School, Henderson

New Hampshire: Susan Newton, Principal, Peterborough Elementary School, Peterborough

New Jersey: Richard Serfass, Assistant Superintendent, Cherry Hill Public Schools, Cherry Hill

New Mexico: Winifred Dresp, Teacher, Picacho Middle School, Las Cruces

New York: Diane Kilfoile, Principal, A.W. Becker Elementary School, Selkirk

North Carolina: Barbara Parramore, Professor of Curriculum and Instruction, College of Education and Psychology, North Carolina State University, Raleigh

North Dakota: Ann T. Clapper, Director, North Dakota Department of Education, Bismarck

Northwest Territories: Peter Grimm, Principal, Princess Alexandra School, Hay River

Ohio: Barbara Denner, Curriculum Director (retired), Gahanna City Schools, Gahanna

Oklahoma: Cheryl Steele, Assistant Superintendent, Mid/Del Public Schools, Midwest City

Ontario, Canada: Evelyn Brown, Superintendent, Muskoka Board of Education, Bracebridge

Oregon: Mary Johnson, Curriculum Coordinator, Corvallis School District, Corvallis

Pennsylvania: John Linden, Assistant Superintendent, School District City of Erie, Erie

Puerto Rico: Sister Vivina Sepulveda, Superintendent of Catholic Schools, Mayaguez

Rhode Island: Marylou Mancini-Gallipeau, Chariho Middle School, Wood River Junction

St. Maarten, Netherlands Antilles: Juliana Hodge-Shipley, Vice Principal, Methodist Agogic Center, Philipsburg

Singapore: Kan Sou Tin, Curriculum Planning Division, Ministry of Education

South Carolina: Rebecca Partlow, Supervisor of Instruction, York District Three, Rock Hill

South Dakota: Wendy Boniauto, Director, South Dakota Curriculum Center, Pierre

Spain: Manuel Wood, Universidad/Las Palmas de Gran, Canary Islands

Tennessee: Pat Ashcraft, Curriculum Coordinator, Chimneyrock Elementary School, Cordova

Texas: Elvis Arterbury, Assistant Superintendent, Beaumont Independent School District, Beaumont

Trinidad & Tobago: Annette Wiltshire, education consultant

United Kingdom: Elizabeth Dunham, Staff Developer, UK District

Utah: Tina Howard, Adjunct Professor, Brigham Young University, Provo

Vermont: Doug Harris, Director, Educational Program Division, National Gardening Association, Burlington

Virgin Islands: Dolores Clendinen, Coordinator of Alternative Education, Department of Education, St. Thomas

Virginia: Lucia Sebastian, Assistant Principal, York County Public Schools

Washington: Rick Schulte, Superintendent, Oak Harbor School District, Oak Harbor

Wisconsin: Sandy Ludeman, Director of Instruction, New Berlin Public Schools, New Berlin

West Virginia: Helen Hazi, West Virginia University, Morgantown

Wyoming: Susan Staldine, Associate Principal, Campbell County High School, Gillette

ASCD Headquarters Staff

Gene R. Carter, *Executive Director*
Diane Berreth, *Deputy Executive Director*
Frank Betts, *Director, Education & Technology Resource Center*
Ronald S. Brandt, *Executive Editor*
John Bralove, *Director, Administrative Services*
Helené Hodges, *Director, Collaborative Ventures*
Susan Nicklas, *Director, Field Services*
Michelle Terry, *Director, Professional Development*

Kevin Adler
Diana Allen
Pam Bailey
Julius Banks
Vickie Bell
Jennifer Beun
Steven Blackwood
Karen Blaker
Gary Bloom
Maritza Bourque
Joan Brandt
Dorothy Brown
Robert Bryan
George Bryant
Colette Burgess
Liz Byrne
Angela Caesar
Kathryn Carswell
Sally Chapman
John Checkley
Katherine Checkley
Raiza Chernault
Sandra Claxton
Lisa Manion Cline
Philip Cohen
Andrea Corsillo
Agnes Crawford
Sandi Cumberland
Elaine Cunningham
Marcia D'Arcangelo
Steve Darnell
Jay DeFranco
Keith Demmons
Becky DeRigge
Michael DeVries
Gloria Dugan
Shiela Ellison
Kathie Felix
Tammy Finley
Gillian Fitzpatrick
Terry Fleming
Christine Fuscellaro
Troy Gooden

Regina Gussie
Nora Gyuk
Dorothy Haines
Susan Hall
Vicki Hancock
Nancy Harrell
Dwayne Hayes
Davene Holland
Julie Houtz
Angela Howard
Debbie Howerton
Peter Inchauteguiz
JoAnn Irick Jones
Mary Jones
Teola Jones
Stephanie Justen
Sandra Kashdan
Leslie Kiernan
Crystal Knight
Michelle Kosloski
Jennifer Lane
John Mackie
Indu Madan
Gina Major
Larry Mann
Jan McCool
Biz McMahon
Clara Meredith
Ron Miletta
Frances Mindel
Nancy Modrak
Cerylle Moffett
Kenny Moir
Karen Monaco
Donna Motley
Jennifer Mulligan
Margaret Murphy
Dina Murray
Kimber Nation
Peter Neal
Mary Beth Nielsen
Jonathan Nobles

John O'Neil
Margaret Oosterman
Jayne Osgood
Millie Outten
Diane Parker
Kelvin Parnell
Margini Patel
Terrence Petty
Carolyn Pool
Ruby Powell
Tina Prack
Pam Price
Lorraine Primeau
Gena Randall
Karen Rasmussen
Hope Redwine
Melody Ridgeway
Mary Riendeau
Judy Rixey
Rita Roberts
Gayle Rockwell
Cordelia Roseboro
Carly Rothman
Jeff Rupp
Marge Scherer
Beth Schweinefuss
Timothy Scott
Judy Seltz
Bob Shannon
Valerie Sprague
Karen Steirer
Lisa Street
Tess Taguas
Judy Walter
Donald Washington
Milton Washington
Vivian West
Kay Whittington
Linda Wilkey
Scott Willis
Carol Wojcik
David Zamora

About ASCD

Founded in 1943, the Association for Supervision and Curriculum Development is a nonpartisan, nonprofit education association with nearly 200,000 members and 66 affiliate groups in the United States and around the world.

Membership in ASCD includes a subscription to the award-winning journal *Educational Leadership*; two newsletters, *Education Update* and *Curriculum Update*; and other products and services.

Following are some of the resources ASCD offers educators—kindergarten through grade 12—as well as others in the education community, including parents, school board members, administrators, and university professors and students. For further information about ASCD, call (703) 549-9110 or fax (703) 548-8725. Internet access: gopher.ascd.org. Or write to ASCD, Information Services, 1250 N. Pitt St., Alexandria, VA 22314.

Advocacy for education issues
Affiliate organizations (U.S. and international)
Assessment resources and guidelines
Audiotape programs
Books on topics listed here—and many others
Book reviews
Catalogues and directories of educational resources
Character education information
Classroom management techniques
Computer-based teaching tools and software
Conferences
Consortiums and collaborations
Curriculum resources
Dimensions of Learning program
Diskette-based educational resources
Dissertation awards
Field-based staff development support
Global education emphasis
Grants information
How-to publications
Institutes
International perspectives
Internet information services

Issues analyses
Journals
Memberships
Multicultural education resources
Multimedia presentations
Networks
Newsletters
Parent involvement resources
Pilot programs
Public information office
Presentations
Professional development workshops
Recognition programs
Research information
Restructuring and school reform plans
Software reviews
Strategic planning support
Supervision and administration resources
Teaching tools and classroom resources
Technology and education information and support
Textbook indexes and summaries
Thinking skills resources
Trainer's manuals and facilitator's guides
Video-based staff development programs
Yearbooks and annual reports